The European Parliament and Supranational Party System

This book examines the impact of increased legislative power and political authority on the internal development of the European Parliament and the supranational party group system. This is done through an analysis of changes in the hierarchical structures that regulate the internal organization of both the EP as a whole and the individual party groups. In addition, the changing pattern of coalition formation between party groups across time and legislative procedure is analyzed. The trends of internal development examined suggest that the increases in EP power that have occurred since the creation of the cooperation procedure by the Single European Act in 1987 have caused a fundamental shift in the character of the European Parliament as a legislative institution. Prior to 1987 the European Parliament, despite direct elections and several small attempts to increase its powers, served primarily as a chamber of debate where much more was discussed than accomplished. Since 1987 the EP has evolved into an effective and influential legislative body with the power to delay, amend, and veto EU legislation.

Dr. Amie Kreppel is an Assistant Professor at the University of Florida. She teaches in the fields of comparative politics, comparative political institutions, and formal theory, including specifically courses on the political institutions of Western Europe and the politics and institutions of the European Union. Her research focuses on the development of political parties and parliaments in Europe and the United States. She has published articles in numerous journals, including *Comparative Political Studies*, the *Journal of Common Market Studies*, the *European Journal of Political Research*, and the *British Journal of Political Studies*. She was recently a Public Policy Scholar at the Woodrow Wilson International Center for Scholars.

Cambridge Studies in Comparative Politics

General Editor

Margaret Levi   *University of Washington, Seattle*

Associate Editors

Robert H. Bates   *Harvard University*
Peter Hall   *Harvard University*
Stephen Hanson   *University of Washington, Seattle*
Peter Lange   *Duke University*
Helen Milner   *Columbia University*
Frances Rosenbluth   *Yale University*
Susan Stokes   *University of Chicago*
Sidney Tarrow   *Cornell University*

Other Books in the Series

List continues on page following Index

This book is gratefully dedicated to my mother
for believing that I could do it,
to George for showing me the path,
and to Zach for keeping me company along the way.

The European Parliament and Supranational Party System

A STUDY IN INSTITUTIONAL DEVELOPMENT

AMIE KREPPEL

University of Florida, Gainesville

CAMBRIDGE
UNIVERSITY PRESS

APR 0 3 2002

PUBLISHED BY THE PRESS SYNDICATE OF THE UNIVERSITY OF CAMBRIDGE
The Pitt Building, Trumpington Street, Cambridge, United Kingdom

CAMBRIDGE UNIVERSITY PRESS
The Edinburgh Building, Cambridge CB2 2RU, UK
40 West 20th Street, New York, NY 10011-4211, USA
10 Stamford Road, Oakleigh, VIC 3166, Australia
Ruiz de Alarcón 13, 28014 Madrid, Spain
Dock House, The Waterfront, Cape Town 8001, South Africa

http://www.cambridge.org

First published 2002

Printed in the United Kingdom at the University Press, Cambridge

Typeface Janson Text 10/13 pt.   *System* QuarkXPress [BTS]

A catalog record for this book is available from the British Library.

Library of Congress Cataloging in Publication Data
Kreppel, Amie, 1968–
    The European Parliament and Supranational Party System : a study in institutional
development / Amie Kreppel.
        p.   cm. – (Cambridge studies in comparative politics)
    Includes bibliographical references and index.
    ISBN 0-521-80625-9 – ISBN 0-521-00079-3 (pb.)
    1. European Parliament.   2. Political parties – European Union countries.
    3. Coalition (Social sciences)   I. Title.   II. Series.
    JN36 .K735   2001
    341.24'24–dc21   2001025495

ISBN   0 521 80625 9   hardback
ISBN   0 521 00079 3   paperback

Contents

Contents

Figures

Tables

Acknowledgments

This book began as my dissertation at UCLA, for which I received much-needed financial assistance from the International Studies and Overseas Program, the Institute for Global Conflict and Cooperation, and the MacArthur Foundation. During the process of revising the manuscript I also received support from the Woodrow Wilson International Center for Scholars. For invaluable help during the research process in Brussels I owe many thanks to innumerable members of the European Parliament, their staff, and the Parliament's secretariat, who met with me, allowed me to interview them, and answered my questions. Special thanks go to Peter Brawn, Francis Jacobs, Michael Shackleton, and Dietmar Nickel, who have always made time to meet with me, discuss my ideas, and often correct my misconceptions. I would also like to thank the amazing network of "fourth-generation" EU scholars who have taught me much and made the journey a lot more enjoyable, with special thanks to Mark Pollack and Simon Hix for their very helpful comments on the manuscript. Other helpful comments on the manuscript have come from Jim Caporaso, Zachary Selden, and George Tsebelis. For keeping me company throughout the writing and much more painful revision process, my thanks (and extra treats) go to Troll and Astro. Finally, for friendship and support in the homestretch, many thanks to Rene Meisner, the canine Quincy.

1

Introduction: The European Parliament and the Institutional Evolution of Legislatures

When the Parliamentary Assembly of the European Economic Community (EEC) was created in 1957 it was perceived as little more than a multinational chamber of Babel. It consisted of 142 Members appointed by the national legislators of the six Member States. It had no direct popular legitimacy, no control over the fledgling budget of the EEC, and no effective ability to influence legislative outcomes.[1] The Assembly was in all senses a consultative body. But over the course of the last quarter-century the Parliamentary Assembly has evolved into a true European Parliament (EP). Directly elected since 1979 with partial (and increasing) control over the budget since 1975 and the ability to delay, amend, and even veto legislation, the European Parliament of today bears little resemblance to the Parliamentary Assembly of old. Today the EP deserves to be considered a "transformative" legislature capable of significantly impacting the decision-making and policy processes of the European Union (Polsby, 1975: 277–296).

This book examines the remarkable institutional development of the European Parliament since its inception in 1957, and particularly since it began its metamorphosis in earnest in the 1970s. It is not the actual increases to the powers of the EP that interest me, but rather the effect of these increases in terms of the internal institutional evolution of the EP as a legislature. In other words, the main question investigated is, What effect did exogenous increases in the powers and influence of the European Parliament have on its internal development? The theoretical models applied assume rational action on the part of the relevant actors

[1] As we shall see, the Assembly had the right to be "consulted" on some matters, but even then its opinion was most often ignored by the true decision makers in the Council.

1

(micro model) when they reform the internal organizational structure of the EP in response to significant environmental (exogenous) changes in EP power and influence (macro model).

A thorough understanding of the internal development of the European Parliament is interesting and important, not only as a case study of institutional development, but also because of the increasingly important role that the EP plays in the creation of legislation and the political life of the European Union (EU). The extent to which the EP is able to exploit its growing powers is largely dependent on its internal development. Without an internal organization capable of efficiently handling the expanding legislative load of the European Union, the EP would have remained a largely inconsequential actor in the policy-making process, despite the significant additions to its official powers that have occurred in recent years. It is important to understand both the extent of the rapid internal evolution of the European Parliament and the impact of increased legislative authority on the direction and character of this development, because these in turn impact the institutional and legislative evolution of the EU as a whole.

The focus of this book is therefore the development of the EP and the supranational party system within it. The primary goal is to trace the internal institutional evolution of the EP and the supranational party groups. Included within this project, however, are two secondary but important goals: The first is to test the applicability and generalizability of models of legislative development rooted in the American congressional context to other national and institutional settings; the second is to suggest some patterns of parliamentary evolution that will be applicable in other new and/or emerging legislative systems. All of these goals are accomplished through an analysis of the impact that external increases to the legislative and political authority of the EP have had on its internal evolution.

A comparison between the internal evolution of the EP and other parliaments would be extremely informative and add to our understanding of the comparability of the "European case." Unfortunately there are not many in-depth analyses of legislative development outside of the American context.[2] As a result, there are no general models of legislative

---

[2] The best example is by Gary Cox (1987), in which he analyzes the internal evolution of the British House of Commons indirectly through an analysis of the rise of political parties within that body.

development that can easily be applied to the EP. This is the motivation behind the two secondary goals of this book.

While there are numerous scholarly studies of the development of the U.S. Congress, most of these are, to a certain extent, context driven and difficult to apply directly in other non-American settings. Two models of institutional evolution are generally applied: the environmental or macro model and the rational actor or micro model. The first focuses on large exogenous changes that effect the role of the legislature. These environmental shifts lead to internal changes to adjust to the new situation. The internal adaptations reflect the character of the external changes; that is, they are fundamentally nonstrategic reactions to actual changes in the demands placed on the legislature.

The rational actor or micro model of legislative development focuses specifically on the character of the internal reactions to external change. Essentially, while the macro model predicts that there will be internal change as a reaction to environmental shifts, the micro model tries to predict what those changes will be based on the *strategic* actions of those with the power to affect change (generally "the majority"). The macro and micro models of institutional development, as frequently applied to the congress, implicitly and explicitly incorporate certain elements of the American system that are not present elsewhere (like a two-party system and single-member districts). By generalizing these models beyond the American (and even the legislative) context it is possible to derive some propositions about institutional development as a result of increased political authority that can be applied more broadly, in particular, the internally centralizing and ideologically moderating effects of granting a multiparty legislature nonhegemonic legislative power. In doing so, this book will hopefully serve as a tentative first step on the long road toward a general theory of institutional development.

Why the European Parliament?

Although the EP is arguably a unique legislative institution, its evolutionary path and the implications of its development may not be. To understand the fundamental transformation of the EP over the last two decades it is necessary to consider some basic differences between different types of legislatures, in particular, the variation in internal organization and external behavior between legislatures that have significant independent legislative authority and those that do not. One need only compare the

British House of Commons to the American Congress to understand the potential differences between these two types of legislatures. The role of political parties, ideology, and the internal organization of each institution are unquestionably different, in large part due to the difference in their independent legislative power.

In a sense the House of Commons and the U.S. Congress represent two ideal types: the chamber of debate and the legislative body, respectively. In the former, most legislative decision making effectively takes place elsewhere, generally within the executive. In the latter, the legislature is one, if not the only, focus of legislative activity. The EP is an example of a legislature fundamentally evolving from one type to the other over a very short period of time.

There is little debate over the fact that the legislative powers and influence of the EP have grown dramatically since its inception, and especially over the last twenty years. The introduction of direct elections as well as the significant treaty revisions of the Single European Act, the Maastricht Treaty, and, most recently, the Amsterdam Treaty have all included provisions to strengthen the legislative role of the EP. The extent to which these reforms have been successful in granting the EP true legislative power remains a topic of much scholarly research and debate (Tsebelis, 1994, 1997; Garrett and Tsebelis, 1996; Moser, 1996; Scully, 1997, Kreppel, 1999b, 2000a) but it is not the central focus of this book. Most observers of the European Union grant that the EP of today bears little resemblance to its predecessors. What have remained largely unacknowledged and unexamined are the internal institutional effects of this transformation.

The history of the EP and its changing legislative role in the larger European Community has been well-documented. There are numerous studies that *describe* the EP, explain how it works, what its actual powers are, and list historical facts and anecdotes (Cocks, 1973; Scalingi, 1980; Bieber, Jacques, and Weiler, 1985; Bieber, Pantalis, and Schoo, 1986; Sbragia, 1992; Nugent, 1994; Westlake, 1994; Corbett and Jacobs et al., 1995). Similar works exist about the party groups, although they are fewer in number (Van Oudenhove, 1965; Pinder and Henig, 1969; Fitzmaurice, 1975; Pridham and Pridham, 1979, 1981; Henig, 1980; Guidi, 1983; Raunio, 1996; Hix and Lord, 1997a). In addition, the history of individual events (such as the introduction of direct elections, the Single European Act (SEA), and the Maastricht and Amsterdam Treaties) that have increased the powers of the EP have also been extensively analyzed both individually and in historical contexts (Bieber, Jacque, and Weiler, 1985; Corbett, 1989; Dinan, 1994; Noel, 1995; Nicoll, 1996; Devuyst, 1999; Moravcsik, 1999).

What we are still missing, however, is an attempt to draw together these diverse aspects to understand the dynamics of the developmental process as a whole. Changes in the focus and nature of the development of the EP's internal organizational structures, as well as the growth of the supra-national party group system *as a result* of the increased ability of the EP to impact legislative outcomes in the EU remain largely unexplored. It is this dynamic and interactive aspect of institutional development that this book addresses through a detailed analysis of the internal evolution of the EP and the party groups across time.

The Approach

The theoretical framework used throughout the book is drawn largely from existing American models of congressional development and is in essence a combination of the environmental (macro) and rational actor (micro) models of institutional evolution. When used in conjunction these models predict that institutional changes will occur when external (environmental) changes permit or require them, and that they will reflect the preferences of those (rational actors) able to control the process of reform. Although these models are designed and generally applied specifically within the American legislative context, this research demonstrates the extent to which it is possible to modify and adapt them to other national settings as well as to other institutions.

Using the combination of these two theoretical approaches is not new (Cooper and Young, 1989; Gamm and Shepsle, 1989; Sinclair, 1989), but it is particularly important for this type of research because it allows the investigation of the *dynamic* process of institutional evolution. The connections between external and internal change are often overlooked in legislative research that is static because it is focused on a specific event or a particular period in time. It is important when looking at the evolutionary process within a legislature to link external changes to internal reforms to understand fully the impact that both have had on the changing character of the institution. In this context it is crucial to examine both the goals of the actors as well as the changing arsenal of tools at their disposal. This can also be understood as changes in the rules of the game.

Combining the macro and micro models in a longitudinal study makes it possible to study the interaction of strategy and changing opportunity. Even if the goals of the actors (Members and party groups) are consistent across time, the variation in the legislative and political powers of the EP suggests that the strategies pursued will change. In essence, every time the role of the EP is modified the tools at the disposal of the party groups, which allow them to pursue their goals, change. As a result, the best possible strategy to achieve their goals is also likely to change.

Fundamentally, all democratic legislatures exist and develop as a result of the interaction between the role of the legislature in the broader political arena, their internal organizational structures, and the party system. None of these factors exists in a vacuum; each evolves in conjunction with the development and growth of the others. Despite its unusual beginnings and supranational character, the rapid and recent nature of the EP's development offers a unique opportunity to study these dynamic relationships.

The Evidence

The specific focus throughout this book is the impact that increased political authority has had on the evolution of the EP, in particular, the effect of increased legislative power on the character of the legislature as a whole (chamber of debate or legislative body) and the relationships between and within the supranational party groups. To what extent does the internal organization of the EP currently resemble that of a chamber of debate or a legislative body? Has this changed over time? If so, when and how? Have the increases in the legislative authority of the EP affected the roles of the various party groups or significantly changed the party system as a whole? What limits do the institutional character of the EU as a whole place on the internal development of the EP?

All of these questions address the fundamental character of the EP and the party groups as well as the roles that they play within the EU legislative process. They are connected to each other by their interactive nature. Whether the EP is a chamber of debate or a legislative body necessarily affects the role of the party groups and their interactions with each other. Similarly, the interactions between the party groups will influence the internal structure of the EP and therefore how it performs its tasks in the larger EU setting. The general constraints of the institutional structure of the EU as a whole also affect the process of internal EP and party group evolution. Each element in the system impacts the others, and a change in one necessarily influences the rest. The questions outlined above are aimed at understanding this influence and the results.

I answer these questions by examining the changing character of the EP's rules of procedure (internal organizational structure), the patterns of coalition formation (party system), the role of ideology in the decision-making process (EU structural influence), and the internal evolution of the supranational party groups themselves all across time. Each of these four topics focuses on a different aspect of the internal structure of the EP. In each case the results of the analysis strongly suggest that the internal evolution of the EP is linked to external increases in its political authority, and that the character of the internal reforms implemented were strategically selected by those within the Parliament capable of controlling the outcomes.

The reason that the acquisition of legislative power has had such a significant impact on the internal evolution of the EP is that it fundamentally altered the ability of both the individual Members and the party groups to achieve their policy goals though direct legislative action. When the EP was created, and indeed for most of its nearly fifty years, its Members had little opportunity to *directly* pursue policy objectives. The EP served as a public, and eventually directly elected, forum of debate. It was an institution that represented "the citizens of Europe" but could do little to directly affect the EU policy process. While the introduction of direct election (1979) was important from a democratic point of view, the real change in the function of the EP did not come until there was significant treaty reform. The Single European Act (SEA) (1987) granted the EP partial decision-making power through the cooperation procedure. The Maastricht (1993) and Amsterdam Treaties (1999) later followed and increased the legislative power of the EP by adding the co-decision (I and II, respectively) procedure.[3]

The opportunity to impact, directly and effectively, policy outcomes had a significant and lasting influence on the internal dynamics between the party groups within the EP. The overall pattern of internal evolution within the EP after the SEA suggests that increasing the decision-making powers of a legislature can lead to the radical transformation of the institution as a whole. In effect the EP has evolved from an ideologically dogmatic, loosely organized chamber of debate to a frequently bipartisan and

---

[3] Each of these events is discussed and described at length in Chapter 4.

hierarchically structured legislative body. But this transformation does not come without costs. As a result, it is important to understand who is able to manipulate the transformation process to their benefit and who loses political influence as a result.

Despite examining four very different areas of internal reform and evolution (the rules, coalitions, ideology, and the party groups) there is a consistent trend of power and influence flowing toward the centralized control of the two largest party groups and away from the smaller groups across the ideological spectrum. Not surprisingly, as suggested by the macro model, internal reforms have been inspired by external changes, and as the micro model would suggest it is precisely these two large groups that have consistently had the power to control the outcomes of reform.

Within the EP no party group has ever held an absolute majority of the seats. There have always been two large party groups, the Party of European Socialists (PES) and the Christian Democratic European Peoples' Party (EPP).[4] Between them they have continuously controlled between 50 and 70% of the seats in the EP. If they work together, the two groups have the potential to be hegemonic. In circumstances that require an absolute majority little can be accomplished without the explicit assent of both.[5] Both internal reforms of the rules of procedure and legislative decision making in the latter stages of the process require the assent of an absolute majority.[6] This means that if the EPP and PES are strategic *and* can find areas of agreement, they can work to manipulate both internal reform and policy outcomes to their benefit. More importantly, it suggests that the other numerous political groups within the EP risk marginalization at a structural as well as an ideological level.[7]

The internal hierarchical organization of a legislature is extremely important and reflects the nature of the institution as a whole. The rules

---

[4] The names of the groups have varied across time. I use the current names throughout to avoid confusion, with the exception of the European People's Party group (EPP). In July 1999, the EPP renamed itself the European Peoples' Party and European Democrats Group (EPP-ED) to incorporate the existence of a broader membership into its name. Because this occurred after the period discussed here, I use the EPP throughout.

[5] This is due not only to their size, but also to the extremely high level of absenteeism in the EP. This is discussed further in Chapters 6 and 7.

[6] This applies to the second reading of the cooperation and co-decision procedures as well as the assent procedure.

[7] Historically there have been between three and twelve party groups in the EP. Since direct elections were introduced in 1979, the number has varied between seven and twelve, with an average of eight or nine party groups.

that determine who can do what when are a crucial aspect of the decision-making process. The character and efficiency of the Parliament are strongly influenced by the rules that structure the day-to-day activities within it. The role of individual Members of the Parliament as well as the relationships between the political parties are defined by the distribution of rights and powers that are established, at least in part, by the internal rules of the legislature.

These internal rules are not static, however. They evolve and change as the role of the institution changes over time. Examinations of the American Congress have demonstrated the extent to which the majority parties within both the House and Senate have used the opportunities presented by external environmental changes to strategically modify the internal organizational structure of the institutions to benefit themselves (Cooper and Young, 1989; Gamm and Shepsle, 1989; Binder, 1996). The Members of the European Parliament have been offered a number of similar opportunities since its inception, including enlargement, direct elections, and the new legislative procedures introduced by the Single European Act and the Maastricht/Amsterdam Treaties. With each external reform the EP was granted increased control and influence over the EU legislative process. And with each external increase in its powers the EP has reformed its rules of procedure to adapt to the new situation. Not surprisingly, given the American experience, these reforms have been increasingly less egalitarian, shifting power toward the two largest groups and away from both individual Members and the smaller groups.

At the same time, patterns of coalition formation between party groups have reflected a similar willingness of the two largest groups to work together despite apparent ideological differences. The level of EPP–PES coalition activity far exceeds anything required by the rules regulating majority requirements and instead reflects the changing character of the EP as an institution (Chapter 7 and Kreppel, 2000b). Just as the two largest groups found it beneficial to work together in restructuring the internal rules of the EP, they have also realized the need for pragmatic coalitions in the legislative arena. Because of the tricephalous nature of the EU legislative process, no ideologically extreme proposal can be adopted.[8] Thus, regardless of the majority requirements of any specific procedure

---

[8] In no case does the EP have hegemonic control over legislative outcomes. Although there are significant variations by legislative procedure, the EP must always work to some extent with both the Commission and the Council to achieve its legislative goals.

or legislative stage, the two groups need to work together to create ideologically moderate, and thus, broadly acceptable proposals. The result is once again the marginalization of the smaller party groups, which are numerically largely unnecessary in the coalition formation process.

Of the four aspects of EP development studied here, only the internal evolution of the party groups themselves has not directly led to a reduction in the role of the smaller party groups in the political life of the EP. On the whole, the party groups have been largely unable to move significantly beyond the developmental stage of loose confederations of like-minded individuals. While it is true that the party groups have a very high level of voting cohesion, it is wrong to assume that this is due primarily to high levels of internal party discipline (see Chapter 8). In fact, the internal decision-making process, and particularly the allocation of benefits within the two largest party groups, is controlled fundamentally by the national delegation leaders. It is possible that this has actually placed more pressure on party group leaders to push for still greater centralization within the structures of the EP to control their members indirectly,[9] with the result once again being the marginalization of the smaller groups.

The overall pattern of internal EP development has been movement away from egalitarian internal structures and strongly ideological coalitions toward increased internal centralization of power and ideological moderation. This has occurred gradually across time as external increases in the legislative and political authority of the EP have given the leaders of the EPP and PES opportunities to strategically reform the internal organizational structures of the EP. Increased legislative powers also gave these two groups an incentive to avoid ideological dogmatism and work together to achieve moderate, broadly acceptable proposals. Together these two trends have led to a highly centralized and largely bipartisan European Parliament that much more closely resembles the U.S. Congress than it does the House of Commons. This transformation suggests that the accumulation of legislative authority by a legislature within a political system that requires moderation may help improve the internal efficiency of the institution and mitigate ideological extremism, but at the cost of marginalizing smaller party groups.

---

[9] I examine the internal evolution of only the two largest groups since these have been present throughout the EP's history and have actively tried to control their members' behavior to one extent or another; see Chapter 8.

This book is divided into three sections. The first section is an introduction to the macro and micro models of legislative development, in which I review their use in the American context and discuss how they can be adapted to non-American and even nonlegislative arenas. More specifically, Chapter 2 is a review of the application of these models to the American Congress and a discussion of the adaptations necessary to apply them to the EP. These adaptations lead to a set of testable hypotheses about the character of internal rules reforms across time. In Chapter 3, I follow a similar process to adapt and apply the macro and micro models of development beyond the legislative context to the parties and the party system as a whole.

In the second section I trace the history of the EP, highlighting those external changes that have led directly to significant internal reforms. The history of the EP is divided into four distinct periods, which roughly reflect the various stages of its development. The early years (1958–1969) include the initial creation and internal organization of the EP and a discussion of the formal role of the EP as established by the Treaties of Rome. The second period (1970–1978) covers the early period of EP development when it was granted partial budgetary control, adapted to the first enlargement, and prepared for direct elections. During the third period (1979–1986) the EP changed yet again, as its membership was doubled by the first direct elections and then later increased still further by the second round of enlargement.[10] Most importantly, it was during this period that the Single European Act was passed, first granting the EP the opportunity to directly participate in the legislative process via the cooperation procedure. Finally, the fourth period of EP evolution (1987–1999) encompasses the expansion of the EP's power through the Maastricht and Amsterdam Treaties, including the addition and subsequent modification of the co-decision procedure as well as the third major enlargement.

The final section presents the empirical evidence and tests the hypotheses developed in Chapters 2 and 3. Chapter 5 examines all proposed reforms to the internal rules of procedure both qualitatively and quantitatively since 1970. I qualitatively assess the character of reforms in the three historical periods covered and categorize amendments based on their intent and result for the quantitative section. Chapter 6 traces the patterns of coalition formation in the EP through a statistical analysis of roll-call

[10] Grouping the accession of Greece in 1981 and Portugal and Spain in 1986 as a single enlargement process.

votes on resolutions between 1980 and 1996, focusing, in particular, on the dramatic changes that occurred in the general character of coalitions before and after the Single European Act. In Chapter 7, I continue the analysis of coalition behavior, focusing instead on the role of ideology in the coalition formation process and in particular on patterns of co-operation and opposition between the EPP and PES. Finally, Chapter 8 examines the internal evolution of the EPP and PES following the model developed in Chapter 5 for the EP as a whole. This includes tracing the evolution of their internal party group rules to determine the extent to which similar patterns of centralization exist. I conclude in Chapter 9 with a discussion of the overall findings and some possible other applications of the model.

2

Theories of Legislative Development and the European Parliament

In this chapter I examine two current models of legislative development that are based primarily on the U.S. Congress. The models each suggest different catalysts for institutional evolution, which, I argue, can be effectively combined to create a more complete understanding of the variables that influence legislative development. The models are then adapted and applied to the European Parliament to create testable hypotheses about the character and direction of its institutional development since 1957.

The Theoretical Models

Theories of legislative development (as opposed to systems of classification) have focused primarily on the U.S. Congress.[1] This has led to several assumptions that are not directly applicable in the European case, in particular, the relationship between the majority and minority parties and between individual representatives and their constituencies. Nonetheless, models of the evolution of the American Congress can help us to understand the development of the European Parliament and how this process has changed over time.

Discussions of the development of the American Congress are frequently divided into two broad categories, based on their assumptions

---

[1] There are numerous studies of legislative classification based on aspects of internal structure and relationships with other political institutions. See, in particular, Blondel (1973, 1990), Loewenburg and Patterson (1979), Shaws and Lee (1979), Mezey (1979), and Norton (1993). This body of work, while comparative in nature, does not really help us to understand the developmental process that leads to a certain type of internal organization other than to note that certain institutional arrangements tend to occur within particular types of political environments.

about what motivates internal change (Cooper and Brady, 1981; Cooper and Young, 1989; Gamm and Shepsle, 1989; Binder, 1996; Katz and Sala, 1996; Koelble, 1996). The two approaches have been called variously macro and micro, environmental and purposive, or sociological and economic; in all cases a similar dichotomy is created between two interpretations of the causes of institutional development and change. The macro model posits that the internal development of a legislature's organizational structure (hierarchy, rules, structure, etc.) is modified as a reaction to changing external demands. In contrast, the micro model argues that the internal rules and organization of the legislature are determined by the individual preferences of a majority of its membership, and change when desired by, and in a manner consistent with, the preferences and powers of the majority.

I briefly discuss each theory and then explain why the dichotomy is perhaps a false one and how the two approaches can be, if not merged, at least connected for a more complete understanding of the process of parliamentary development. The notion that the dichotomy created by these two approaches is not only unnecessary but, in fact, potentially detrimental to a better understanding of legislative evolution is not original to me. There are several studies that explicitly point out the need to address both approaches (Cooper and Young, 1989; Gamm and Shepsle, 1989; Sinclair, 1989). In addition, there are other analyses of congressional development that implicitly incorporate both types of theory without a formal endorsement of either (Smith, 1989; Stewart, 1992). What I demonstrate through an analysis of the internal development of the EP is that both approaches not only can, but also should, be incorporated into any analysis of parliamentary evolution for a full understanding of the causes and character of internal development. At the end of this discussion I briefly examine recent, more formally oriented theories about the influence and evolution of institutions to show how this project fits within the broader literature on the impact of institutions on the policy process.

The Macro Model

The macro model invokes an essentially environmental theory, which holds that internal institutional modification and development can be understood as a response to increased responsibilities due to changing external realities, or more simply, "institutions develop as they adapt to new circumstances and new demands placed on them" (Gamm and

Shepsle, 1989: 42). According to this model, internal revisions are frequently enacted to improve legislative efficiency or address extenuating and mutable external variables (Cooper and Brady, 1981; Cooper and Young, 1989). This model finds its roots in the seminal study by Nelson Polsby on the institutionalization of the U.S. Congress (Polsby, 1968). Polsby analyzed the U.S. Congress and found that as the legislative workload and membership of the Congress increased, it developed internal structures that helped to improve efficiency and successfully tackle the elevated workload. The changes included specialized committees, increased procedural restrictions, and more partisan approaches to congressional activity. Implicit in Polsby's analysis is the conclusion that the benefits reaped by increased internal development are *collective* in nature. He specifically cites increased power and efficiency of the institution as well as higher levels of professionalization as results of internal development inspired by increased external demands (Polsby, 1968: 166). A much more recent discussion of parliamentary change notes that the cost of *not* adapting to environmental changes is essentially institutional failure and eventual replacement (Copeland and Patterson, 1994: 152–153). This clearly identifies institutional adaptation as a collective good for Members since the other option is marginalization. Thus, in some sense, internal institutional reforms that are inspired by a need to address increased external demands are collective goods to the extent that they are successful.

What the macro theory of legislative development lacks, however, is a successful method of predicting the *character* of the internal reforms that result from these increased external demands. It is hard to imagine any situation for which there is one singular solution. In most (if not all) cases the solution itself will be a subject for debate and potential political tension. One need not even invoke the self-interest of Members to conclude that there are likely to be many potential solutions suggested by any externally created problem of increased demand. How a legislature chooses among the universe of potential solutions is the question broadly addressed by the micro model of legislative development, although it is rarely framed in precisely those terms because of the artificial separation between the two approaches that frequently exists in the literature.

The Micro Model

Micro or purposive explanations of legislative development assume that changes to the internal structures of the legislature are conscious rational actions by individual Members pursuing some goal or preference (frequently defined in terms of self-interest). As a result there is no expectation that resulting changes will benefit all members (be collective goods). Instead, internal reforms are likely to benefit only the majority required to successfully acquire them. This approach suggests that internal institutional change can be used as a tool by the majority to create rules and structures that benefit them to the potential detriment of the minority (Cooper and Young, 1989; Gamm and Shepsle, 1989; Remington and Smith, 1995; Binder 1996). Accordingly, internal revision need not be a reaction to increasing or changing external demands (though these often serve as a useful excuse) and are not expected to be collective goods.

The underlying notion of member activity being premised on some form of self-interest has existed for some time. The "electoral connection" of David Mayhew (1974) is now taken for granted and is fundamentally rooted in notions of Member self-interest. There have, however, been significant variations within the general micro, or perhaps more accurately, rational approach. What links together these potentially disparate theories is the underlying notion that Members' actions are informed by their preferences (or interests), and that we must understand these if we are to understand the process of institutional development as a whole.

What the micro model does not do is explicitly connect internal revisions to the broader political environment. This does not mean that those who invoke the micro model ignore the larger picture (they generally do not); it means that the theory itself has no structured way of incorporating external realities into the predictive model. While it may not be necessary for there to be external changes that increase demands (as in the macro model), the larger environmental setting, and any changes to it, must affect at some level the goals of individual members and, more importantly, the opportunities available to achieve them. Since these are the bases of the micro model, it should formally incorporate the significance of the broader political arena.

The macro and micro models are integrally connected to the extent that the former predicts when change will occur and the latter predicts the nature of that change. When combined they have the potential to add significantly to our understanding of when and how institutions develop. My use of these two models to gain a better understanding of the development of the European Parliament will be based on the awareness that both are significant and that neither can tell the whole story alone.

The macro and micro explanations of legislative development are certainly not the only theoretical examinations of institutions, their roles, and their development. Positive legislative theory based more specifically on rational choice and game theory also examines the evolution and impact of formal institutions.[2] These theories are generally divided into two categories: theories of information and theories of exchange (Shepsle and Weingast, 1995). In a sense this dichotomy maps back onto the previously described difference between macro models of collective goods type reforms and micro models of rational manipulation, respectively. Theories of information argue that institutions develop in general to promote the work of the legislature (or institution) through the creation of information networks that allow accurate and effective decision making by the body as a whole (Krehbiel, 1991). So, for example, committees within a legislature exist to allow members to develop expertise and free the legislature from excessive outside influence. The expertise of committee members is then used to arrive at policy proposals that will accurately represent the median of the entire body.[3]

On the other side, theories of exchange argue, in a manner similar to the general micro approach, that institutions serve to permit individuals or groups to gain something from working within them. Perhaps it would be better to say that institutions are *created* to allow gains from exchange to accrue rather than to produce a collective good, like information. Again using the creation and dominance of committees within a legislature as an example, theories of exchange argue that strong committees allow members control over decision making in those legislative arenas that most concern them (if they serve on the appropriate committee).[4] The committee system thus allows for the creation of numerous specialized fiefdoms in which Members can press for their specialized interests, regardless of the overall cost (often leading to the much-maligned legislative logroll in the American context). If everyone's specialized interests are

---

[2] For an excellent review of this literature and its development over the last quarter-century see Shepsle and Weingast (1995).

[3] This is an extreme oversimplification of the model but does hit the main point, i.e., that the internal institutional structure of committees benefits the entire legislature (a collective good) rather than some smaller subsection that is able to use the system to its advantage.

[4] It should be noted that both theories of information and theories of exchange are based almost entirely on the example of the U.S. Congress and as a result reflect many of the peculiarities of the American system (such as the dominance of committees within the legislature).

fulfilled, the end result is not the collective good of well-informed policy creation, but a budget deficit (Fiorina, 1987).

In the end, the debate between existence and role of information institutions and exchange institutions may be as false a dichotomy as that which exists between the macro and micro theories of institutional development. It seems more likely that the two are most often combined so that the basic necessary information is provided to prevent loss of institutional power, but that the internal structures created are also used to benefit those who are able to manipulate their creation and use. In other words, the need for information may serve as a justification for the creation of nonegalitarian internal legislative institutions in the same way that exogenous increases in the legislative role of a legislature may serve as the excuse for internal reforms that benefit only some subsection of the membership.

Although theories of information and exchange are useful and to some extent applicable to the internal development of the EP, I will use the broader macro and micro theories throughout with reference to the connection to the other theories when they are specifically pertinent. Before we can use the macro and micro theories to create precise predictions about the nature of EP development, however, it will be necessary to first make some adaptations to these basic models to fit the European situation.

The Macro Model Applied

Of the two approaches, the macro is the more easily applied to the case of the European Parliament. This is because there is little implicit in the general argument that is based on the specific characteristics of the U.S. Congress. The general macro approach does not specify the nature of external changes or when they will or will not warrant reciprocal internal legislative reforms. To add to the predictive value of the macro model, the basic approach has been modified somewhat by the inclusion of an approximate measure for when the chain reaction of development will occur. This is done through the definition of "critical moments," when external or environmental changes are large enough to necessitate internal reform (Copeland and Patterson, 1994). A brief glance at the history of the EP suggests four potential "critical moments" when the nature of the EP as a political institution was clearly redefined.[5] The first was the 1970 Budget

---

[5] Martin Westlake (1994: 137) cites the same four key moments as critical in the developmental process of the EP.

Act, which granted the EP partial control over EU finances (fully implemented in 1975), and the second was the introduction of direct elections for members of the EP in 1976 (implemented for the first time in 1979). The third and fourth critical moments involved treaty revisions, which added new legislative procedures and increased the potential of the EP to affect policy outcomes. The Single European Act (1986 – enacted in 1987) introduced the cooperation procedure and the Maastricht Treaty (1992 – enacted in 1993) introduced the co-decision procedure, which was later modified by the Amsterdam Treaty (1997 – enacted in 1999; see Chapter 4). Although there have been numerous small revisions and additions to the EP's status and powers, these represent the most significant external changes that could fulfill the macro model requirement of notably changing (increasing) the demands placed on the internal institutional structures of the EP.

An application of the macro model to the development of the EP can be made through a simple chronological analysis of these four events and the timing and nature of the internal evolution of the EP. A thorough understanding of these four events should help us to predict the nature of the internal reforms. At a very basic level, the internal revisions of the EP should have addressed the needs created by these external changes; otherwise the EP would have lost ground as a legislative institution and not increased its relative power (Copeland and Patterson, 1994). Second, the cumulative effects of these external developments need to be understood since this is what determines the nature of the EP as an institution across the years. This suggests that a useful application of the macro approach needs to do more than just describe the new demands placed on the Parliament; it needs to explain their significance in terms of the overall nature of the EP as a legislative institution.

The macro approach is largely descriptive, in that it does not predict the specific nature of internal change (although Polsby [1968] and Copeland et al. [1994] describe only collective goods). Despite this, it does have some marginal predictive capabilities. It does, for example, predict that internal modifications *follow* external changes in demand. Thus, the bulk of internal development since the creation of the EP should follow closely on the heels of these large external alterations of its role within the EU. Internal developments should also clearly address the potential problems of efficiency created by new powers. Implicitly, the model also predicts that internal revisions should at some level be collective goods in that all Members benefit from maintaining the ability of the EP to function effectively. This understanding of the macro model leads to the following hypotheses, which can be tested against the actual internal evolution of the EP:

- *Hypothesis 1*: Developments in the internal organization and structure of the legislature should follow chronologically large changes to its role and responsibilities within the larger political environment.
- *Hypothesis 1a*: Changes to the internal organization and structures of the legislature should be related to and address the environmental modifications that necessitated them and, to the extent that they benefit the institution as a whole, they should be collective goods.

The Micro Model Applied

Application of the micro model to the development of the European Parliament presents more of a problem. There are two potential barriers to its application to the EP. First, the European Parliament is still in the process of development, not only as regards its internal organization, but also in terms of its relationship vis-à-vis the other institutions of the EU. While the general nature and extent of the external powers of the American Congress have remained largely stable for over a century, the legislative authority and powers of the EP are in a state of constant evolution and flux. In the forty years since it was created it has moved from a consultative assembly with no powers over purse or legislation to a legislative body with budgetary control over a substantial (and increasing) percentage of the budget, conditional agenda-setting powers (Tsebelis, 1994, 1996), and veto power on many issues of primary importance within the Union.[6]

Second, the EP cannot be clearly divided into majority and minority or Government and Opposition. There is no government to support in the traditional sense, and no single party group within the EP controls an absolute majority of the seats. While there are significant ideological differences among the party groups, it is not the case that one side governs independently while the other adopts the role of loyal opposition. This makes it impossible to speak of "the majority;" instead, there are a myriad of potential coalitions in the EP that potentially vary not only by topic

---

[6] Including internal market regulations, the free movement of workers, guidelines for trans-European networks, and the framework programs for research.

20

and legislative procedure, but also across time (Kreppel and Tsebelis, 1999; Brzinski, 1995). As a result we must find some substitute for "the majority" based on our understanding of the role that the majority plays in the congressional setting.

Since the micro model requires that we understand the *preferences* and *interests* of "the majority" in the legislature to understand why particular internal revisions were made, we must apply the following adaptations. First, the internal development of the EP should be divided into three distinct periods, because its institutional nature, and as a result its ability to influence policy outcomes, has varied significantly. The first period spans from the first plenary session in 1958 until the institution of direct elections for MEPs in 1979. The second period runs from 1979 through the introduction of the Single European Act in 1986, and the third from the implementation of the SEA to the implementation of the Maastricht Treaty (1993). During each of these three periods the EP has had a different role (both self-perceived and real) within the EU as a whole. The result is that during each of these periods the EP was in a different state of development in terms of its political and legislative authority and powers. Consequently, while the goals of the MEPs may have remained constant, their ability to achieve them varied considerably. As a result, despite Members and party groups maintaining the same preferences, their actions are likely to vary significantly during the different periods examined here. This suggests that each stage of EP evolution should be analyzed separately to incorporate its changing political role and policy influence within the EU as a whole.

The second adaptation of the purposive model is an abandonment of the minority–majority dichotomy, which is inappropriate in the EP setting. In its place we will use a large party group–small party group dichotomy. This substitution is not as dramatic as it might seem, because the underlying logic remains the same. In the U.S. Congress the majority is able to manipulate the rules to its benefit while the minority is not. In a similar way, in the EP the large party groups are the only ones that can hope to form effective majorities and successfully modify internal structures to their benefit. The two largest party groups in the EP have consistently been the Socialists (PES) and the Christian Democratic People's Party (EPP). Together they have always accounted for between 50 and 70% of the total EP membership. This fact, when combined with generally high rates of absenteeism (Kreppel and Tsebelis, 1999; Brzinski, 1995) and the requirement of an absolute majority to amend the rules, means that the agreement of both large groups is necessary for any successful revision of the rules. The difference between this and a standard majority–minority dichotomy is significant, however, in that it informs the types of internal revisions that we should expect to see. Within the EP we should antici- pate changes that benefit any large party as opposed to changes that benefit only the majority party.

The next hurdle in applying the micro model of legislative development to the EP lies in trying to discern the goals or preferences of MEPs. While most of the American literature has focused on the "electoral connection," as originally described by Mayhew, as the underlying force behind legislative action, a similar connection does not exist in the European Parliament for several reasons. During the first period (1958–1979) MEPs were appointed from within their national legislatures, not directly elected. There was no direct tie between voters and MEPs, and because of the relative impotency of the EP there was little interest in the activities of MEPs by their national party leaders. Concepts such as "position taking" and "constituency services" are simply inapplicable during this period.

The situation does not change significantly during the second period (1979–1986). While it is true that after 1979 MEPs were directly elected and could conceivably claim some link to their constituents, there were a number of reasons why the electoral connection still would not be an accurate interpretation of MEP actions during this period. Candidacy for the EP is based on party lists, and not individual single member dis- tricts (except in the UK).[7] Lists are created by national (not EP) party leaders, and the issues driving campaigns have been overwhelmingly national as opposed to European in orientation (Lodge, 1984; Nieder- mayer, 1984; Reif, 1985; Bieber, Pantalis, and Schoo 1986; Fitzmaurice, 1988; Corbett, 1989; Westlake, 1994). The general perception of the EP as a relatively unimportant aspect of EU policy making was still common throughout the second period, so what MEPs did was of little importance to their national party leaders (Scalingi, 1980; Robinson and Bray, 1986; Sbragia, 1992; Westlake, 1994; Corbett and Jacobs et al., 1995). The sit- uation has changed somewhat since 1986. The EP has gained in legisla- tive authority since 1987, and it is now recognized as having, at least potentially, a significant role in the EU legislative process. The electoral connection still, however, cannot serve as the primary driving force for

---

[7] Beginning with the June 1999 elections, the proportional method was used to elect MEPs in the UK as well.

parliamentary actions in the EP to the extent that it is in the U.S. Congress. Despite direct election, the typical ties between elected and electors do not exist in the European context. With the partial exception of Great Britain, where MEPs were elected in single member districts between 1979 and 1999, there is little to connect individual MEPs to their constituency. Even ties to party labels are obscured by the mixture of national parties joining a single supranational party group.[8]

In the absence of an electoral connection, what determines MEP preferences and activities? If, in keeping with rational choice aspects of the micro model, we assume that individual Members want to maximize their potential benefits, how is this achieved in the EP? Since re-election is not something that MEPs can effectively control by their parliamentary behavior, the next best possible universal goal is policy objectives.[9] It is credible that this is, in fact, why most Members have joined the EP. The manner in which Members pursue this goal may differ significantly, however, depending on the historical period of EP development and the arena of political action.

During the first two periods of its evolution (1958–1986) the EP was largely devoid of any influence over policy outcomes. MEPs had only partial control over the budget and some weak powers in regards to relations with third party countries (non-EU nations). The only potential for the EP to impact policy outcomes was through the relatively ineffective "consultation" procedure, which only required that the Council wait for an opinion by the EP, not that it incorporate that opinion.[10] It seems probable that during this period of impotence nearly all MEPs wanted to increase the power and authority of the EP so that they could subsequently achieve their desired policy objectives. Most MEPs were pro-federalist and

---

[8] For example, in the 1989–1994 legislature both the Italian Liberals and the Republicans were members of the Liberal Group in the EP, despite the Republicans leaving the governing coalition and joining the opposition at the national level. In addition, the short-lived nature of many of the groups has led to general confusion at the national level. Only the EPP, the PES, and the ELDR have been organized as party groups throughout the history of the EP, and even these groups have all changed their names at least once.

[9] This is also frequently referred to in the American Congress literature as a fundamental goal of Members of Congress. In fact, the re-election goal is sometimes considered only as a necessary predecessor to the realization of policy goals.

[10] An important Court of Justice decision in 1980 (Isoglucose 138/79 and 139/79) held that the Council did indeed have to wait for the EP to issue an opinion, although they still were not required to pay any heed to it. This is discussed further in Chapter 4.

ostensibly joined the EP to impact the process of European integration (Van Oudenhouve, 1965; Westlake, 1994: 100). Even those who were less ardent supporters of an eventual European Union of States most likely felt restrained in the pursuit of their goals by the impotency of the EP as a political actor. The general desire to increase the relative legislative and political influence of the EP can be used as a substitute for the missing "electoral connection" stipulated by the micro theories of legislative development during the first two periods of EP development.[11] It must remain clear, however, that the underlying goal remained the achievement of policy objectives; EP power was a necessary first step to achieve this end.[12] Expansion of the legislative authority of the EP could potentially be obtained in many ways, including increasing internal efficiency (to best use the meager powers that it did have) and trying to increase its power when and where possible through simple assertions of right.[13]

Applied in this scenario, the micro model suggests the following path of internal development. Once legislative power is achieved (albeit to a limited extent) the differences between MEPs and party groups should begin to be more significant. Influence over EP decisions and the internal decision-making process will become increasingly important as the potential to impact EU legislative outcomes increases and differences in policy objectives take center stage. As a result, the power to control the agenda, individual appointments, and even action on the floor of the Parliament all should become more contentious and coveted as EP power in general increases. The previous collegial character of the internal organization (the result of a collective goal of increased EP power) will deteriorate as individuals and groups turn their attention toward the achievement of relative power within the EP so as to pursue their various and often competing policy goals.

Essentially, the micro model suggests that once the powers of the EP increase, so should the internal divisiveness within the EP. As a result we

---

[11] In a sense this is similar to the standard re-election goal if we consider that both are pre-conditions for the eventual achievement of policy goals.

[12] In effect, this suggests that increases in the legislative power and authority of the EP were viewed as a means to an end rather than an end in themselves. This is an exaggeration to the extent that many federalists viewed the extension of the EP's powers as a fundamental ingredient to the achievement of a true and democratic European Union.

[13] For example, the Rules of Procedure (RoP) provide for questions to be addressed to the Commission and the Council despite the fact that the Treaties mention only questions being addressed to the Commission.

should expect to see clear signs of these changes in the nature of internal organizational developments that occur. During periods of general consensus, when the near universal goal is an improvement in the condition of the Parliament vis-à-vis the other institutions of EU, we should witness internal developments that are collective goods benefiting all members as they increase the status of the Parliament. Once consensus breaks down, internal power struggles should become significant. As a result we should expect to see internal changes and developments that benefit some political groups more than, and possibly to the detriment of, others. Changes to the internal organizational structures of the European Parliament will focus less on the good of the institution as a whole and more on particularistic benefits, limited to those who are able to control the developmental process. In the case of the EP this means the larger party groups.

The purposive (micro) model, as well as our understanding of MEP preferences during the different evolutionary periods of the EP, suggests the following hypotheses about EP internal development:

- *Hypothesis 2*: In the absence of an ability to successfully impact legislative outcomes (policy goals), Members will join together to work toward the strengthening of the legislature as a political institution (legislative efficiency and power). Reforms will be collective goods (in that they will benefit the legislature as a whole) and will not explicitly benefit one subsection of Members over the others.
- *Hypothesis 2a*: When the potential to impact legislative outcomes is realized, internal reforms will no longer be primarily collective goods, but will instead tend to benefit the subsection of the legislature's membership that can control voting outcomes. As a result, consensus among Members about the internal structure and development of the legislature will deteriorate.[14]

Testing the Models

An examination of the existing literature on the evolution of legislatures has suggested two models of development that, with some adaptations, can be applied to an analysis of the European Parliament. A combination

[14] Note that the initial desire to increase the power of the legislature should remain since this is still in everyone's best interest.

of the two models leads to predictions about the timing and type of internal organizational development experienced by the EP. These models can be tested through a comparison of their predictions to what has actually occurred. I outline here how I propose to test, and what evidence will be considered to support each of the hypotheses outlined above.

I study the changing character of the internal development of the European Parliament through an analysis of its Rules of Procedure (RoP) and their evolution over the past forty years. The Treaty that established the European Communities and the EP expressly allowed the new assembly to create its own set of internal rules and structures, with very few explicit restrictions. The formal organizational structure and hierarchy of the EP is established and modified via the Rules of Procedure (RoP). Although there are numerous informal norms that significantly impact the functioning of the EP as an institution, the bulk of the EP's internal structure is determined by the Rules (Bowler and Farrell, 1999).[15]

Because the structures of the EP are decided endogenously, they offer a useful window into the nature of the institution as a whole. The breadth and level of complexity of the Rules of Procedure and the hierarchical structures they create offer a helpful measurement of overall internal development. Rules can be egalitarian or inegalitarian. Changes to the organizational and hierarchical structures of the EP can be sincere efforts to effectively incorporate new tasks and increase overall efficiency, but they can also be strategic attempts to manipulate outcomes to benefit some subsection of MEPs. In this way an analysis of the rules is extremely helpful in charting not only the internal development of the EP, but also the applicability and usefulness of the macro and micro models.

Testing the Macro Model

The macro model assumes that internal revisions will be direct responses to exogenous changes, which somehow impact the activity of the legislature. As a result, revisions can be expected to follow external changes and be collective goods. To test this model I examine the chronology of events

---

[15] The most important of the informal norms will also be discussed because many have eventually been incorporated into the official rules. As we shall see in Chapter 5, the formal inclusion into the rules of many previous norms was a distinct trend in the period just after the first direct election of the European Parliament.

and determine if, as predicted, internal reforms follow external changes, and attempt to specifically address the new circumstance created by the external change. In addition, I try to establish the extent to which these revisions were collective goods, or whether they were more beneficial to some subsection of EP members.

To determine whether revisions to the RoP were direct responses to environmental changes, and the extent to which they were at least perceived to be collective goods, I examine their character and breadth. This is based on debates within the EP as well as official documentation about the proposed changes from the EP and the other institutions of the Community. The analysis of the nature of the EP's response to these external revisions is based on the actual changes to the rules proposed by the Committee on Rules, including the explanatory statement provided by the *Rapporteur* and the debates in plenary.[16]

Testing the Micro Model

The micro theory of legislative development predicts that individuals within a legislature act in a purposive way to fulfill specific goals. This suggests that when it is in the interests of the "majority" to manipulate the internal rules or organizational structures of the institution, it will do so. A corollary to this argument is that when everyone's best interests are served by consensual action everyone will work together to achieve collective goods. The application of this model to the European Parliament predicts that, in the absence of EP political or legislative authority, all MEPs will be better off working to increase the power of the EP (since participation in a lame duck legislature is most likely not very rewarding politically or personally). Once political power is achieved, differences in policy goals will create internal divisions, and the type of self-interested manipulation of rules and internal structures predicted by Hypothesis 2a will occur.

To test the applicability of this model I examine all rules and revisions proposed by the Rules Committee between 1970 and 1994 to determine if

---

[16] A *Rapporteur* is an individual assigned to each proposal or resolution that goes through committee. The *Rapporteur* works essentially as a chair for an individual piece of legislation. He or she is responsible for drafting the proposal/resolution and ensuring that as far as possible the views of all members of the relevant committee have been incorporated. The *Rapporteur* also frequently meets with the relevant Commission official to ensure cooperation between the Commission and the EP as far as possible.

they are egalitarian in nature or benefit some subsection of EP member-ship. There is general agreement in the literature that, prior to the Single European Act (SEA), the EP had little or no impact on policy making, although there is some dispute about the extent of its impact after the SEA (Tsebelis, 1994, 1995, 1996; Moser, 1996; Hubschmidt and Moser, 1997). If the micro model is an accurate explanation of internal EP reform, we should find that changes to the rules or internal structures of the EP were generally collective goods (benefitting the institution rather than individ-ual Members) prior to 1987 and increasingly less egalitarian afterwards. I have suggested above that internal revisions that were not collective goods were most likely to benefit the larger party groups.[17]

If this model is a true representation of what has occurred in the EP, we should also expect that votes on institutional matters prior to 1987 were largely noncontroversial, while votes on changes after that date were more contentious and divided, according to who benefited and who did not. To test this hypothesis I also examine the level of agreement in the Com-mittee on Rules during each historical period. We should expect a high level of committee unity during the first period and increasingly lower overall rates in the second and third periods. Additionally, where amend-ments increase the power of the larger parties we should expect to find a high rate of success if, in fact, these party groups are acting in their own self-interest by forming coalitions across ideological lines to pursue mutu-ally beneficial institutional reforms.

Conclusions

The European Parliament has evolved dramatically over the last forty years and in particular since 1987. The specific nature of this evolution has remained largely unstudied. Despite growing interest in the European Parliament as a legislative actor, little work has been done on the internal development that has allowed it to play a significant role in the EU leg-islative process. Regardless of the treaty revisions of 1987, 1993, and 1999, and the addition of new legislative powers, if the EP had failed to evolve internally as an institution, its impact on the policy output of the EU would have remained minimal.

---

[17] In particular, the European People's Party (EPP) and the Party of European Socialists (PES), since these two together control enough seats to be able to achieve any mutually beneficial outcome.

The goal of this research is to address this lacuna through an examination of the development of the European Parliament as a legislative body. In particular, I analyze the connections between the role of the EP within the broader political environment and the character of its internal development and the role of the party groups within the Parliament as a whole. To investigate these relationships, two models of legislative development founded largely in the literature on the American Congress are applied to the European Parliament. Because of the existence of several fundamental differences between the EP and the U.S. Congress, the macro and micro models are adapted to be applicable to the institutional realities of the EP. These modified theories are then used to develop a series of testable hypotheses about the timing and character of internal EP evolution. The application of the macro and micro models helps not only to determine the impact of exogenous increases in EP authority on its internal development, but also to demonstrate the applicability of these models of institutional reform beyond the context of the American Congress.

3

The Development of the Party Group System and the Party Groups

Although the macro and micro models of development find their origin in analyses of the evolution of the American Congress, it is possible to expand them beyond the American and even beyond the legislative contexts. The modifications necessary to apply these models of development to the European Parliament were discussed in Chapter 2. In this chapter I adapt them to an analysis of the evolution of the supranational party group system and the internal development of the party groups themselves. There is a great deal of literature on both political parties and party systems. I believe, however, that an application of the macro and micro models can further expand our understanding of the developmental process of parties and party systems. By applying these models of development we can focus on the impact that external changes (increases) in legislative power have had on the internal organization of the party groups and their interactions with each other.

I address first the development of the party system and then the internal evolution of the supranational party groups. In each case I first briefly discuss some of the traditional literature. I then move on to explain how the macro and micro models can be adapted to be applicable in each case. Finally, I use the macro and micro models to derive hypotheses about the character of party system and party group development and outline how I plan to test these hypotheses.

The Development of the Party Group System

Traditional analyses of party systems tend to focus on the number of parties within a system, the character of interparty competition, and the level of ideological polarization (Duverger, 1954; Sartori, 1976;

Panebianco, 1982). While all of these are important aspects of existing party systems, they do not directly address the interactions between parties or the actual *development* of the party system. The focus of these studies tends to be on static definitions and classifications, not models of dynamic evolution and change. Nonetheless, these descriptions of party systems help in understanding the nature and importance of variations in a party system that can occur across time. It will therefore be useful to briefly review some of the types of party systems defined by this body of work.

Traditional Analysis of Party Systems

The most basic element of any party system is the number of parties present, followed closely by their location on the traditional left–right ideological spectrum, and their interactions with each other. The standard classifications are one-party systems, two-party systems, and multiparty systems. The first are generally understood to be nondemocratic because the minimum requirements for democracy cannot be met in the absence of free and competitive elections (Dahl, 1956). Two-party systems are generally associated with majoritarian electoral systems and strong executives (Duverger, 1954; Lijphart, 1984).[1] Finally, there are multiparty systems. Common throughout Western Europe, these generally have more than three viable political parties and a proportional list-based electoral system. Multiparty systems are almost always parliamentary systems (with France being a partial exception), while two-party systems can be either parliamentary (UK) or presidential (USA) systems.

While the simple counting and coding of parties present and active within the system is not particularly informative on its own, when the various aspects of a party system are combined the information gathered can be quite useful. For example, certain types of party systems may be inherently unstable, in particular, "fractured" and "polarized" systems (Sartori, 1976). In the former, the party system consists of numerous small parties, none of which are able to form the basis of a stable governing coalition leading to political instability. In the latter case, the political parties are located only on the extremes of the left–right spectrum, leaving the center vacant. Also essential is the absence of a norm of political

---

[1] There are certainly exceptions to these generalizations; Austria is a notable one.

compromise and cooperation between the ideological left and right.[2] Political polarization is not limited to multiparty or two-party systems, and examples of each type exist.[3] Extreme party system polarization can lead to ideological dogmatism and government, or even regime, instability (Sartori, 1976). A healthy party system, on the other hand, is one in which the ideological center is occupied, party fractionalization is kept to a minimum, and there are opportunities for alternation in power between the various parties or coalitions.

In contrast to polarized party systems are "bi-partisan" and "consociational" systems. These definitions are generally applied to party behavior within a parliament or legislature only, while the term "polarized" frequently refers to activity within the electoral arena as well. Bipartisan party systems generally occur in two-party systems and are frequently characterized by high levels of interparty cooperation. A multiparty system in which there are two primary or dominant parties with a high level of coordination and compromise can also be categorized as a bipartisan system.[4] The term "consociational" or consensus usually refers to systems in which there is a high level of interparty cooperation across ethnic or religious as well as ideological lines (Lijphart, 1975, 1984). These systems occur almost exclusively in federal systems or countries with significant internal ethnic/religious divisions.

The literature describing party systems is vast; topics vary depending on the particular type of system studied, from consociational (Lijphart) to polarized (Sartori) and from stagnant to unstable, but generally speaking the focus is on description and classification of existing systems more than explaining development or change within a system. Knowing the number of parties within a system, their ideological location, and the possibilities for alternation in power can reveal a good deal about the level of democracy and stability of the political system as a whole, but they do not directly address the developmental process that interests us here.

As a result we return to the previous models of legislative development, adapting them to the process of party system, instead of parliamentary, development. This task is made somewhat easier in the European case

---

[2] These definitions are loosely taken from Sartori (1976). Similar discussions of political polarization can also be found in Panebianco (1982) and Morlino (1980, 1981).

[3] Prior to 1994, Italy was the quintessential polarized multiparty system, while the UK can be described as an example of a weakly polarized two-party system.

[4] This possibility is extremely important in terms of our understanding of the supranational party system after 1987, as we shall see in Chapters 6 and 7.

by the fact that the supranational party group system exists almost entirely within the European Parliament.[5] While this makes broad comparisons with other party systems more difficult, it simplifies our task of applying the macro and micro models. Because competition between the supranational party groups is almost nonexistent at the electoral level, only the legislative sphere of action needs to be studied.[6] I examine the ability of both the macro and micro models to explain the character and timing of changes in the supranational party group system. This includes formulating testable hypotheses about party group development and the connections between parliamentary and party system evolution.

The Macro Model Applied

The fact that the supranational party system exists almost exclusively within the EP and the resulting legislative focus of party group activity means that the development of the party system will be significantly influenced by changes in the legislative powers of the EP. As a result, the history of the party system, like the Parliament, can usefully be divided into distinct periods. The analysis here will examine the development of the party group system only *after* the first direct elections, because the dual mandate prior to direct elections effectively limited the ability of the party groups and the group system to develop fully. As a result, the analysis will be divided into only two periods: 1979–1986 and 1987–1996, or, in other words, before and after the attainment of legislative influence. During the period from 1958 to 1986, the EP was generally understood to be a relatively impotent actor in the legislative process. Although there were several incremental increases in EP power throughout the period from 1970 to 1985, none were significant enough to effectively change the relative institutional stature of the EP as a legislative body (Robinson and Webb, 1985).

---

[5] There are European Parties organized outside of the EP, but these are weak and depend almost entirely on the EP groups for funding and organizational staff. For more on the supranational party federations see Ladrech (1996, 1997) and Hix and Lord (1997).

[6] Individual MEPs are elected on the basis of lists drawn up by their *national* parties. Rarely is there any mention of the European party groups, and in fact there is no a priori requirement that any elected MEP join a specific supranational group (although the national group might assert certain pressures). Only two of the supranational groups can even claim members from all fifteen member states of the EU.

After the implementation of the Single European Act and the introduction of the cooperation procedure (and again after the Maastricht and Amsterdam Treaties created/modified, respectively, the co-decision procedure) the ability of the EP to impact legislative outcomes increased substantially. The addition of these two new legislative procedures, each of which represented a qualitative leap forward in the perceived political power of the EP, substantially changed the character of the EP as an institution. It is unlikely that the supranational party system remained unchanged by the transformation of the EP from consultative assembly to influential legislature.

The macro model predicts that internal development should occur as a response to external change. When applied to the development of the party group system this means that increases in the legislative and political roles of the European Parliament should affect the development of the party group system. Once again, this aspect of the model provides clear hypotheses about the timing of the developmental process, in particular, that the internal EP response should follow the external change chronologically and address the new political situation. The second aspect of the macro model, however, is more difficult to apply in regard to the party group system. While it is possible to imagine changes to the internal development of a legislature that are common goods (increased legislative efficiency), it is more difficult to envision changes to a party system that could be classified similarly. Party systems consist of individual parties that are, almost by definition, in competition with one another. Because, by their very nature, political parties are competitive with one another, there is little potential for the creation of true public goods.[7] To avoid stretching the model beyond recognition it seems best to examine only the primary prediction, which leads to the following hypothesis:

- *Hypothesis 3*: The development of the party group system should follow chronologically, and be related to large changes to the role and responsibilities of the European Parliament within the larger political environment.

---

[7] It has been frequently noted that one of the primary functions of political parties is to compete both in the electoral and the legislative arenas. See, in particular, Lawson (1976) and Ware (1996).

The Micro Model Applied

Any application of the micro model requires some understanding about the goals of the relevant actors. It was stated previously that Members of the EP pursue their goals using the tools and information available to them. As their tools change, I predicted that their actions would change to make the best use of their new tools. The same should be true of the party groups. Thus, while the goal of influence over EU policy outputs remained consistent, we should expect to see very different actions pursued to achieve that end as the tools available to the party groups changed after the Single European Act and Maastricht Treaty reforms.

Initially, when the EP was largely unable to directly influence policy outcomes, the legislative actions of the party groups were primarily limited to publicizing and increasing support for issues that they felt were important (Raunio, 1996). These could range from European social policy to human rights abuses in Bangladesh.[8] The intent was to further group policy goals through the only avenue available: increased public and political attention. Broad consensus among the party groups was not necessary to achieve this goal. In fact, it was frequently true that the more extreme positions were the most successful in garnering the media's attention.[9] The impact of this strategy on eventual policy outcomes was not negligible. In many cases the Commission and the Council ultimately adopted proposals on issues that originated in the EP if the EP had demonstrated that there was public support for their position. Even the Single European Act is commonly acknowledged to trace its origins back to the 1984 Draft Treaty on European Union, an EP initiative.[10]

Following the passage of the SEA and the Maastricht Treaty, the ability of the EP to directly influence EU legislation was greatly increased, however, the new procedures did not grant the EP unilateral powers. The extent of EP influence was tied to the extent to which it could work effectively with the Commission and Council *and* reach a consensus internally.

[8] There is no restriction to the scope of EP "own initiative" resolutions. Over time, however, the increased legislative burden of the EP has led to a reduction in their overall number.

[9] This is discussed by Raunio (1996: chapters 4–5), who notes the importance of press attention to many MEPs and party groups.

[10] The EP's Institutional Affairs Committee, led and inspired by Altiero Spinelli and his famous "Crocodile Club," created the European Parliament's 1984 Draft Treaty on the European Union.

The rules regulating voting in the new procedures alone required new methods of cooperation between the party groups if the EP was to effectively exert any increased influence over policy outcomes.[11] Some adjustment in political tactics was essential if the groups were to realize the full potential of the additional powers granted to the EP by the new legislative procedures.

I suggest that a fundamental shift in the character of the supranational party system and the nature of the EP as an institution occurred as a consequence of the dramatic increase in the potential legislative role of the EP. The result was the existence of a fundamentally different kind of Parliament before and after the SEA. During the first phase the EP was constrained to giving its opinion without an effective avenue of independent influence over legislative outcomes. Groups were free to be "irresponsible" (in Sartori's terms) because they could take any position they desired, since there was little chance of their proposals being fully implemented.[12] As a result, the groups within the EP were more likely to tend toward ideological extremes and dogmatism. This tendency was reinforced by the fact that precisely these types of positions tended to capture the attention of the media and the public. The result was a fractured and polarized party system in which there was little need for compromise or cooperation between party groups.[13]

However, as the EP acquired the power to impact legislative outcomes, the political groups could no longer afford ideological dogmatism if the EP was to maximize its new powers. Once the domain of parliamentary influence was increased to include the legislative arena, it became necessary for the groups to create legislative proposals that would be moderate enough to gain acceptance by both the Commission and the Council. This led the groups away from dogmatism and extremism toward methods of

[11] Both the cooperation and the co-decision procedures require absolute majorities within the EP to pass amendments, veto or reject proposals, and accept modified proposals during the latter stages (second and third readings).

[12] This concept is applied in particular to the Italian Communist Party (prior to its name change and internal split), which was the second largest party in Italy for over forty years without ever fully joining the governing coalition. The perceived "anti-systemic" nature of the Communist party made it an impossible coalition partner, but also freed it from ever having to actually implement its campaign promises (Sartori, 1976).

[13] As we shall see later, the proliferation of political groups between 1979 and 1992 was also due to changes in the internal rules, which made it more beneficial to form a group than remain independent, with only marginally increased benefits going to the larger groups.

compromise and moderation to take full advantage of their newly established powers. This impetus toward compromise was increased still further by the formal restrictions of the new legislative procedures, which required absolute majorities in the final stages of parliamentary action, in effect requiring the two largest parties to cooperate in the final stages of the legislative process.[14]

Once the potential for the EP to directly impact legislative outcomes was achieved, the actions of the party groups had to change to best pursue the predominant goal of legislative influence and the achievement of policy objectives. The connection between increased EP legislative power and the party group system suggests the following hypothesis:

- *Hypothesis 4*: Party groups will act to maximize the probability that their policy goals will be realized. Their actions will reflect the political tools at their disposal and the legislative rules or restrictions imposed on them.

This hypothesis predicts a shift from a dogmatic party system based primarily on strict ideological concerns to an increasingly pragmatic body focused on the successful creation of broadly acceptable and enforceable public policy. The transition is a dramatic one, comparable to the transformation of the British House of Commons into the American House of Representatives. Although the EP is still considerably less powerful than the American House, it shares many characteristics, not the least of which is the need to create legislation that is acceptable to the two other independent institutions. Bipartisanship is a common occurrence in the American Congress, while it is almost unheard of in the British House of Commons. Ideological compromise can thus be the result of more power, not less, if that power is not unconditional.

Testing the Models

The confinement of the European supranational party system to the parliamentary realm simplifies the task of selecting the best way to study its development. The distance between the party groups within the EP and the process by which individual members are elected limits

---

[14] Levels of absenteeism in the EP have been consistently high, often close to 50%, making the absolute majority requirement much more difficult to obtain (Brzinski, 1995; Kreppel and Tsebelis, 1999).

any study of the evolution of the party system as a whole to activity that occurs within the legislature itself. Given this limitation, an examination of coalition formation between the various party groups offers an excellent method of studying the development of the party system as a whole. The types of coalitions formed addresses questions of polarization and fractionalization as well as the internal stability and consolidation of the party system.

Coalitions within the EP are unusual because they can vary from one vote to the next without fear of government instability. Because the executive (the Commission) is independent of the EP, repeated variation in party coalitions has no impact on its duration or perceived viability. The potential for widely fluctuating coalitions offers an excellent opportunity to study the supranational party system without external constraints. Political groups within the EP can be created and dissolved at will, aside from the numerical requirements for group formation established in the Rules of Procedure. Coalitions can vary across time, legislative procedure, or even by topic. These potential variations are examined through an analysis of 300 roll-call votes occurring between 1980 and 1996 on resolutions, and between 1987 and 1996 and 1994 and 1996 under the cooperation and co-decision procedures, respectively.

Testing the Macro Model

The application of the macro model to the development of the supranational party system is comparatively straightforward. The model predicts that change will occur as a result of broader environmental shifts. I have continued with the previous assumption that the most important environmental changes were those that increased the legislative power and authority of the European Parliament. I focus in particular on the qualitative changes that occurred with the introduction of the cooperation procedure after the adoption of the Single European Act in 1986 and the co-decision procedure introduced by the Maastricht Treaty.

If the macro model is a useful tool for understanding the development of the party group system, we should see significant changes in the types of coalitions formed after the adoption of the Single European Act. The macro model does not help us to predict what type of shifts we should see; for this we must once again turn to the micro model.

Testing the Micro Model

Before we can apply the micro model to the evolution of the party group system, we have to determine the goals of the parties themselves. Traditional discussions of political parties tend to assume that the achievement of political power is the primary goal of most parties. Whether this desire is based on a benign wish to be able to implement the policies desired by their electorate or a more pernicious desire for power, the "electoral connection" is generally considered to hold first place among party goals. For the party groups of the European Parliament this preliminary step is less important because it is largely out of their control (see the discussion in Chapter 2). As a result, the pursuit of policy objectives becomes the primary goal of the party groups as well as individual Members more generally. How this goal is achieved, however, once again varies depending on the legislative power of the EP, or the tools available to the groups.

If Hypothesis 4 is correct, we should expect to see a shift away from the type of polarized system described by Sartori toward a more bipartisan system, in which parties work together across ideological barriers to achieve viable legislative outcomes. We should expect this because cooperation rather than conflict became the most effective path to policy influence after the implementation of the SEA. This does not mean that ideology is no longer an important determinant of voting behavior after 1987; rather, it is mitigated by the pragmatic desire to impact EU policy outcomes (Kreppel, 2000b). This may be particularly true in the European setting because the fundamental issue of much legislation is often the level of integration, which tends to cut across traditional left–right ideological barriers.[15]

The Internal Development of the Party Groups

Although the macro and micro models of legislative development were not designed to explain the development of political parties within a legislature, they may serve as a valuable tool here as well. In fact, the basic theses of these models (that organizations respond to environmental shifts

---

[15] This should not be confused with the level of regulation, which, although related to integration, is not synonymous. See Kreppel and Tsebelis (1999) for a discussion of the interplay between the left–right and regulatory axis in the European context.

[macro] and that these responses will generally be to the benefit of those who are most able to manipulate the internal adjustment process [micro]) are implicit in many of the established works on political party development. In particular, studies of political parties that examine the process of transformation from cadre to mass-based (Duverger, 1954; Ostrogorski, 1964) and those that analyze the impact of shifting social cleavages (Lipset and Rokkan, 1967) make implicit use of the macro model of development. Other studies, which focus on the connections between parliamentary and party development (Cox, 1987) and legislative power and party power (Cox and McCubbins, 1993), implicitly invoke the micro model. I briefly discuss these previous studies of political party development, drawing out the implicit uses of the macro and micro models. I then explicitly apply the macro and micro models to the internal development of the party groups of the European Parliament. Finally, I outline some hypotheses of party group development predicted by the application of these models to the party groups of the European Parliament, and how I plan to test them.

Traditional Studies of Political Parties

In his classic *Political Parties*, Maurice Duverger charts the evolution of political parties from cadre to mass-based (Duverger, 1954).[16] The transformation from parties focused primarily on activity within the Parliament to parties that were able to effectively incorporate the new voting masses into their internal organizational structure was neither automatic nor simple. Duverger notes that political parties were forced to adapt to the introduction of universal suffrage (an environmental change), not only by broadening their electoral appeal to a much larger and more varied public, but also by creating internal organizational structures capable of incorporating and exploiting an expanding membership (pp. 62–71).

This shift of focus required a complete revision of the previous norm of small groups of loosely connected individuals working together without recourse to structured rules or internal hierarchies. As the membership and electorates of parties increased, they were forced to create more complex internal structures to organize themselves and their work. New

---

[16] It is an interesting historical note that Maurice Duverger was not only a Member of the EP, but was also the first MEP to be elected outside of his own country. He was elected to the EP on the Italian Communist slate.

strategies had to be adopted that incorporated and effectively utilized large numbers of new members anxious to participate fully in the electoral process. Those political parties that were able to adapt to, and even take advantage of, the new social environment were able to survive and flourish; others that were less flexible were doomed to political marginalization. In other words, parties that reacted strategically to the vast increase in the voting public by incorporating new members fully into the party were able to turn universal suffrage to their electoral benefit. Those parties that maintained their previous behavioral norms, or which were simply unable to evolve, were generally punished in the electoral sphere.[17]

The macro model is easily perceived in Duverger's description of party transformation since the historical metamorphosis of political parties was clearly connected to an environmental change: the introduction of universal suffrage. A theoretical understanding of the precise manner in which political parties reacted to this specific external change is less important for our purposes than the fact that some adaptation was needed and pursued. The micro model is also present to the extent that the reforms pursued by the parties were aimed at maximizing their electoral potential through the organization of the newly created voting masses.

In a similar way, the work by Seymour Lipset and Stein Rokkan on the role of social cleavages in determining the nature of a party system also implicitly relies on the macro model of development (Lipset and Rokkan, 1967). Their basic model of party system development relies on the notion of social cleavages, which divide society and serve as the building blocks of political party formation. By determining what the primary dividing lines in society are, it is possible to understand the character and breadth of a society's party system. As social cleavages shift and new social, economic, and religious divisions become paramount in society two changes are possible within the party system: Either new political parties are born that correspond to the social groups defined by the emerging cleavage, or the established parties expand and adapt in an attempt to incorporate the new social division. In either case, the implicit theory is once again based on the general macro model that broad environmental changes force transformations within the party system as a whole as well as the individual political parties.

---

[17] This analysis assumes that (re-)election is a (if not the) primary goal of all parties (cadre or mass) since election is a prerequisite of political power and the ability to achieve political/policy goals.

The rational actor aspect of the Lipset and Rokkan model of party system development and change is less obvious but nonetheless present. As new issues emerge, which divide society in a manner not consistent with the existing political landscape, the ability of established parties to incorporate them into their agenda becomes crucial. When a new social cleavage merely adds a dimension to the political debate (environmental issues), as opposed to dividing existing parties (slavery in the United States, and to a lesser extent EU membership in Britain) there is a fair amount of room for strategic action on the part of existing parties. If existing parties can co-opt newly salient issue areas, they will be able to block the establishment of a new party and protect their own membership.[18] The birth of a new political party catering specifically to an emerging political/social cleavage that is either ignored or deeply divides the traditional parties is likely to cost existing parties electoral support, sometimes to the point of near extinction and replacement by the new party.[19]

Thus, the micro model suggests that those parties that can co-opt new issues and prevent emerging parties will do so to avoid a potentially fatal loss of electoral support. Unfortunately, although useful because of the implicit invocation of the micro model, the focus of this work, like Duverger's, is on the electoral arena. Although interesting in a broader sense, theories of electoral strategy are largely inapplicable to the EP for the reasons given earlier. The micro or rational choice model of organizational development suggests that political parties should respond strategically to the new political environment *where possible*. This response can be in terms of both their external and internal actions. Because the electoral arena is not particularly relevant to the supranational party groups of the EP, the focus of their reform is likely to be internally oriented, and thus is not covered directly by either of these works.

There are numerous other studies of political party and party system development (Michels, 1962; Ostrogorski, 1964), almost all of which incorporate the macro and/or micro models of development to some extent, although in most cases the arguments are made implicitly rather

[18] A recent example is the emergence of Green parties across Western Europe. In many countries, as soon as Green parties began to win substantial electoral support the established parties attempted to incorporate "green" issues into their own platforms to avoid losing members and electoral support.

[19] The classic example is the Labour Party's rise to power in the United Kingdom at the cost of the Liberal party's historic dominance, largely as a result of the former incorporating the working masses into an effective political party.

than explicitly, and most often reference is to the electoral activities of parties rather than to their internal development. There is at least one notable to exception to this.

In his book, *The Efficient Secret*, Gary Cox makes explicit use of both models of party development (although he does not label them macro and micro) in reference to the internal development of British political parties (Cox, 1987). This work examines how an environmental change (increased legislative load) led to the centralization of power in the executive and the resultant impact on the evolution of the political parties. The emergence of strong, highly disciplined political parties is explained through an analysis of the interaction between party rank-and-file and party elite in the government. As the executive increased its control over the initiation of legislation (under the guise of increased efficiency) rank-and-file party members were forced to bargain with party leadership to get their own bills on the agenda and successfully through the Parliament. The result was a strengthening of the party elite with respect to rank-and-file membership. The book makes clear, however, that the decision of the party elite to restrict the ability of rank-and-file members to present proposals was a strategic maneuver to strengthen party discipline thinly veiled as an attempt to increase efficiency (Cox, 1987: 45–67). Thus, we have an external change (increased legislative load) leading to the internal development of the parties, as predicted by the macro model, and the type of strategic internal response by the party elite predicted by the micro model.

The Macro Model Applied

As was the case for the EP itself, the explicit application of the macro and micro models of development to the internal evolution of the party groups requires some adaptation to the specific situation within the EP. Their application will be useful, however, in that they will help us to predict what type of internal development we should expect the party groups to experience, and when.

The macro model is once again the easier model to apply because of its focus on the effects of environmental shifts, which are not linked to the original American context of the theory. The four critical moments in the development of the European Parliament outlined in Chapter 2 can be used here as well. The impact of these four historical events on the internal development of the groups may be significantly different for the groups than it was for the EP as a whole. While the substantial increases in legislative authority that arose from the Single European Act and Maastricht were of primary importance for the EP, the introduction of direct elections probably caused more fundamental transformations within the party groups. Direct elections not only more than doubled the membership of the EP, they also greatly increased the heterogeneity of the groups because it was no longer necessary that MEPs also be members of the governing coalition within their national legislatures. The result was not only an increase in the total number of party groups, but also an increase in the number of national party delegations represented within each group. In addition, the significant increase in the size of the groups required different organizational structures than the collegial pre-election party groups had used.

An application of the macro model to the internal development of the party groups leads to hypotheses that are very similar to those discussed in Chapter 2 in reference to the development of the EP as a whole. As in that case, these hypotheses can be tested by a simple chronological comparison between the timing of the critical moments and the internal development of the groups. We should expect that the internal evolution of the groups will be influenced by large external changes, in particular, the introduction of direct elections, which, in a sense, is very similar to the introduction of universal suffrage discussed by Duverger.

- *Hypothesis 5*: Developments in the internal organization and structure of the party groups should follow chronologically large changes to the role and responsibilities of the legislature within the larger political environment.
- *Hypothesis 5a*: Changes to the internal organization and structures of the party groups should be related to and address the environmental modifications that necessitated them.

As was the case in our discussion of the development of the EP as a whole, the macro model is useful in understanding the development of the political party groups only in so far as it helps to predict *when* changes will occur. The model is largely silent about what type of development we should expect beyond noting that internal changes should address the environmental events that inspired them. To gain a better understanding of what types of internal reforms will be pursued by the party groups it is necessary to use the micro, or strategic, model of development.

The Micro Model Applied

Political parties have many potential goals, depending on the limitations imposed by their political surroundings. It is generally assumed that parties want to attain power and control of the government. In a democratic system it is assumed that, once in power, parties will pursue the policy objectives they espoused during elections. In this sense the final objective is not power per se but control over legislative outcomes that most interests parties. The level of power accessible to the parties will influence their actions as they pursue this goal. Despite the unique supranational and indirect nature of the European party groups, the same general tenets should hold true for them as well.

The supranational party groups are marginal actors in the electoral arena and have only limited control over the executive.[20] As a result, the primary arena for organized party group action in the EU is within the European Parliament. This is the only direct access that the supranational political groups have to EU legislation and their only avenue of influence over policy outcomes.[21] As a result, changes in the power and influence of the EP in the legislative process are likely to affect the activity and internal organization of the party groups to some extent.

While some of the traditional goals of political parties, such as interest aggregation and linkage, are tenuous in the case of the party groups due to their indirect nature, the goal of achieving policy objectives is both present and fundamental. An additional objective is the attainment of relative power within the EP itself to the extent that this aids in the achievement of policy goals.[22] In effect, these are the only goals applicable to the

---

[20] The party groups do present supranational manifestos during EP elections. In addition, many groups participate in international and European party organizations such as the Socialist International. In both cases, the level of activity is minor compared to what occurs within the European Parliament. Control over the executive is limited to a vote of censure for the entire Commission.

[21] Robert Ladrech (1997) suggests that recently there has been a growing tendency to try and coordinate the actions of some of the party groups in the EP (particularly the EPP and the PES) and like-minded members of the Commission (and occasionally even the Council). To the extent that this is effective it would represent another opportunity for party groups to influence policy in the EU. It might also represent a foothold for the supranational party organizations outside the EP to get involved.

[22] Power within the legislature is often cited as a potential goal of legislators, although this is frequently indirectly connected to the primary goal of re-election (Mayhew, 1974).

party groups since they cannot attain power outside the EP and have little opportunity to serve as direct links between the masses and the government (being distant from both). Given these two potential goals and the assumptions of the micro model, how is the internal development and organization of the party groups likely to change as the EP gains influence over legislative outcomes?

When the EP was without direct legislative power and unable to effectively influence policy outcomes, the party groups had little need or desire to exert strict control over their membership. When the actions of Members and even the EP itself had only marginal influence over policy outcomes, there would have been little interest in strict party control over rank-and-file Member actions. Thus, during the years before the EP gained direct influence over legislative outcomes the internal structure of the party groups should have been relatively amorphous, with weak constraints over Member behavior. This would have been particularly true prior to direct elections.

There are several reasons to expect this to change once the EP gained significant legislative authority. First, the ability of the EP as an institution to affect policy outcomes meant that the party groups now had access to legislative influence. The potential to achieve policy goals is likely to have galvanized the party groups and made internal cohesion and coordination far more important. Second, internal competition for positions of authority within the EP became much more intense over time. Although EP membership more than quadrupled (from 142 to 626 between 1958 and 1995) the number of internal posts remained close to constant. The number of EP vice presidents increased from eight to fourteen and committee chairmanships have increased from thirteen to twenty.[23] The result is a much higher level of internal competition for these positions. As a partial offset, the number of *Rapporteurships* has increased steadily over time as a result of the increasing legislative load of the EP due to the new cooperation and codecision procedures (Corbett et al., 1995: 211).

The allocation of all of these positions, as we shall see, is far from simple. The bulk of studies of the European Parliament state that these positions are distributed amongst the groups on the basis of size using the d'Hondt method of proportional distribution (Westlake, 1994; Corbett

---

[23] In addition there are a number of subcommittees, and there have been a few temporary committees since 1994.

et al., 1995). This suggests that the party elite are able to select amongst their membership who should get a given position. The RoP of the EP pertaining to the EP hierarchy state only that:

The President, Vice Presidents, and Quaestors shall be elected by secret ballot in accordance with the provisions of Rule 136. Nominations shall be with consent. They may only be made by a political group or by at least thirty-two Members.

In the Election of the President, Vice Presidents, and Quaestors, account should be taken of the need to ensure an overall fair representation of Member States and political views (Rule 13, 1999).

Thus they imply that the groups make nominations, with attention to the fair representation of their national delegations. In practice, at least since 1989, who will fill the post of president, and generally the vice presidents as well, is decided ahead of time by the two largest groups (Westlake, 1994: 186–187).[24]

As far as committee chairmanships are concerned the official Rules of Procedure call for these positions to be decided through elections within the committees themselves:

At the first committee meeting after the election of committee members pursuant to Rule 152, the committee shall elect a bureau consisting of a chairman and one, two or three vice chairmen who shall be elected in separate ballots (Rule 157, 1999).

In reality, however, here too there is generally an agreement reached ahead of time within the Conference of Presidents, and the actual election process within the committees is for appearances sake only.[25]

Apparent party group control (through the Conference of Presidents) over the distribution of internal EP and committee leadership positions means that the group leaders had the potential power, as well as the incentives, to increase internal group discipline and organization as the legislative power of the EP grew. An application of the micro model to internal party group development leads to the following hypotheses:

---

[24] This practice was officially ended in July 1999, when the EPP and the Liberal group formed a coalition against the PES and agreed to rotate the presidency between them, excluding the Socialists.

[25] For example, in 1994 an agreement in the Conference of Presidents between the group leaders called for a member of the Forza Europa to become chair of the Energy Committee. When the committee met as called for in the rules it elected a Socialist member instead. Socialist members of the committee were chastised, the elected member withdrew his candidacy, and the Forza Europa candidate was later duly elected.

- *Hypothesis 6*: When the Parliament is without legislative authority or the ability to impact policy outcomes there will be little incentive for the political party leaders to organize and discipline their members.
- *Hypothesis 6a*: Once the Parliament obtains legislative authority and influence the political party elite will have greater incentives to discipline their Members and attain internal cohesion. Internal organizational structures that regulate Member activity and the development and use of benefits and sanctions against Members will increase.

Testing the Models

Although the previous literature on the development of political parties are not directly applicable to the internal development of the supranational party groups in the EP (with the partial exception of the work by Cox), they do serve as useful indicators of what sort of evolution we should expect. The application of the macro and micro models helped to narrow these expectations into specific predictions based on an understanding of the particular political realities of the European Parliament. Unfortunately, testing these predictions is extremely difficult, because of the lack of consistent historical information about even the largest of the party groups. In the absence of an ability to pursue rigorous analytical testing, much of the analysis will be based on a series of interviews conducted with both Members of the European Parliament and the staff of the group secretariats.[26]

The Macro Model Tested

The macro model predicts only that internal developments will follow from and be a response to external environmental changes. The same critical moments that were crucial in the development of the Parliament as a whole should also be key in the internal evolution of the party groups. In particular, the introduction of direct elections will effect the party groups because of the dramatic expansion of the groups that followed in terms of both size and diversity. Increases in the legislative authority of the EP will

---

[26] A total of over sixty interviews were conducted between February–May 1996, November–December 1996, and March 1998. In all cases the anonymity of the interviewee was guaranteed.

also be significant, because of the increased need for internal party discipline and group cohesion (voting requirements). The desire for internal group unity was most likely also enhanced by the increased ability of the EP to impact legislative outcomes.

To test the predictions of the macro model I examine the available versions of the party group rules of the two largest groups, the Party of European Socialist (PES) and the European Peoples' Party (EPP). Both of these groups have existed consistently since the creation of the EP (albeit with several name changes over time). I was not able to compile a complete set of Rules for both groups, in particular, neither group secretariat had copies of any group rules dating before 1975. For the EPP group I have all versions of the Rules since 1975, and for the Socialist group I have the 1977, 1986, 1989, 1991, and 1996 versions.[27]

Within the rules of each group I look for examples of significant internal development, in particular, the expansion and formalization of the group's internal organizational structure through the creation of new internal posts (treasurer, whip etc.) and the formalization of previous norms through their incorporation into the rules. By comparing the development of the internal rules of the groups with the external evolution of the EP as a whole, the influence of the "critical moments" of EP development can be examined. Since my data-set does not include any Rules prior to 1970, the effect of the acquisition of partial control over the budget cannot be analyzed. The other three critical moments are all included.

The Micro Model Tested

The micro model is much more difficult to test. In effect, if Hypotheses 6 and 6a are correct, we should expect to see the group elite attempting to restrict the activities of individual Members more and more frequently. This can be done through the manipulation of the group's Rules, but also through the rules of the EP as a whole. Additionally, there is the possibility that Members are not coerced by any formal rules, but instead by informal norms. In the latter case it is difficult to definitively connect restrictions on individual Member activities to a concerted effort on the part of the group elite to control their rank-and-file Members.

---

[27] It is not clear how many intermediary versions there may have been that are missing from my set.

In addition to looking at the internal Rules of the groups (which, as previously noted, are sparse) the use of benefits and sanctions to control group members can be analyzed. In the absence of an ability to directly impact an individual Member's chances of re-election, it seems likely that group leaders would turn to the distribution of benefits and sanctions within the EP to influence Member behavior. In particular, the distribution of positions within the internal EP hierarchy (president, vice presidents, and quaestors), Committee leadership positions and *Rapporteurships* should reflect the party elite's satisfaction with its members. This follows the general understanding of the activities of American Congressional party leadership where direct control over re-election is similarly limited (Cox and McCubbins, 1993).

In this case, party group leaders should distribute positions to Members on the basis of whether or not an individual voted the party line consistently and, in the case of the EP, participated on a regular basis.[28] This is tested through a comparison of individual voting records and the distribution of benefits such as *Rapporteurships* under the cooperation and co-decision procedures between 1987 and 1996 and committee chairmanships between 1979 and 1996. If Hypotheses 6 and 6a are correct, we should see an increasing tendency to award those Members who consistently vote the party line and regularly attend the plenary with key positions within the EP. Because the analysis of roll-call votes cannot begin until after direct elections, this will be a test primarily of the impact of increased legislative power (through the addition of the cooperation and co-decision procedures).[29]

Conclusions

The development of the supranational party system and the party groups within the EP are both fundamental and interesting aspects of EP evolution; both, however, have remained largely ignored by the current literature on the EP. Traditional theories of party system and internal party development tend to focus on the electoral arena, which is largely

---

[28] Throughout my interviews group leaders consistently cited the poor attendance records of their members (not voting against the party line) as the biggest problem facing the groups and the EP as a whole.

[29] The analysis begins after 1979 because of the institution of electronic voting in 1980. Roll-call votes prior to 1980 were extremely rare and did not have the same function has they have had since. See Chapter 5 for a discussion of the strategic use of roll-call votes.

inapplicable to the EP supranational party groups. As a result, the macro and micro models of institutional development are modified and applied to analyze their evolution.

Voting records between 1980 and 1996 are used to study both the evolution of the party group system and to add some insight to the use of benefits and sanctions by group leaders to influence individual Member activity. The informal nature of many of the groups' operating procedures makes a large-scale, rigorous analytical study of the internal evolution of the party groups impossible. This problem is compounded by the unavailability of many of the groups' internal historical documents. However, an analysis of the internal Rules of the PES and EPP since 1975 is used to gain useful information about the internal development of these groups. Due to the lack of internal rules prior to 1975, only the impact of direct elections and the addition of the cooperation and co-decision procedures on the internal evolution of the party groups are examined.

The analysis of the party system also suffers from the problems of missing data since the analysis is based primarily on voting records since 1980. As a result, the impact of only the final two "critical moments" in the life of the EP on the party system are analyzed fully. Together, these analyses help to determine the extent to which the party system and the party groups of the EP have evolved over time, the influence that broad environmental changes have had on this process, and the applicability of the macro and micro models beyond the legislative sphere.

4

The History of the European Parliament

The position of the European Parliament (EP) within the broader European community has changed significantly over time. As the competencies and breadth of the European Communities, and then the European Union, expanded, the EP pressed for, and adapted to, increases in its powers. Before we explore the adaptive process of the EP it will be helpful to review the evolution of the EU as a whole and the changing role of the EP within it.

A full understanding of the history of the EP requires that we examine its immediate predecessor, the Common Assembly (CA) of the European Coal and Steel Community, and the political environment that led to the initial creation of the European Economic Community (EEC). Following this, the general history of the EP will be divided and discussed in four sections: the early years (1958–1969), which include the initial organization of the Parliament and the institutional role of the EP as established by the Treaties of Rome; the first period of development (1970–1978), during which the EP gained partial control over the budget and direct elections were established; the second period of development (1979–1986), when the first direct elections were held, the EP's power of delay was reinforced, and the Single European Act was created; and, finally, the most recent period of development (1987–1999), which includes the acquisition of true legislative power by the EP through the implementation and reform of the cooperation and co-decision procedures. I focus in particular on the political role of the EP and its relationship vis-à-vis the other Community institutions during each of these periods.

It is important to remember that other international assemblies that existed at the time that the Common Assembly (the EP's predecessor) was created were clearly not legislative bodies. Most had minimal powers of consultation and little else. They were organized along national rather than ideological lines and, more often than not, debated and discussed far more than they were able to accomplish. The Treaty of Paris, and later the Treaties of Rome, created a European Assembly that looked as if it would follow the same general model. Over the course of time, however, two crucial events occurred that dramatically changed the nature of the EP and the path of its institutional development: the creation of political party groups and the eventual acquisition of true, independent, legislative authority. The first occurred almost immediately; the second took thirty years. Together these two events have been the principal determinants of EP development and the transformation from consultative assembly to legislative body.

The Predecessor: The Common Assembly of the ECSC (1950–1957)

In the years immediately following the Second World War there were many "federalist" movements within Europe. The main goal of these burgeoning organizations was to somehow create common bonds between the countries of Europe, which would mitigate the return of nationalism and help prevent another war. Many early attempts at pan-European organization faltered and disappeared. Those that succeeded tended to become amorphous because of their attempts to include everyone and everything within a single blanket organization (The Council of Europe, The OECD). The narrow focus of the European Coal and Steel Community was a reaction to the perceived failure of many of the broader international organizations to bind the nations of Europe together.

The specific focus of the Coal and Steel Community originated out of the conflict between France and Germany over the Saar and Ruhr regions, which had been intensifying since the end of the war. In March of 1950, German Chancellor Konrad Adenauer made overtures toward France with the idea of linking France and Germany in a manner similar to the unsuccessful Anglo-French union of 1940. This solution was not well received in France, but it did spark the imagination of Jean Monnet, who was then Commissioner for the first French "National Plan." Monnet viewed the increasing tension between France and Germany over coal and steel production as detrimental to the economic and social well-being of both countries. As a result, he suggested to Robert Schuman, the Foreign Minister of France, a plan that would unite the coal and steel industries of

France and Germany and create an independent authority to govern coal and steel production. Monnet's plan was presented to Schuman and French Prime Minister Bidault on May 3, 1950; Schuman announced the plan publicly just six days later.

Originally, the plan included Britain in the common coal and steel pool; however, Britain's reticence over the creation of an "independent" supranational authority led it to retreat from the talks, which eventually led to the creation of the European Coal and Steel Community (ECSC). The new Community was extended beyond just France and Germany, however, through the inclusion of Italy, Belgium, the Netherlands, and Luxembourg.[1] The six governments hammered out the details of the new community throughout the summer of 1950 and spent another year ratifying the Treaty in their home legislatures. The European Coal and Steel Community was officially ratified in April of 1951 and came into existence in August 1952.

The institutional organization of the new Community was centered around the "High Authority," which was a truly supranational institution with significant controls over the production and distribution of Europe's coal and steel. To balance the power of the supranational High Authority, a nationally oriented Council of Ministers was added during the treaty negotiations. As an additional bulwark against supranational tyranny, a High Court was created to adjudicate in case of disputes or appeals by Members of the coal and steel industries. The Common Assembly of the Coal and Steel Community, although not mentioned by Schuman when he initially announced the project, had been part of Monnet's original plan. The Assembly was included primarily because the Council of Europe had a consultative Assembly and Monnet felt that the absence of a similar institution in the new coal and steel community would be detrimental to public acceptance of the new Community (Mayne, 1962, 1968; Monnet, 1978).

The Common Assembly (CA) was not, however, viewed as a viable counterbalance to the High Authority and, in fact, the Common Assembly received very little attention during the initial negotiations that created the ECSC. Despite its origins in Monnet's early draft proposal, the Common Assembly was mentioned in only ten of the over one hundred

---

[1] Monnet (1978) notes in his memoirs that the extension of the new Coal and Steel Community to other countries was a last minute addition.

articles of the ECSC Treaty (Articles 20–25, 38, 78, 94, and 95). As a result, the Common Assembly had very limited and ill-defined supervisory powers. It was an appointed body consisting of representatives selected from their national parliaments.[2] The CA had no direct legislative authority and could censure the High Authority only when the annual program was presented to it, and then only by a vote of 2/3 of its membership and an absolute majority of the votes cast. The overall weakness of the Common Assembly was partially mitigated by the close ties that it developed with the High Authority since both were "supranational" institutions and generally favorable toward increased integration between the Member States.

In spite of its weakness relative to the national parliaments of the Member States, the Common Assembly was fundamentally different than the other international assemblies of the time. It was the first to be legally guaranteed specific powers (such as the power of censure over the High Authority), even if these were extremely weak when compared to those of the national parliaments. It was also the first to organize itself on the basis of *ideological affinity*, as opposed to *national identity*. The election of the new Assembly's first president, during its constituent session, was decided along ideological and not national lines.[3] In June 1953, only six months after its inception, the Members of the new Common Assembly agreed to sit according to their ideological affinity rather than alphabetically or by national identity.[4] The internal development of the Assembly was furthered during its second meeting (in January 1953) by the creation of six internal committees, which roughly mirrored the organizational structure of the High Assembly.

Notwithstanding its political weakness compared to the High Authority and the Council, the Common Assembly began to look like the national

[2] The Paris Treaties allowed for Members of the Common Assembly to be directly elected but permitted each Member State to decide for themselves how their members would be chosen. In the end all of the Member States opted for appointing their representatives from within their own national legislature.

[3] The Belgian Socialist, Paul-Henri Spaak, declared that he would not run against the German Christian Democrat von Bretano unless *all* Socialist Members agreed to support his candidacy. In the end he won with the support of all of the Socialists, including the Germans, who were forced to vote against the German candidate.

[4] Members sat alphabetically in the Council of Europe and by nationality in the General Assembly of the United Nations.

parliaments that its Members were familiar with. By the end of its first year the Assembly could boast of three organized supranational political groups (Christian Democrats, Socialists, and Liberals) and an internal organizational structure that included an executive, a preliminary set of Rules of Procedure, an organizational Bureau, and six committees. The full potential of the Common Assembly will never be known because it existed for only five years before it was supplanted by the European Parliamentary Assembly of the newly formed European Economic Community and Euratom.

The Creation of the European Economic Community (1955–1958)

After two abortive attempts to expand the Coal and Steel Community into new arenas (the European Political Community and the European Defense Community), the further integration of Europe was successfully initiated by Belgium, The Netherlands, and Luxembourg through the "Benelux Memorandum" of May 18, 1955. The memorandum, drafted largely by Belgian Prime Minister and ex-president of the Common Assembly, Paul-Henri Spaak, called on the other countries of the Coal and Steel Community to join together and further European integration through the expansion of supranational cooperation. The memorandum declared that such a step was "indispensable for maintaining Europe's position in the world, for restoring its influence and prestige and for securing a constantly rising standard of living for its people" (Benelux Memorandum, point 1).

The memorandum called for cooperation in the fields of energy (with special attention paid to atomic energy), social policy, and, particularly, the economic arena beyond the coal and steel industries. The reaction of the other Member States was both positive and quick. By June 1955 the foreign ministers of all six Member States were able to adopt a resolution calling for the further integration of Europe ("Resolution Adopted at Messina by the Foreign Ministers of the Member States of the ECSC"). The resolution called for the six Member States of the Coal and Steel Community to meet and draft a new treaty with the goal of broad European cooperation in the economic, atomic, and social arenas. The intergovernmental discussions were led by Spaak and eventually resulted in the adoption of two separate treaties. One treaty dealt with increased economic integration between the Member States and the creation of an internal free market (the EEC Treaty), and the other focused on atomic energy and its development and peaceful use within Europe (the Euratom Treaty).[5]

The decision to create two distinct organizations arose out of the preferences of the various Member States. France, in particular, was interested in an atomic energy community but was initially quite opposed to an economic community. Germany's preferences were the exact opposite. In the end both communities were established as a compromise. On March 25, 1957, the six Member States signed the final Treaties establishing the European Economic Community and Euratom. These two new communities joined the previous Coal and Steel Community to form the European Communities, although their institutional organization was significantly different from that of their predecessor.

Within the Coal and Steel Community the High Authority reigned supreme. It was an extremely powerful supranational body, which the nationally oriented Council could only restrain, not control. Much care was taken during the creation of the two new communities to reverse the balance of power. While the High Authority officially remained for the Coal and Steel Community, a new Commission was created for each of the new Communities. The Commissions, while still supranational, were less autonomous than the High Authority, with the intergovernmental Councils holding much more relative power. Until 1967 there were, in fact, three separate Councils and Commissions, one for each community.[6] When the new communities were added it was decided to create a single Assembly and a single European Court of Justice (ECJ) for all three communities.[7] Thus, the previous Common Assembly of the Coal and Steel Community was dissolved and a new, enlarged (from 78 to 142 Members) "European Parliamentary Assembly" was established.[8]

---

[5] The specific call for integration in the arena of social policy was largely lost in the shuffle, although there were aspects of social policy integrated into the EEC Treaty.

[6] In 1965, a merger treaty was passed that unified the six separate institutions into one Commission and one Council, with the Commission still retaining the previous powers of the High Authority in regard to matters related to coal and steel. The Treaty was not fully implemented until 1967.

[7] The Common Assembly pressed for a single parliamentary body, believing that this would increase its relative power within the Communities.

[8] The official name for the European Parliament was European Parliamentary Assembly, although it was referred to throughout the Rome Treaties as "the Assembly." In 1962, the Parliament changed its name to the European Parliament. This was not officially recognized by the other institutions until the Single European Act, which was the first official document to refer to the Parliament by that name. I use "European Parliament" or EP throughout unless referring to the previous Common Assembly.

The new European Parliament (EP) was by no means, however, a wholly new or original institution. The EP met for the first time on March 19, 1958, only twenty days after the last session of the Common Assembly. Over one-third of the Members of the new Parliament had also been Members of the Common Assembly.[9] The first president of the new Parliament was Robert Schuman, a veteran of European affairs and an original proponent of the Coal and Steel Community. The provisional Rules of Procedure for the new Parliament were the previous Rules of the Common Assembly, all of which led to a very smooth transition and a rapid process of initial internal organization. This said, however, the new parliament was significantly different from the previous Common Assembly in several important ways.

The most significant difference between the old Common Assembly and the new European Parliament was that while Members of the Common Assembly *could* be elected directly, the new Treaties *required* that the Members of the European Parliament be elected directly. The new Treaty called on the EP to draft a plan for universal direct elections [EEC Treaty Article 138(3) and Euratom Treaty Article 108(3). Article 21 of the ECSC Treaty was also amended accordingly]. An additional increase in the political authority of the newly established European Parliament was that its power of censure over the Commission (previously the High Authority) was no longer limited to the annual report. The EP could now move to censure the executive at any time, over any issue, although the previous voting requirements were still in force.[10] Both of the new Treaties also formally included the new Parliament in the legislative process, albeit tangentially, by including a consultation procedure for some policy areas. For legislation falling under a few specific articles the Council was required by the Treaties to consult the Parliament and get its opinion. However, there was no requirement that the Council act on the European Parliament's suggestions, and in most cases the consultation process was little more than empty symbolism (see Figure 4.1).[11]

---

[9] Fifty of the 142 Members had served in the previous Common Assembly.

[10] Neither the European Parliament nor the previous Common Assembly has ever successfully called for the censure of the Commission, although several attempts have been made. The closest thing to a successful vote of censure occurred in 1999, when the entire Santer Commission resigned after allegations of widespread mismanagement (made largely by the European Parliament) led to threats of a censure vote that looked like it might be successful.

[11] In fact, the Council often made its final decision before the EP had issued an opinion, thus negating the Parliament's role altogether. The Court of Justice ruled in 1980

Figure 4.1   Consultation Procedure (January 1958–Present)

All things considered, the new European Parliament was a step forward compared to the previous Common Assembly, but not as big a step as had been hoped for. During the two years between the Benelux memorandum and the final ratification of the Rome Treaties, the Members of the Common Assembly, together with those more supportive of the federalist ideal, had lobbied hard to increase the role and responsibilities of the new legislature. The goal had been a new European Parliament modeled after the national parliaments of the Member States. The reality fell far short of this ideal. The powers of the EP, while greater than those of the Common Assembly, were still minute when compared to those of the Council and Commission. In 1958, the Members of the new European

(Isoglucose case 138/79 and 139/79) that this was not permissible and required that in all cases where consultation is required by the Treaties the Council must wait for the EP's opinion before making final decisions. This is discussed further below.

Parliament were still appointed by their national parliaments, had no direct influence over legislative output, and had no control over the limited budget of the new Communities. The new Parliament spent the first ten years of its existence battling fruitlessly against this situation.

The Early Years (1958–1968)

The ten years following the Rome Treaties were difficult for the new European Community as a whole. The full implementation of the Treaties was to occur in three stages, with the final stage beginning in 1966. As it happened, full implementation was effectively blocked until the Single European Act (SEA) approximately twenty years later. These years were particularly frustrating for the European Parliament, which had hoped to quickly move beyond the meager powers allocated to it in the Treaties. In the end, the Parliament was largely unsuccessful during its first decade.

One of the first goals of the new Parliament was the fulfillment of the Treaty's call for the direct election of its Members. To achieve this end the European Parliament drafted its first proposal on direct elections (the Dehousse Report) in May 1961. The report outlined a common uniform electoral procedure for all six Member States and a schedule for implementation. The Council largely ignored this proposal, as well as the two that followed in 1963 and 1969. Thus, while the European Parliament responded to the Treaties' requirement that the Assembly "draw up proposals for election by direct universal suffrage in accordance with a uniform electoral procedure in all Member States," the Council failed to act unanimously to "lay down the appropriate procedures" and "recommend them to the Member States for adoption in accordance with their respective constitutional requirements" (Article 138 Treaty of Rome). In fact, there was very little action on the part of the Council to fulfill the Treaty requirements.

Stymied as regards their direct election, Members of the European Parliament attempted to improve their relative institutional position through increased internal organization and informal extensions of the few powers granted to the Assembly in the Treaties. Internally, the Parliament formalized many of the previous norms of the Common Assembly. It incorporated the party groups formally into the rules and began to use the groups as a basis of internal organization. As a part of its internal push for an increased role in the Community the EP incorporated into its Rules of Procedure several powers not officially granted to it by the Treaties. In particular, the Parliament called on the president of the Commission to present an annual program formally to the Parliament to garner its approval and requested that the Council respond to parliamentary questions and report to the EP regularly on Community activities.

Throughout these early years the Parliament attempted to use the consultative powers granted to it by the Treaties in the most extensive way possible. Since the Treaties allowed the Commission to incorporate the Parliament's suggestions (Article 149(2)) into its proposals, the parliament began in the early 1960s to request that the Commission do so on a regular basis. In 1964, the Parliament formally requested that the Commission report on its adoption of recommended changes and explain any failure to incorporate the Parliament's suggestions. In a resolution passed in October 1966, the Parliament further decided that it would formally request that the Commission incorporate its proposed changes to proposals in the final Commission text according to Art. 149(2) and, in the case of especially important legislation, arranged for the appropriate committee to follow up and determine the final action of the Commission.

The Parliament also tried to increase its authority and influence within the Community by publicly redefining itself. In March 1962, the Parliament passed a resolution to formally rename the "Assembly" of the Treaties the "European Parliament." Although the resolution passed with a large majority within the Parliament itself, the name change was largely ignored by the other institutions of the European Communities. Within the media the name change was more successful and in time the Assembly came to be referred to as the European Parliament in all but the most official documents. It was not until the Single European Act, nearly twenty-five years later, that the Council officially recognized the Parliament's name change.

Throughout the first decade of its life the new European Parliament was largely unsuccessful in its quest for increased power and legislative authority. This was particularly frustrating because the dual mandate prior to direct elections meant that Members all had experience within their national parliaments. While there was some variation in the relative power of the national parliaments of the six Member States, all were significantly more influential than the European Parliament. This meant that all Members of the EP understood their relative weakness and inability to impact directly the development of the new European Community as a whole. The constant battle for more influence suffered in particular from the return to power of General Charles de Gaulle in France.

Although the original concept of an integrated Europe was introduced and initiated by two French men (Monnet and Schuman), France was in no way completely unified behind a supranational Europe. In fact, it was the French National Assembly that had defeated the proposed European Defense Community in 1953 (despite it also being a French proposal). When General de Gaulle returned to power in 1958 he was strongly opposed to an overtly supranational European Community. From the outset he strongly distrusted the very pro-federalist president of the Commission, the German Walter Hallstein, and this distrust only grew over time (de Gaulle, 1971: 148). Although de Gaulle had come to power after the ratification of the Rome Treaties, he successfully stymied their full implementation for twenty years.

The first attempt to mitigate the supranational aspects of the Treaties was launched by de Gaulle in a 1960 press conference when he declared that "the rebuilding of Europe – that is, its unification – is clearly essential." But also that it was necessary to be "guided by realities" and the reality was that "the pillar upon which Europe can be built are in fact, the States" (Press Conference, September 5, 1960). The eventual result of de Gaulle's declaration was the formation of a committee made up of six representatives of the Member States with the express task of creating a proposal for formalized political (and social) cooperation between the six Member States. This committee came to be known as the Fouchet Committee, after its chair, Christian Fouchet, the French ambassador to Denmark.

Initially there was a fair amount of support for the new initiative by both the Parliament and the Member States. As the new proposal developed, however, the smaller states, and the Netherlands in particular, began to fear Franco-German hegemony and suspect de Gaulle of trying to supplant the Rome Treaties. The result was a compromise proposal that departed significantly from de Gaulle's original plan. As a result, de Gaulle felt that the French delegation had made too many concessions and took it upon himself to rewrite the plan, disregarding many of the compromises that had been so meticulously constructed during the previous months. The new plan, labeled Fouchet II, was a severe disappointment to the other members of the Community, who felt that they had been betrayed by France and, in particular, by de Gaulle.

The result was predictable: The other members of the Council refused to accept the Fouchet II plan and instead tabled a new plan independently of France in 1962. By this time, however, momentum had been lost and nothing came of the new plan. Not to be dissuaded, de Gaulle also presented a new plan for multilateral cooperation between just France, Italy, and Germany (the "big three"). Italy, however, decided against joining for fear of upsetting the Benelux countries. The result was the 1963 Franco-German Treaty of Friendship and Reconciliation, which institutionalized the previous *rapprochement* between France and Germany.

Throughout this period the Parliament tried to influence and support increased supranational cooperation. In 1961, the EP passed a resolution in support of the proposed Fouchet Committee and declared "its readiness to place its experience at the disposal of the Governments of Member States in the search for the best means of achieving real and complete political unity" (Battista Report, Doc. 62, 1961). Needless to say, neither the Fouchet Committee nor the individual Member States took the Parliament up on its generous offer. In fact, de Gaulle was vehemently opposed to precisely the Parliament's interpretation of the Fouchet project as an attempt to increase "political unity." From the beginning de Gaulle's goal had been to limit supranationalism and (some felt), in particular, to prevent the implementation of the final stage of European integration outlined in the Rome Treaties, which required the implementation of majority voting in the Council (Spaak, 1967: 14; Monnet, 1978: 482–483). De Gaulle definitively achieved this goal in 1966 with the Luxembourg Compromise, which essentially continued the previous unanimity requirement in the Council if a Member State declared that it had a "vital national interest" at stake.[12]

The Luxembourg Compromise originated out of a dispute between de Gaulle and Commission President Hallstein. In an attempt to finance the growing Common Agricultural Policy, the Commission proposed that the Community make the transition to "own finances" three years ahead of schedule in 1967, rather than 1970.[13] The Commission proposal not only called for the Member States to give up their export levies early; it also shifted budgetary control to the Commission and European Parliament. To make matters worse, Hallstein presented his plan to the European Parliament before the Council. The result was immediate. De Gaulle

---

[12] For a more detailed discussion of the Luxembourg Compromise and its strategic significance, see Tsebelis and Kreppel (1998).

[13] Previously the Community had been funded solely by Member State contributions. Beginning in 1970, a series of agricultural levies were to be the basis of "own finances," which would form the basis of a community budget.

decried the usurpation of power by the Commission and Hallstein in particular. The other Member States did not immediately support de Gaulle's position or reject outright the Commission's proposal. The crisis came to a head once the deadline for an agreement on the funding of the Common Agricultural Policy (CAP) had passed without successful compromise between France and the other Member States. On July 1, 1965, de Gaulle recalled the French representative and boycotted all Council meetings initiating the "empty chair" crisis.

The other Member States continued to function as best as they could without France, but little could be achieved without French participation. In a desperate attempt to put an end to the crisis and convince France to rejoin the Community a compromise was reached at the January 28–29, 1966, Council meeting. The other five Member States agreed to an interim financing of the CAP, which did not call for "own resources" and a concomitant increase in the power of the Commission and Parliament. More importantly, the Member States "agreed to disagree" and, after restating their support for qualified majority voting and the full implementation of the treaties, agreed to the Luxembourg Compromise.

During the Luxembourg Council meeting the remaining five Member States called for every attempt to be made when important national issues were at stake to reach a compromise acceptable to all Members within a reasonable amount of time. This implied that when unanimity was not possible, decision would be taken by majority vote. The French delegation, however, stated that "when very important issues are at stake, discussions must be continued until unanimous agreement is reached." The Compromise between the Five and France stated that "the six delegations note that there is a divergence of views on what should be done in the event of a failure to reach complete agreement. However they consider that this divergence does not prevent the Community's work being resumed in accordance with the normal procedure" (*Compromis de Luxembourg* Bull. 3/66, author's translation from the original French).

The impact of the Luxembourg Compromise was vast. The Treaties were to be fully implemented beginning January 1, 1966. This meant qualified majority voting in the Council in most areas. This was *never* implemented because of the French boycott. By agreeing to the Luxembourg Compromise the other Member States effectively agreed to abide by unanimous decision making in the Council in spite of the Rome Treaties. The full impact of this was not discovered until the Single

European Act re-instituted the Treaty and opened the door to qualified majority voting.

The French boycott of the Council included a clear indication of de Gaulle's position on the relative power and political role of the EP as well. One of the primary French arguments against the Commission's plan had been the increase in parliamentary power that would result from partial control over the budget. Despite all of its efforts throughout its first ten years, the European Parliament was unable to improve either its position relative to the other EEC institutions or its reputation as a responsible political actor. Although the Parliament did its best to organize itself along the lines of the national parliaments, its appointed nature and limited powers kept it from being perceived as an effective legislature. Despite these setbacks, the Parliament continued to press for greater powers and the implementation of direct elections as provided for in the treaties. During the 1970s the Parliament was much more successful. Although the EP still failed to achieve its ultimate goal of significant legislative influence, it did make numerous steps forward in the 1970s, including direct elections and partial budgetary authority.

The First Period of Development (1969–1978)

The early 1970s were a period of renewed hope and excitement in the European Communities. The departure of de Gaulle from the political scene opened the door to both the enlargement of the Community and the completion of its institutions as foreseen by the Rome Treaties.[14] The first significant action of de Gaulle's successor, Georges Pompidou, was to call for a summit of the national leaders of the Member States to begin to chart out the future of Europe. The Hague Summit of 1969 was made famous by Pompidou's concluding speech, in which he called for the "completion, deepening, and enlargement" of the European Community. Specifically he called for the full enactment of the Treaties, which had been effectively postponed by the Luxembourg Compromise. This meant not only the introduction of majority voting in the Council, but also the eventual introduction of direct elections for the European Parliament.

Unfortunately, although the decade began auspiciously, changes in national governments, several international events, and widespread

---

[14] De Gaulle had vetoed British entry into the Community twice (1963 and 1967), much to the dismay of the other five Member States.

economic hardship severely restricted the extent to which Pompidou's call to action was implemented. Despite the "eurosclerosis" of the mid-seventies, however, the European Parliament was able to achieve two of its primary goals: partial control over the budgetary process and the direct election of its Members. The first arose directly from the 1969 Summit; the agreement to hold direct elections did not occur for another five years, despite the active support of German Chancellor Willy Brandt during the Hague Summit.

The first clear result of the Hague Summit was an agreement to resolve the community's dilemma over the CAP through self-financing. The same dilemma that had previously led to the French boycott was this time easily resolved with the creation of a plan that was not very dissimilar from that espoused by Hallstein five years earlier. The community was to have its "own resources" collected from national levies on agricultural products and duties on industrial goods imported into the Community. In addition, a national contribution of not more than 1% of revenues from the Community-wide Value Added Tax (VAT) was to be contributed to the Community's coffers. The new budgetary process provided a moderate role for the European Parliament while still maintaining the dominance of the Council.

The budget of the Community was broken down into two sections: compulsory and noncompulsory spending. The former consisted primarily of the CAP, which also accounted for roughly 90% of the Community's budget during this period. Compulsory spending was defined as that which arose directly from legislation already in effect. The Parliament had little or no control or impact over this portion of the budget. Instead, the Parliament was given partial control over the remaining "noncompulsory" portions of the budget as well as the ability to increase or decrease the overall budget within certain restricted margins. The Budget Act was adopted by the Council in September 1970 and quickly ratified by all of the Member States. The new Budget Act was not to be implemented until 1975, and by then an additional set of rules and amendments were adopted that also granted the Parliament the power of discharge and added a "conciliation procedure" for future bills with significant financial impact.[15]

[15] See in particular resolutions 2 and 3 annexed to the Treaty of 22 April 1970 and the Joint Declaration of 4 March 1975 on the conciliation procedure. The budgetary process is incorporated into Articles 199–209, EEC Treaty.

The revised Budget Act also added the requirement that the President of the Parliament sign the budget for it to be officially adopted.[16]

President de Gaulle's retreat from the political scene also opened the door to British entry into the Community. Although Britain had rejected the offer to join the Community when it was first created in 1958, it had made two attempts to join during the 1960s that had both been vetoed by de Gaulle. The door to Community enlargement was opened by Pompidou during the Hague Summit, despite his previous support of de Gaulle's veto. This was due, in part, to the dramatic shift in France's economic circumstances during the late sixties, and in part to the movement of the new German Chancellor, Willy Brandt, toward the East with the introduction of his *ostpolitik* policy. Brandt wished to open political dialogue with the East and, in particular, East Germany. Fearing not only German economic hegemony but also a steady drift towards the East, Pompidou and others supported the entry of Britain into the Community as a possible counterbalance.

Unfortunately, British entry was not viewed favorably by many within its borders. Both the Labor and Conservative Parties were torn over the question of entry into the EEC. Entry negotiations began in June 1970, when the Conservatives, led by Heath, were in office. However, by the time that British entry was official on January 1, 1973, the Conservative government was in deep trouble and in 1974 the Labour Party, led by Wilson, came to power and forced the re-negotiation of British entry. The re-negotiation was extremely contentious. It lasted nearly eleven months and focused primarily on Britain's budget contribution and its relationship with the Commonwealth. An eventual resolution was reached that included special arrangements for British trade with the Commonwealth and a budget "correcting mechanism" that was intended to insure that no Member paid too much into the Community budget. Immediately following this agreement Wilson called for an exceptional national referendum to decide whether the United Kingdom would remain within the EEC. Although the results of the referendum supported continued membership, Britain's role within the Community has remained largely contentious.

---

[16] This increased the power of the EP, although it was mitigated by a provision that called for the funding of all compulsory expenditures on a monthly basis based on the previous year's budget until a new budget could be agreed to if the president failed to sign.

British entry may have been the most difficult, but it was not the only country to join the EEC during this period. Norway, Ireland, and Denmark all went through the negotiation process at the same time. Norway eventually decided not to join (after a national referendum barely rejected entry), but the other two countries joined, resulting in a Community of nine instead of six. For the European Parliament this meant an increase in the number of Members from 142 to 198 as well as the addition of two more languages (Gaelic was not considered an official Community language). Most importantly, however, British entry meant the incorporation of a very distinct parliamentary tradition into the general *melange* of continental parliamentary experience. Almost immediately the British contingent made itself felt through the addition of a formal "question time" and nonformal whipping procedures within the party groups. The new Conservative British members formed their own political group and demonstrated a level of internal organization not previously known within the Parliament.[17]

Along with the creation of the Community's own resources and the enlargement of the Community, the 1969 Hague Summit revitalized the old idea of organized meetings between the heads of state at regular intervals to discuss broad political issues not necessarily falling specifically within the economic jurisdiction of the Community. Pompidou suggested a formalized process of foreign policy coordination through regular meetings of the foreign ministers of the Member States. Although this reminded many of the Fouchet Plan previously supported by de Gaulle, the other Member States were not opposed to the general idea and agreed to the creation of the "Davignon Committee" to study the possibilities. The Committee's report was submitted to the Council in May 1970. The report called for biannual meetings of the foreign ministers of the Member States (with the possibility of more frequent meetings between their political directors). Pompidou had originally called for the creation of a formal secretariat (located in Paris). The Davignon Report avoided the potential for conflict that this might create by suggesting instead that the current presidency of the Council act as president of the foreign ministers meeting in European Political Cooperation (EPC) and provide any incidental support required.

---

[17] The British Labor Members boycotted the EP until after the successful referendum of 1975 confirmed British entry in the Community. Once they began participating in the EP, they joined the Socialist group.

Even though the EPC lacked the institutional foundations that many federalists would have preferred, it was important in that it opened the door to *political* cooperation between the Member States and helped expand the jurisdiction of the European Community as a whole. The concept of political cooperation was extended still further by an agreement during the December 1974 Paris Summit to institutionalize summit meetings. The result was an agreement to hold meetings between the national leaders of the Member States three times a year in what were to be known as "European Councils." The extension of the Community into the political arena in a clearly intergovernmental way oddly worked in the Parliament's favor. It was decided during the same summit that the shift toward intergovernmentalism within the area of political and foreign policy cooperation should be balanced by the direct election of the European Parliament (Point 12, final *Communiqué*, Paris Summit, 1974). The Member States tentatively agreed to hold direct elections in May or June of 1978, although this was later delayed until 1979 to accommodate the British.

Although the Parliament finally achieved partial control over the budget and the promise of direct elections, it was less successful with regard to its constant push for increased legislative authority. Throughout the 1970s a series of reports were commissioned and completed that focused on the institutions of the Community and the Parliament in particular. The Vedel Report, the first in this string, and the only one dedicated exclusively to the question of increased EP power, was completed in April 1972.

The Vedel Report was organized by the Commission after the Hague Summit as a response to the increased budgetary powers of the EP and the call for a European Monetary Union (EMU).[18] The task of the Committee was to study what powers should be granted to the EP and what the likely effect of an expansion of EP power in the legislative arena

---

[18] At the same time as the Davignon committee was formed to study European Political Cooperation, a second committee under Pierre Werner was organized to examine and make proposals for the European Monetary Union (EMU). Although initially successful in creating the "snake"(an anti-inflationary agreement between Member States), the system faltered and failed shortly after its creation. It was partially replaced by the European Monetary System and the Exchange Rate Mechanism in 1979. The relative success of the ERM was in large part responsible for allowing further action toward the creation of a single currency in the 1990s. The question of a true European Monetary Union was not officially revisited until the 1992 Maastricht Treaty, which set the stage for the single currency and the "Eurozone."

would be (Vedel Report: Introduction, paragraphs [a] and [b]). The Vedel Report called for the power of the Parliament to be increased to "co-decision" with the Council through a two-stage transition process (Vedel Report, Chapter IV, Section II, 1–2). The Parliament was also to be consulted on all international agreements and, after the second stage of implementation, its assent would be required for these as well (Vedel Report, Chapter IV, Section II, 4). Although the report was moderate in its recommendations compared to what the Parliament might have liked, nothing ever came of its suggestions.[19]

Other reports that failed to inspire significant Community reform included the Tindemans Report (January 1976), requested of then Belgian Prime Minister Leo Tindemans by the Council during the 1974 Paris Summit; the Spierenburg Report on the Commission (September 1979), initiated by Commission President Roy Jenkins; and the report of the Three Wisemen (October 1979) on Community reform without Treaty revision, proposed by French President Giscard. In each of these reports the institutions of the Community and their relationships with one another were analyzed with an eye toward creating a more effective interinstitutional working environment. As the breadth of Community action increased, the tenor of the reports grew more anxious. It became clear that the Community could not continue to develop and expand with the effective unanimity restriction created by the Luxembourg Compromise and the extreme imbalance of power between the institutions in favor of the Council.

Unfortunately for the EP, despite all of the reports and the good intentions of many within the Community, significant reform of the institutions was not, and perhaps could not have been, immediately forthcoming. The economic crisis in France, the political instability in Britain, and the malaise of the Commission (which had yet to recover from de Gaulle's attacks) combined to make any substantial reform of the Community's institutions impossible. Thanks to a general improvement in the economy and the concerted effort of the many within the Community, this situation changed in the early 1980s, and by 1985 the Community was well on its way to institutional reform and a new level of European integration.

---

[19] It should be noted though that many of the powers suggested were ultimately granted to the Parliament in the SEA, Maastricht, and Amsterdam Treaties, although no official references to the report were made.

The Second Period (1979–1986)

The first direct elections in and of themselves were not the watershed that many (especially within the European Parliament) had hoped. In the event, European elections were finally held June 7–10, 1979. Although the Parliament's original proposal had been to have all of the voting occur on one day, the Council decided that a four-day voting period would better suit the varying traditions among the Member States. Despite a great deal of active campaigning and press attention, voter turnout for the landmark elections was generally much lower than expected, ranging from a low of 33% in Great Britain to a high of 85% in Italy, with an overall average of 63%.[20] In all cases turnout was significantly lower than the average turnout for national elections.

Notwithstanding what might have been perceived as apathy on the part of the European voter, the newly elected Members of Parliament took their seats with a great deal of excitement and energy. There were a considerable number of previously appointed Members who ran and won seats in the new directly elected Parliament (European Parliament, 1986). This allowed for a certain amount of continuity despite the significant influx of new Members with no political experience at the European level. One of the first tasks facing the new Parliament was its own internal reorganization. With direct elections the total membership of the EP more than doubled, growing from 198 to 410. The numerical requirements and organizational structure of the previously appointed Parliament could not be maintained given this increase in membership. Several attempts by the previously appointed EP to revise its Rules of Procedure in accordance with the imminent changes failed, leaving the task to the newly elected Members. A far more contentious process than originally expected, an entirely new and reorganized set of Rules of Procedure was finally adopted only in 1981, over two years after the first attempt by the previous Parliament (see Chapter 5).

Even though direct elections did not result in the sudden transformation of the European Parliament into an effective legislative body, it did subtly change its political authority relative to the other Community institutions. The Commission, although also generally pro-integrationist, was still an appointed body with no direct connection to the citizens of

---

[20] Turnout was 61% in France, 91% in Belgium, 89% in Luxembourg, 47% in Denmark, 65% in Germany, 64% in Ireland, and 58% in The Netherlands.

Europe at all. Council members, although responsible to their national parliaments, were not directly responsible to the electorate either. This gave the European Parliament a unique distinction: Not only was it directly responsible to the people of Europe, but its direct election also meant that it was much more representative of population in terms of ideological breadth. Neither the Council nor the Commission could be said to represent the opposition within their home countries. The Court of Justice recognized this unique aspect of the European Parliament in an extremely important ruling in 1980.

Just after the first direct elections the Council passed a final directive without waiting on the opinion of the EP, even though the Treaties required the Council to solicit the EP's opinion (consultation procedure). The European Parliament took the Council to Court, declaring that it had ignored the Treaty and its provisions. The European Court of Justice, in the landmark "Isoglucose" case, agreed with the Parliament and declared the legislation invalid, forcing the Commission and Council to begin again. In its ruling the ECJ stated that the Treaty provisions that require the Council to consult with the EP are

the means which allow the Parliament to play an actual part in the legislative process of the Community. Such a power represents an essential factor in the institutional balance intended by the Treaties. Although limited, it reflects at Community level the fundamental principle that the people should take part in the exercise of power through the intermediary of a representative assembly. (European Court of Justice case 138/79 and 139/79)

The unique position of the European Parliament as the only Community institution directly responsible to the people of Europe made it essential that the Council abide by the Treaties and wait for its opinion.

While the ECJ ruling was in itself an important official recognition of the unique role of the Parliament, the Isoglucose case was made more important by the use that the Parliament made of it. During the actual case in question the EP had already debated the issue and all that was needed was a final vote on the resolution as a whole, but instead the vote had been postponed and the proposal sent back to committee. This process was formalized during the general revision of the rules that was occurring at the same time. Essentially the EP granted itself, through its internal rules, the power of legislative delay. The new rules allowed the Parliament to make its proposed amendments and forward them to the Commission. If the Commission responded that it would be unable to incorporate them into its text as per Article 149(2) of the Treaties, then the Parliament could simply refer the matter back to committee before the final vote, holding up the whole legislative process. Although only an indirect and negative power that was primarily useful when there was a strict deadline, the power of delay derived from the Isoglucose ruling significantly increased the bargaining power of the European Parliament vis-à-vis the other European institutions.

Although the Isoglucose case and the resulting power of delay that it granted to the European Parliament were important, the Parliament still pushed for greater legislative authority. They argued that the EP was the only direct representative of the people of Europe and as such should have a greater influence on the legislative output of the Community. This sentiment increased still further with the accession of three new states. In 1981, Greece joined the Community, followed five years later, in 1986, by Portugal and Spain. All three countries had recently suffered under totalitarian rule and were somewhat wary of a Community system in which the only democratically elected body was subjugated to the legislative will of the other institutions. The new Members joined in the Parliament's longstanding battle for increased legislative and political authority.

The Members of Parliament were not alone in feeling that the EP's powers should be increased. In 1981, the Genscher–Colombo Plan, sponsored by two members of the Council, Hans-Dietrich Genscher, then German Foreign Minister, and Italian Foreign Minister Emilio Colombo, was presented to the Council as a program for further Community development. The plan not only advocated "more effective decision-making structures" and greater Community involvement in external affairs, but also an increased role for the European Parliament in both Community and European Political Cooperation (EPC) affairs (EC Bull. 11/1981: 88). While the central focus of the plan was European cooperation on foreign policy and security issues, and not the relative power of the EP, it did explicitly list eight ways in which the powers and role of the EP should be expanded. These included biannual reports from the Council on progress made toward "European Union," consultation on international agreements and further accession treaties, and consultation between the Council and the EP on the appointment of the Commission President (EC Bull. 11/1981: 89).

The Genscher–Colombo Plan was submitted to the Member States in November 1981 and ultimately ended in the Stuttgart Solemn Declaration signed on June 19, 1983. The Solemn Declaration was a watered down version of the original plan, but it did include some increases in the role of the Parliament. In particular, the declaration recognized that "the Assembly of the European Communities has an essential role to play in the development of the European Union" (EC Bull. 6/1983: 26). The plan also called for the Parliament to be consulted prior to the appointment of the Commission President and prior to "the conclusions of any significant international agreements by the Community and the accession of a state to the European Community" (EC Bull. 6/1983: 27). Relations between the EP and the other institutions were strengthened through the requirement that the Council Presidency report to the Parliament regularly on European Political Cooperation, and at the beginning of its term in office.[21] The Commission was also called on to present its annual program to the Parliament for debate and vote.

The European Parliament was still not satisfied with its role within the Communities, or the continued reliance on unanimity within the Council. One of the strongest proponents of institutional reform was the Italian Altiero Spinelli. A long-time federalist, Spinelli began to organize meetings with others within the Parliament who shared his views. This eventually came to be known as the "Crocodile Club," after the name of the restaurant in Strasbourg where the group generally met during the Parliament's week-long plenary sessions. The Crocodile Club was eventually institutionalized within the EP through the creation of a Committee on Institutional Affairs, with Spinelli as chair, in July 1981.[22] The new committee set out almost immediately to draft its own plan for the creation of a new "European Union."[23] The new program was called the "Draft Treaty Establishing the European Union." The Draft Treaty proposed a merger of the political and the economic realms under one treaty. Structurally, the Draft Treaty called for the institutions to remain very much the way they were; however, additional voting procedures were added to allow for a variety of different decision-making possibilities, depending on the particular topic and arena of the debate. In particular, those areas explicitly

---

[21] The presidency of the Council rotates in a fixed order on a biannual basis between the Member States.

[22] The addition of the new committee was included in the 1981 general revision of the rules.

[23] The term European Union was first used by French President Giscard in the final *communiqué* following the 1976 summit. He declared, rather prematurely, that a new "European Union" would be achieved by the end of the decade (1980). This clearly did not come to pass, but the term stuck and was eventually realized in 1992 with the Maastricht Treaty on European Union.

74

covered by the Rome Treaty or those more effectively dealt with at the Community level were to be decided through "common-action," or majority rule, with increased participation of the Parliament. Other areas, and in particular those previously dealt with in the European Council or EPC, were to be resolved through "cooperation" or unanimous consent (EC Bull. 2/1984: 11, point 10.1).

The EP passed the Draft Treaty on February 14, 1984; however, it was never ratified or endorsed by the Member States. Instead, it eventually served as a partial rough draft for the Single European Act (SEA), which was eventually passed in 1985 and came into effect in 1987. Part of the impetus that kept the Draft Treaty from becoming merely another failed attempt at reform came from the unexpected support of French President Francois Mitterrand. Spinelli, who was serving as *Rapporteur* for the Draft Treaty, made a public statement directly calling on Mitterrand and France to support institutional reform (Burgess, 1989: 184–185). Mitterrand responded (to the surprise of many) by giving a speech before the European Parliament less than four months later. In his speech, Mitterrand called for institutional reform in the EC, including an enlarged legislative role for the European Parliament and more restricted use of the veto in the Council of Ministers (EC Bull. 5/1984: 137–138).

French support guaranteed that the Draft Treaty would not simply be ignored by the other member states. At the June 1984 European Council meeting at Fontainebleau, the European Council agreed to convene two ad hoc committees on the European Union. The more important of the two committees was given the task of making "suggestions for the improvement of the operation of European cooperation in both the Community field and that of political, or any other co-operation" (Keatinge and Murphy, 1987: 217). This committee came to be known as the Dooge Committee, after its chair, majority leader of the Irish Senate, James Dooge. Because of what many perceived to be the importance of the committee, it was also known as Spaak II, after the Spaak committee that had prepared the original draft of the Treaties of Rome in 1956.

The final version of the Dooge Committee's report was delivered to the European Council at its 1985 meeting in Milan (previous drafts had been submitted at the Dublin summit in December 1984 and the Brussels Council meeting in March 1985). The proposal called explicitly for the "adoption of the new general principle that decisions must be taken by a qualified or simple majority" within the Council and for the Parliament to share "joint decision making" powers with the Council (Report of the

Ad Hoc Committee to the European Council, March 1985, part III, section A, point iv, subparagraph [a] and Section C paragraph [a]). The committee was divided, however, with the Danish, British, and Greek representatives clearly opposed to the majority position, which supported an end to unanimity. Interestingly, there was less conflict over the proposed increases in the legislative role of the EP (footnotes 25–27 and subparagraph [b]).

The proposal also included a section on implementation, suggesting that an intergovernmental conference be convened to create a draft treaty on European Union that would take account of the *acquis communautaire*, the Stuttgart Solemn Declaration, the Dooge Report, and the European Parliament's Draft Treaty (Report of the Ad Hoc Committee to the European Council, March 1985, part IV). The same minority of countries opposed to majority voting also opposed the proposal to convene an Intergovernmental Conference (IGC) (see footnote 36 to the report of the Ad Hoc Committee). Despite the continued opposition by the British, Danes, and Greeks, an IGC was called by the European Council at the Milan meeting in June 1985 (EC Bull. 7/8, 1985: 7–11).

The IGC covered numerous policy areas. One of the most controversial was the question of majority voting in the Council. Both the Genscher–Colombo Plan and the European Parliament's Draft Treaty called on the Council to abide by the provisions established in the Rome Treaties, which clearly called for qualified majority voting on a large number of topics (Art 149, Rome Treaty). In other words, both the Parliament and some Member States were calling for a renunciation of the Luxembourg Compromise. In addition, the national parliaments of Italy and Germany passed resolutions calling for nothing less than "EP/Council co-decision and generalized majority voting" (Camera dei Deputati, 29.11.85, and Bundestag – 10 Wahlperiode – 181 Sitzung 5.12.85, Drucksache 10/4088). To these demands were added those of the European Peoples Party (EPP), a majority of the Socialists and the Liberals, who "made an appeal to extend majority voting and the powers of the European Parliament" (*Agence Europe*, no. 4202, 12/13.11.85: 4). The Commission also added its support for "increased use of majority voting in the Council of Ministers and new procedures of co-decision for the European Parliament" (Burgess, 1989: 204).

While the demand for increases in the legislative role of the Parliament was widespread, there was no guarantee that it would be achieved because of the requirement of unanimity in the IGC and the eventual need for national ratification. Britain, Denmark, and Greece continued to oppose radical treaty revisions and the imposition of majority rule. On the other side, the Italian representatives threatened to veto any proposal that did not satisfy the European Parliament (Corbett, 1987: 241), and the French and Germans had already demonstrated their desire to move Europe toward further integration, which included a stronger EP and majority voting within the Council. In the end a compromise was reached and the Single European Act was adopted. The SEA made a commitment to qualified majority voting for most of the single market program, as well as allowing the future expansion of areas of majority decision making to be decided on by unanimous consent, but most importantly for the EP it added the cooperation procedure to the legislative arsenal.

The European Parliament was initially quite discouraged by the outcome of the Single European Act (Westlake, 1995: 138). Despite its promise to base the new Single European Act on previous plans and studies, very little of the Parliament's own Draft Treaty had found its way into the final version of the SEA. The new legislative procedure was generally viewed as a weak substitute for true co-decision and was not initially expected to have a significant effect on the EP's ability to influence Community legislation. In reality, the combination of the new cooperation procedure and the institution of majority voting in the Council combined to dramatically increase the role of the Parliament in the legislative process.

The Third Period of Development (1987–1996)

The Single European Act was signed in February 1986 and went into effect in July 1987. The SEA was important for the European Parliament in several respects. It was the first official document to recognize the EP's chosen name, which had been a bone of contention between the Council and the Parliament since the latter had changed its name twenty-five years earlier. The SEA also granted the Parliament veto power over the accession or association of new states. The previous Stuttgart Solemn Declaration (1983) had only made a commitment to "consult" or confer with the Parliament without actually granting it any official powers. By far, however, the most important increase in the EP's power was the addition of the cooperation procedure for certain legislative topics, which gave the EP the power to amend legislation directly (see Figure 4.2).

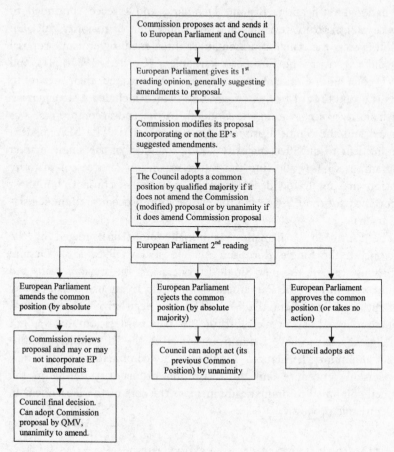

Figure 4.2 Cooperation Procedure (July 1987–Present)

The new legislative procedure added a second reading to the previous consultation procedure and allowed the EP to directly impact legislative outcomes through its amendments. The Cooperation procedure includes seven steps. In the first stage the Commission initiates legislation and sends it to both the EP and the Council. The Parliament then (after referral to the appropriate committee) holds a first reading, during which a simple majority can adopt amendments and the proposal as a whole. After the Parliament's first reading the initiative goes back to the Commission, which can revise its original proposal by adopting any or all of the EP's amendments.[24] The Council then decides on a Common Position (CP) based on the Commission's (possibly revised) proposal. The Council can adopt the Commission's proposal by qualified majority, but unanimity is required to modify it (including any EP amendments incorporated into the Commission's revised proposal). In the fifth step, the EP is once again given the opportunity to amend the proposal in light of the Council's Common Position. By its own rules the EP can offer amendments only if they were adopted by the EP previously (during the first reading) or if the text of the proposal had been significantly revised so as to be substantively different from what existed during the first reading.[25] If the EP feels that its views are wholly ignored or that the proposal for whatever reason should not pass, it can, by an absolute majority of its members, reject the proposal. A rejection by the EP can only be overturned by a unanimous vote in the Council.[26] After the EP's second reading the previous process is repeated. The Commission reviews the proposal and decides to adopt the EP's amendments or not (with explanations) and sends the proposal to the Council. In the final stage the Council can once again adopt the Commission proposal by qualified majority or change it by unanimity.[27] The decision of the Council during the second reading of the proposal is final.

The European Parliament, although pleased that it had gained some increase in its legislative authority, was generally not satisfied with the new procedures. The cooperation procedure still required that the EP garner the support of the Commission and this frustrated the EP, which desired independent legislative authority. This frustration was mitigated somewhat by the fact that "although the Parliament was still practically dependent on the Commission, the Commission was politically dependent on the Parliament" as a result of the latter's direct election (Westlake, 1994: 25). The result was a kind of symbiotic relationship, and although the

---

[24] The Commission is then supposed to tell the EP which amendments it can and cannot adopt and then explain why, but this does not always occur.

[25] Originally Rule 51 (Rules of Procedure 4th edition, June 1987), currently Rule 80 in the 14th edition, 1999. The EP can, however, offer modified versions of previous amendments in an attempt to bargain with the other institutions.

[26] If the Council is unable to overturn the rejection, then the Commission must re-introduce the proposal and the entire process must begin again.

[27] It should be noted that the Council could adopt any EP amendment not adopted by the Commission by unanimity.

Table 4.1. *EP Amendments Adopted by the Commission and Council* (*July 1987–December 1993*) *Under the Cooperation Procedure Before Implementation of the Co-Decision Procedure*

	First Reading	Second Reading
European Parliament Amendments	4,572	1,074
Amendments Adopted by Commission	2,499 (55%)	475 (44%)
Amendments Adopted by Council	1,966 (43%)	253 (24%)

Source: Adapted from Corbett et al., 1995: 199.

Table 4.2. *EP Amendments Adopted by the Commission and Council* (*July 1987–July 1997*) *Under the Cooperation Procedure*

	First Reading	Second Reading
European Parliament Amendments	6,008	1,593
Amendments Adopted by Commission	3,244 (54%) + 360 (6% partially)	685 (43%) + 64 (4% partially)
Amendments Adopted by Council	2,463 (41%) + 240 (4% partially)	335 (21%) + 48 (3% partially)

Source: Adapted from Maurer, 1998: 42.

Commission did not accept all of the EP's amendments, it did incorporate a significantly large percentage into its proposals, forcing the Council to do the same unless it could unanimously amend the Commission proposal (Tables 4.1 and 4.2).

Not satisfied with the progress made in the Single European Act, the Parliament immediately began to press for a new Intergovernmental Conference, during which the entire constitutional design of the Communities would be revised to create a more equal role for the Parliament. A series of reports on various aspects of the Community were produced, including the Toussaint Report on the "democratic deficit," the Catherwood Report on "the cost of non-Europe," the De Gucht Report on fundamental rights, and the Graziani Report on the impact of the Single European Act after one year. All of these reports set the stage for the Herman Report, which essentially outlined a new path toward European Union and called on the Parliament itself to establish a new draft constitution toward this end.

Understandably, neither the Commission nor the Member States were initially eager to begin the process of constitutional revision again so shortly after the SEA. Unfortunately, the requirements of the Single Act and the Single Market that it created forced the Member States to once again consider Treaty revisions. A main concern of the SEA had been the creation of a single European market and the absolute end to trade barriers of all kinds (not just tariffs). As time passed many Member States began to conclude that the single internal market could not be completed without stronger monetary ties between the Member States and most likely a single currency (Corbett et al., 1995: 303). During the 1989 European Council in Madrid the Member States agreed to hold another IGC to begin in 1990. The scope of the new IGC was initially restricted to discussions of economic and monetary union only.

The Parliament tried to expand the scope of the forthcoming IGC to include political union (and institutional reform) by appealing directly to the national governments and parliaments of the Member States. The European Parliament met with the national parliaments in Rome in November 1990 in what came to be known as the "Rome Assizes." During this meeting, and in its discussions with the national governments, the EP once again pressed for extended majority voting in the Council, increased legislative authority for itself, and the creation of a tangible European Union based on democratic principles and the notion of a European citizenry. The proposals of the Parliament were organized within the Martin Report, which was adopted in November 1989.

Through constant pressure the Parliament was able to gradually gain some Member State support for its proposals and the idea of broadening the 1990 IGC to include the topic of further political union. Both the Italian (a long-standing supporter of the EP) and the Belgian Parliaments publicly supported the EP's proposals. This was followed in April 1990 by a joint statement from German Chancellor Kohl and French President Mitterand calling on the other Member States to create a second IGC to deal specifically with questions of furthering European political integration.[28] The result was the decision at the June 1990 Dublin summit to convene a second IGC "to transform the Community from an entity mainly based on economic integration and political cooperation into a union of political

---

[28] The move to deepen European integration was, in part, also inspired by the events occurring in Eastern Europe and the likely reunification of Germany. For a more detailed discussion of the impact of these events, see Dinan (1994: 157–193).

nature, including common foreign and security policy" (Bull EC 6/1990: 7). The European Parliament's Martin Report served as a partial agenda for the IGC, thanks in part to the overwhelming support that it garnered at the Rome Assizes just one month before the IGC was convened.[29]

The European Parliament was able to participate to a much greater extent in the creation of the Maastricht Treaty, which arose out of these IGCs, than it had in the previous run-up to the Single European Act. An interinstitutional conference was created that met once a month and consisted of ministerial representatives of the twelve Member States and twelve MEPs as well as representatives from the Commission. In addition, the president of the Parliament was able to address the IGC meetings on several occasions and deliver the EP's opinion on the future development of a politically unified Europe. A separate delegation from the Parliament also continued to put pressure on the Member States through individual meetings with national leaders.

The Maastricht Treaty was signed in 1991, but it was not officially ratified until 1992 (because of an initial negative vote by the Danes during a national ratification referendum) and not fully implemented until November 1993.[30] The new Treaty created a new "European Union" to replace the previous European Communities. The new Treaty marked a much more decisive departure from the previous European Communities than the SEA had. The Maastricht Treaty marked the first time that integration was pursued in political as well as economic arenas. The previous European Councils and Summits, which had always existed outside the scope of the Community and the Treaties of Rome, were incorporated into the new European Union. The Maastricht Treaty officially brought European political and defense cooperation under the same roof as economic cooperation. It also officially recognized the concept of a European citizenry for the first time, as well as the need for European political parties. On the economic front, deadlines for a European Monetary Union and a single currency were created that forced a higher level of economic coordination between the Member States than ever before.

[29] The Rome Assizes adopted the Martin Report by a vote of 150 to 13. The Assizes consisted of members of all of the national parliaments of the Member States (2/3) and Members of the EP (1/3).

[30] As a result of the Danish "no" vote the terms of entry for Denmark were modified to incorporate a series of "opt-outs," which then permitted them to join the new European Union created by the Treaty.

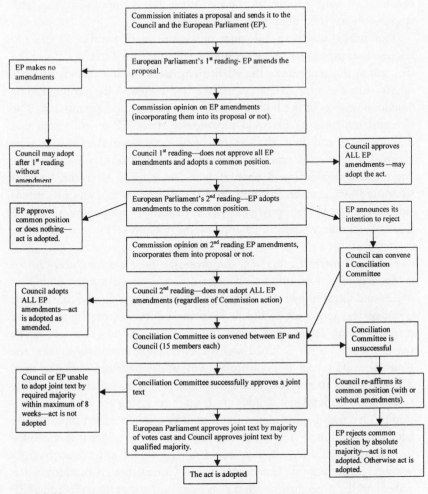

Figure 4.3 Co-Decision Procedure I (November 1993–April 1999)

For the European Parliament, the biggest change introduced by the Maastricht Treaty was the addition of the co-decision procedure, which gave it absolute veto power in some areas of legislation. The new legislative procedure was more complicated than the cooperation procedure introduced by the SEA because of the creation of a "conciliation committee" and the possibility for a third reading (see Figure 4.3). As in the consultation and cooperation procedures, the Commission was still responsible for the initiation of all proposals.[31]

The initial stages of the new procedure were similar to the old cooperation procedure. A new proposal was forwarded to the EP and the Council at the same time; the Parliament made its first reading amendments after the appropriate committee had reviewed the proposal. The amended version of the bill was then forwarded to the Commission. The Commission once again could incorporate those EP amendments that it approved of and then send the (modified) proposal to the Council. The Council adopted a Common Position (qualified majority to adopt the commission proposal and unanimity to amend it). After the Council submitted its Common Position the EP could either announce its intention to reject the proposal (absolute majority), adopt the Common Position (simple majority), or amend the Common Position (absolute majority).

If the EP intended to reject the proposal, the Council could call for a "Conciliation Committee," which consisted of an equal number of MEPs and Council members.[32] If a joint proposal was agreed to, then the proposal was sent back to the floor of the EP for approval (an absolute majority being required to reject the proposal). If no accord could be reached between the Council and the EP during conciliation, then the Council could revert to its previous Common Position (modified or not). The EP could then either definitively veto the proposal (by an absolute majority of its members) or adopt it. If upon receiving the Common Position the EP merely amended it (no intention to reject), the proposal went back to the Council. The Council could then either adopt it as amended (by qualified majority) or, if it could not or would not adopt the EP's version (including all amendments), a Conciliation Committee was called and the procedure continued as described above for an intended EP rejection.[33]

There are two key aspects of the co-decision procedure that differ significantly from the consultation or even the cooperation procedure. The first is the obvious ability of the EP to definitively veto legislation if

[31] The Maastricht Treaty did officially grant the EP the power to request that the Commission introduce a bill on a particular topic. The Council already had this right.

[32] This was initially twelve of each, but it was increased to fifteen after the 1995 enlargement.

[33] As we shall see, the Amsterdam Treaty substantially simplified this procedure.

it is not satisfied with the final draft. The ability to veto legislation is a negative power and thus not very useful when the EP prefers the Council's proposal to the status quo; however, it does provide the EP with a powerful bargaining tool when the Council desires or needs legislation to be approved in a timely manner. The Council can not simply ignore the position of the Parliament if it wishes to see a proposal passed. The second aspect is the diminished role of the Commission as a result of the increased cooperation required between the EP and the Council (Tsebelis and Garrett, 2001; Kreppel, 2000a).

Under both the consultation and cooperation procedures the Commission is the primary path to legislative influence for the EP. During the consultation procedure the only way that the EP can influence legislative outcomes is if the Commission incorporates its proposals into the legislation through the use of Article 149(2). During the cooperation procedure the EP can hope for the Council to incorporate its amendments independent of the Commission, but this is generally unlikely, given the need for unanimity in the Council and the generally anti-integrationist stance of its members.[34] Successful EP amendments are generally incorporated by the Commission into the amended proposal sent to the Council, making them easier to adopt than reject (Tsebelis, Jensen, Kalandrakis, and Kreppel, forthcoming). Although the Commission plays the role of intermediary during the first and second rounds of the co-decision procedure, it is largely left out of the loop afterward. Cooperation during the second round of the co-decision procedure and in the Conciliation Committee must occur between the Council and the EP if a proposal is to be successful. This new arrangement creates a somewhat more equal balance between the legislative branches, although the EP is still the weakest of the three.

Although the most important, the new co-decision procedure was not the only addition to the powers of the EP included in the Maastricht Treaty. By including foreign and security policy within the broad structure of the new European Union, the Treaty gave the EP some limited input in these arenas as well. The power of assent granted to the EP in the SEA was modified by the Maastricht Treaty to include all "important"

[34] The Commission and the EP are generally perceived to be in favor of increased integration while the Council prefers less, caring more about the protection of national sovereignty. As a result, in a one-dimensional model the commission usually lies between the Council and the EP (closer to the latter). This makes it unlikely that the Council would unanimously adopt anything not also supported by the Commission. It occurs, but rarely. There is evidence to suggest that this may be changing, however (Kreppel, 2000a).

Table 4.3. *EP Membership and Languages Used 1951–2000*

Year	# of MEPs	# Member States	# Languages Used
1951—Common Assembly	78	6	4
1957—European Parliament	142	6	4
1973—Denmark, Ireland, and UK Join	198	9	6
1979—Direct Elections	410	9	6
1981—Greece Joins	434	10	7
1986—Spain and Portugal Join	518	12	9
1991—German Unification	579	12	11
1995—Austria, Finland, and Sweden Join	626	15	11

international agreements. These were defined as those with important budgetary implications, requiring a formal institutional framework, or which require the amendment of Community legislation under the co-decision procedure (Corbett et al., 1995: 216). The new Treaty also changed the absolute majority requirement within the EP for all assent procedures dealing with association agreements to a simple majority requirement. In large part the decision to revise the majority requirements was due to the frequent inability of the EP to muster sufficient votes due to high absenteeism rather than its opposition to the proposed association agreement.

In addition to the changes wrought by the Maastricht Treaty, the internal evolution of the EP was also challenged by the next wave of EU expansion. In 1990, German reunification increased the membership of the EP and forced a general re-evaluation of seat distribution amongst the Member States.[35] In 1995, the European Union expanded still further, with the accession of Austria, Finland, and Sweden swelling the ranks of the EP to 626.[36] The 1995 expansion of the EU not only increased the EP numerically (so much so that it could no longer fit in its old hemicycle), but it also added two additional languages to the already overwhelmed translation services of the EP (see Table 4.3).[37] Despite the added complexity of

---

[35] Initially the East German Members had no voting privileges. Once reunification was complete, the allocation of seats in the EP was re-calculated and the total membership increased to 567.

[36] Norway once again started the accession process but decided in the end not to join.

[37] All official documents and debates in the EP now have to be translated simultaneously into eleven different languages.

Table 4.4. *EP Amendments Adopted by the Commission and Council (November 1993–1997) Under the Co-Decision Procedure*

	First Reading	Second Reading
EP Amendments Adopted by Commission	52.5% (+3.9% in part)	61% (+1.9% in part)
EP Amendments Adopted by Council	42.7% (+3.7% in part)	46.9% (+12.5% compromise text)

Source: European Parliament's Website at
http://www.europarl.eu.int/dg2/conciliation/rep96-97/en/annex2en.

Members from four new countries (including the East Germans), the EP has continued to successfully exploit its new legislative powers.

By the end of 1996, the European Parliament had clearly learned to use its additional powers effectively. The percentage of EP amendments adopted by the other institutions was significantly higher than had been the case under either the consultation or cooperation procedures (Table 4.4). The Commission, despite its reduced role in the procedure as a whole, adopted a higher percentage of EP amendments under the co-decision procedure than under the cooperation procedure. Relations between the Council and the EP have continued to improve as a result of the increased contact initiated by the co-decision procedure (Earnshaw and Judge, 1996; Kreppel, 2000a). The balance of power between the three legislative branches of the EU, while still far from equal, no longer resemble the "bicephelous" community of the 1970s and 1980s.

Although the Maastricht Treaty was probably the most significant treaty reform since the creation of the EEC in 1957, it was by no means the final attempt to reform the institutions and competencies of the EU. Less than three years after the implementation of the Maastricht Treaty another intergovernmental conference was called to face the problems associated with the deepening and enlarging of the EU. This resulted in the Amsterdam Treaty (adopted in 1997 and ratified in 1999). Although the focus of the Amsterdam Treaty was not specifically on re-evaluating the powers of the European Parliament, it did effectively increase these through a restructuring of the legislative processes.[38] The co-decision procedure was

[38] Originally the main goal of the Intergovernmental Conference (IGC) that led to the Amsterdam Treaty was the institutional reform of the EU that would allow for future enlargement and deeper integration. Many of these reforms proved too contentious and

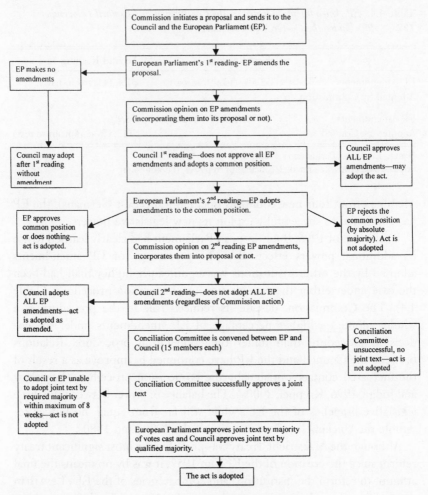

Figure 4.4 Co-Decision Procedure II (Since May 1999)

simplified to exclude the initial "intention to reject" stage, and, more importantly, the ability of the Council to simply revert to its previous Common Position (with or without revisions) if the Conciliation Committee was unable to achieve a compromise was removed (see Figure 4.4). Now, if the Council and the EP are unable to agree in Conciliation,

further reform was put off for the future. At the time of writing another IGC is meeting to try, once again, to resolve the very difficult issues around reform of the Commission and weighted voting in the Council, among other possible reforms.

the proposal simply dies and the entire process must begin again with a new Commission initiative. This is significant because it emphasizes the equality of the EP and the Council in conciliation and because it removes the potential unilateral agenda-setting power of the Council in the final stage of the procedure (Tsebelis, 1997; Tsebelis and Garrett, 1997). A less significant result of the Amsterdam Treaty was the official limitation of the EP to 700 Members, which means that there will have to be a redistribution of seats among the Member States at the next enlargement.[39]

In the nearly thirty years following the first significant increase in its powers (the 1970 Budget Act), the EP has been transformed from a consultative assembly to a true legislative body. This metamorphosis did not occur automatically, and it would not have occurred without the continuous effort on the part of the EP itself. Through what one observer has called "*petite pas* and quantum leaps" the European Parliament has successfully achieved most of the reforms that it sought over the years (Westlake, 1994: 30). Its Members are directly elected (as stipulated by the treaties); it has the power to delay, amend, and even veto legislation; and it has even gained an indirect power of legislative initiative since the Maastricht Treaty. Although much has been accomplished during the last thirty years, the development of the Parliament is still far from complete. In spite of all of the increases in its power, the EP is still the weaker partner in the legislative triumvirate of the European Union. Many of its new powers are negative and can only slow down or stop the legislative process.[40] This is problematic given the common belief that the Parliament generally desires action (and increased integration) more than the other legislative institutions.

The Parliament's future role in the emerging European Union is still not clear. History has demonstrated, however, that it is unlikely that the EP will accept its position without continued battle. The extension of the EU to new policy and geographic areas is likely to highlight the uniquely

---

[39] It was decided by the member states at the Nice Summit in December 2000 that the number of MEPs should be increased to 734 to accommodate a redistribution of MEPs among the current members and in light of future enlargements.

[40] The power of delay from the Isoglucose Case and the power to reject bills under the cooperation procedure and definitively veto them under the co-decision procedure are methods of slowing down or halting the legislative process. Since generally the EP prefers more integration, it will rarely prefer no legislation (and no further integration) to whatever the Council and the Commission offer.

democratic nature of the EP and offer another opportunity for its Members to press for increased power.

Now that we have a better understanding of the changing role of the European Parliament within the political environment of the European Union, we can test the ability of the macro and micro models of legislative development to explain or predict the EP's path of internal evolution. In the next four chapters we will focus on the impact that increases in the political and legislative power have had on the character of the development of the EP and the supranational party groups.

5

The Internal Development of the European Parliament: From Collegiality to Conflict

As Chapter 4 has clearly demonstrated, the European Parliament has only recently been successful in its long struggle for the attainment of true political power. A result of the EP's long history of legislative impotence has been a notable lack of scholarly interest in its internal development and organizational mechanisms, including the activity and interaction of the party groups. The earliest discussions of the Parliament consisted primarily of comparisons between the new institution and the national parliaments of the Member-States and tended, almost inevitably, to conclude that the EP was both politically handicapped and institutionally immature (Dehousse, 1967; Bubba, 1970; Fitzmaurice, 1978; Henig, 1979). There were some excellent descriptions of the party groups during the early years of the Parliament and during the run-up to, and immediately following, the first direct elections in 1979 (Van Oudenhove, 1965; Pinder and Henig, 1969; Fitzmaurice, 1975). The focus of these works, however, tended to be the traditional counting of parties and locating them along the left–right spectrum. Little was said about their internal development or their interactions with one another beyond noting their comparative weakness. Unfortunately, the failure of the EP to immediately become a significant political actor following direct elections discouraged further studies of both the internal structures of the EP and the party groups.

Even the best of the subsequent analyses of the European Union have generally included little more than a descriptive chapter about the EP (Dinan, 1994; Nugent, 1994). Modern analyses of the European Union very rarely delve into the internal operating procedures of the EP beyond a brief description of the hierarchical structures. No attempt is made to analyze how these structures have developed across time. Most usually

91

note the existence of the party groups but rarely move beyond describing their number and ideological (as opposed to national) orientation (Guéguen, 1992; Peters, 1992; Nicoll and Salmon, 1994; Welsh, 1996). In a few cases, attention has been given to the perceived weakness of the party groups and their tendency toward broad consensus building across significant ideological differences (Westlake, 1994).[1] A recent analysis of the political parties in the European Union discusses the party groups in the EP and their interactions with the national and federal party organizations at length, but it fails to address their interactions with one another or how these have varied over time (Hix and Lord, 1997). The next four chapters try to address the existing lacunae in our understanding of the internal development of the EP, the party groups, and the relationships between them through extensive qualitative and quantitative analyses to test the hypotheses suggested in Chapters 2 and 3.

The Internal Development of the European Parliament

The application of the micro and macro models of institutional development to the European Parliament led to several hypotheses about the impact of external increases in legislative power and authority on internal organizational development. The fundamental underlying principal of the micro or purposive theory of legislative development is rational action. Individual Members of a parliament attempt to shape the institutional structure of their legislature in a manner that maximizes their ability to achieve their goals (whatever they may be). A broad interpretation of the macro model suggests that internal changes will in some way reflect the timing and nature of external environmental shifts. In Chapter 2, I suggested that the two theories could, and should, be connected to help us to understand the impact that changes in the broader political environment have on the strategies of the different actors within the legislature.

The application of the macro model led to predictions about the timing of internal reforms and suggested that these will chronologically follow exogenous changes to the powers and political role of the EP and will

---

[1] Two frequent examples of party groups' weakness are their lack of control over electoral lists, which are determined by the national parties, and the extensive use of the d'Hondt method for the distribution of internal political offices. This is discussed at length in Chapter 8.

directly address these changes. The micro model instead focused on the character of internal reform, suggesting that when the EP was largely powerless reforms would be collegial. However, once the EP gained substantial power, and a new ability to effect policy outcomes (the goals of the Members and party groups), internal reforms would be inegalitarian, benefiting only those with the power to ensure their adoption. As a result, it is important to remember how the powers of the EP and its potential influence over legislative outcomes have changed.

In this chapter I test the ability of the environmental and rational actor (macro and micro) models of legislative development to explain the changing character of the internal organizational structures of the European Parliament. I test the macro model first, through an examination of the general trends and major revisions of the EP's Rules of Procedure (RoP), to see if they are connected chronologically to changes in the relative power of the EP vis-à-vis the other EU institutions. Next, I test the prediction of the micro model that individual actors will pursue the internal changes that offer them the best opportunity to realize their goals (policy objectives). To do this I use a quantitative analysis of individual modifications of the RoP proposed by the Committee on Rules to further substantiate what the general trends imply about the changing character of rules revisions. As the tools available to Members and party groups change in sync with the development of the EP as an institution, we should see a shift in the types of internal organizational changes pursued. As the legislative power of the EP increases we should see a departure from generally egalitarian amendments to ones that increase the relative power of some Members over others. This trend should be positively correlated to the further expansion of EP power. If my understanding of changing Member goals and the effects of increased legislative power are not correct, the above patterns will not be evident.

Testing the Macro and Micro Explanations of Internal Reform

The powers of the EP did not increase consistently over time. There have been four "critical moments" in the EP's history; consequently, it will be useful to divide the years covered here into three distinct periods representing the different stages of the EP's external political development.[2] By

---

[2] See Chapter 4 for more information about the EP's developmental history and Chapter 2 for a discussion of the four "critical moments."

following the impact of these environmental changes on the internal development of the EP we can test both the macro and micro models simultaneously. We should expect revisions to the internal structures of the EP to follow exogenous changes to the power of the EP, and that the nature of these revisions should vary as the potential of Members to achieve their goals changes.

The political year in the EP begins in March instead of January; as a result, years listed here will run from the second day of the March plenary session through the first day of the March plenary of the following year. The analysis of changes to the Rules of Procedure begins in 1970, when the first significant increase in EP power since its creation in 1958 occurred. The first period includes March 1970 through March 1979. This encompasses the introduction of the Budgetary Act and the decision to hold direct elections, although the elections themselves did not occur until June of 1979. The second period runs from March 1979 through March 1986. This includes the realization of direct elections as well as the agreement of the Single European Act, which was not implemented until 1987. It also includes the Stuttgart Solemn Declaration (1983), which, without amending the Treaties, promised to allow the EP greater participation in international agreements. The third and final period is from March 1986 through March of 1996. This comprises the enactment of the SEA as well as the creation and enactment of the Maastricht Treaty on European Union.[3] The official versions of all of the Rules of Procedure used during this research are listed in Appendix A.

The powers of the EP were obviously significantly different in each of these periods. I demonstrate that the internal structures (rules) also varied notably during these three periods. To do this I discuss the internal structure of the EP during each period and the revisions made as a result of the new political/institutional situation. A summary of some important structural changes is presented in Appendix B.[4] I also describe the process used to examine these changes statistically, and the results of the data analysis.

---

[3] I do not include rules revisions that occurred as a result of the Amsterdam Treaty, which was not fully ratified and implemented until 1999.

[4] The tables do not include changes that were directly tied to increased powers; instead they focus on the shifting balance of power within the EP's organizational structures.

The Macro Model Applied

In 1970, when this analysis begins, the EP consisted of 142 Members representing six different countries (Belgium, France, Germany, Italy, Luxembourg, and The Netherlands). Members were appointed by their national legislatures, of which they were also members (thus, all Members of the European Parliament [MEPs] had a dual mandate). There were four political groups in 1970, three of which had been formed in the first year of the EP (1958) and were essentially extensions from the previous Common Assembly of the European Coal and Steel Community (ECSC). These were the Christian Democratic Group, the Socialist Group, and the Liberal Group. The fourth group was the European Democratic Alliance, a neo-Gaullist group consisting primarily of French MEPs. The group was created in 1965, after an internal split within the Liberal group.

In 1970, the EP was organized in much the same way as its predecessor, the Common Assembly. There was a Bureau, which consisted of a president and eight vice presidents. There was also an enlarged Bureau, which included the president, vice presidents, and the political group chairs. The enlarged Bureau was responsible for preparing the draft agenda and supervising the internal organization of the EP, and it dealt with most internal administrative questions as well. (rule 12, RoP 1968/72).

The role of the political groups in the enlarged Bureau was not their only one; however, in 1970 their role in the internal organization of the Parliament was not usually formalized in the rules. There had been a conscious decision by the Members of the European Parliament from the beginning to organize themselves primarily by ideological affinity as opposed to national identity, although the latter could not be ignored (EP Debates, March, 1958). It was decided, for example, from the outset that MEPs would sit according to ideological affinity, not nationality, as was the case in the other transnational assemblies of the time. There were unofficial norms, which allowed political group chairs to submit lists to the president with their suggestions for committee assignments. In addition, committee chairs and *Rapporteurships* were generally divided amongst the political groups according to the d'Hondt system, despite the fact that there was no mention of such a system in the rules. Rule 37(2) only stated that proposals (drawn up by the Bureau) should be designed "to ensure fair representation of Member States and of political views." No mention was made of the groups themselves.

In fact, in the 1968 (French) and 1972 (English) editions of the Rules of Procedure (RoP) the political groups were mentioned just ten times in six different rules (out of a total of fifty-four rules).[5] There were very few instances when a group could act as a group officially. Most of the time, when mention was made of the political groups, it was terms of consulting with them, not allowing them to participate actively in parliamentary life. Rule 47(1) was a rare example of a power being granted to a group that was not allowed to a single individual, a trend that was to become prevalent later on. Rule 47 stated that "questions may be put to the Commission or Council by a committee, *a political group*, or five or more representatives." It should be noted, however, that at this time at least fourteen MEPs were necessary to form a group, so it was much easier to achieve the five-member requirement than political group status. The number of individual Members required to perform an activity that could be performed by any political group was to be a controversial issue throughout the Parliament's development.

The European Parliament in 1970 had no control over the legislative output of the European Union (then the European Economic Community or EEC). In May of 1970 the EP was granted some control over the budget as a result of the creation of independent Community financing (see Chapter 4). Overall, however, the EP had little opportunity to impact political outcomes. As a result, the EP served primarily as a debate chamber in which "own initiative" resolutions and opinions were discussed at length, but little of practical significance was achieved. This had a significant impact on the manner in which it chose to organize itself internally.

There were two major environmental changes ("critical moments") that should have been impetuses toward structural revision during this period, according to the macro model: the Budget Act of 1970 (implemented and revised in 1975) and the Council's decision to introduce direct elections for MEPs in 1976 (not realized until 1979). Interestingly, despite some technical revisions to incorporate the budgetary process into its rules, the addition of partial control over the purse does not appear to have had a significant impact on the character of the EP's internal structure. Instead, the increase in membership that resulted from the accession Treaties of 1973 (the UK, Ireland, and Denmark) called attention to the laxity of the EP's internal structures. The addition of the British, Irish, and Danish Members

---

[5] The specific rules that mentioned the party groups were 5(3), 7(7), 27(2), 28(1), 28(2), 28(3), 31(2), 47(1), 47(2), and 47(4).

increased total membership of the EP from 142 to 198, but increased numbers were not the sole cause of a general tightening of the EP's Rules of Procedure. The British Members brought with them experiences from the House of Commons, and they wished to incorporate these experiences into the general organizational structure of the EP. The most notable case of this is the introduction of "Question Time," which gave the MEPs the opportunity to discuss important matters with members of the Council and Commission in full plenary (Rule 47a, introduced in 1973).

The general trend of internal reform during the first period (1970–1979) was increased precision in the rules. Several previous norms (such as the election of the president by acclamation instead of secret ballot) were officially incorporated into the rules. There was a significant trend toward the centralization of power into the hands of the president or the Bureau and enlarged Bureau. A number of previous norms about the role of the political groups were institutionalized (such as the nomination of officers). On the whole, however, there were few attempts to significantly consolidate the power of the political groups relative to individual or nonaffiliated members. The number of rules was not significantly increased, although the general level of specificity within each rule generally was.

My application of the macro model predicted that internal revisions would follow exogenous changes and be collective goods to the extent that they benefited the institution as a whole. During the first period this appears to have occurred. The acquisition of partial control over the purse did not lead to broad internal revisions, but only the minimum necessary to allow for the EP to fulfill its responsibilities under the new procedure. The Council's decision to hold direct elections led to several unsuccessful attempts to substantially revise the EP's RoP by the 1979 deadline (see the quantitative discussion below). Even these proposed revisions, however, were largely focused on incorporating the reality of direct elections and the doubling of the EP's membership into the rules.

During the second period (1979–1986), the rules underwent significant and wide-reaching reform. The realization of direct elections and the resultant end of the double mandate led to a succession of attempts to reform the rules.[6] In the end, an entirely new set of rules was created. The

---

[6] Some countries continued to allow the double mandate, but on the whole, since direct elections, few MEPs have held concurrent positions within their national parliaments. Many MEPs continue to hold local office, particularly the French Members, who are also frequently mayors in their hometowns.

total number of rules increased from 54 to 116, but, most importantly, activity in whole new areas was formalized through incorporation into the rules. Sections dedicated to the reorganization of the legislative process joined obvious additions dealing with direct elections. New procedures for decision making (such as the possible delegation of decision making to committees) were added to improve efficiency on the floor. New kinds of committees were given official recognition (committees of inquiry and temporary committees).

At the same time, as the internal structures of the EP were being better defined and increased (as predicted by the macro model), there was a general shift toward the consolidation of the political groups' power not clearly attributable to any objective need of the Parliament as a whole. The ability of individuals to select their own replacements on committees was usurped by the political groups. Political groups were able to act in ways that individual Members could not in an increasing number of cases on the floor of the plenary (early end of debate, request for adjournment, etc.). During the same period, a huge battle was waged over the minimum number of Members required to form a political group. It is significant that in the end the small groups (ten Members) were able to maintain their status as groups if Members represented three Member States.[7] Several attempts were also made to reduce the level of obstruction caused by individuals and small groups through the reduction and restriction of the powers available to them (points of order were redefined and requirements for prior notification for "explanations of vote" or requests for roll-call votes were added).

On the whole, the rules during the second period, particularly after the general revision of 1981, were substantially more precise and well-organized (an index was added for the first time). Activities that had not been discussed in the previous versions of the Rules of Procedure were addressed (seating arrangements in plenary and own initiative reports, among others). The internal organization of the EP was rationalized; committees were given additional powers to make decisions at the same time as the authority of the president was being increased (decisions on vote outcomes could not be questioned and power over the catego-

[7] The original proposal had suggested a doubling of the requirements since the membership of the EP had doubled. This was fought against by the small group for the Technical Coordination of Independent Members led by Marco Pannella. Through extreme obstructionism the group was able to obtain a compromise and retain group status.

rization of "questions" was delegated to the president). The realization of direct elections and resulting increase in both the membership of the EP and the amount of time that members had to dedicate to the activities of the EP were clearly the motivation behind many of the changes included in the 1981 general revision of the rules. The timing and nature of many of these revisions closely follow the predictions of the macro model, however, another trend in internal revisions that is prominent during the second period is not predicted, and cannot be explained, by the macro model because of the nonegalitarian nature of the reforms.

Throughout the second period, and particularly after the 1981 reforms, the political groups became a more significant force in the activities of the plenary. Frequently, although not exclusively, increases in the powers of the party groups occurred to the detriment of the rights and powers of individual and nonaffiliated Members. These reforms, though often made in the name of greater efficiency, were in no way clearly mandated by the environmental shifts occurring at the time (the implementation of direct elections and the adoption of the SEA). Furthermore, they were clearly not public goods since the ability of individual members and especially nonaffiliated members to act was severely restricted. Thus, while the macro model can help to explain some of the internal revisions of the second period, there are others that are clearly beyond its purview. To understand these revisions it will be necessary to invoke the micro model of legislative development in the next section.

The third and final period (1986–1996) marked both a continuation and a break from the trends established in the second period. Between 1986 and 1994 the legislative powers of the EP increased dramatically. Both the cooperation and the co-decision procedures gave the EP the opportunity to impact the legislative outcomes of the EU. The need to incorporate these additional procedures and the subsequent increase in the power of the EP were significant for its internal organization.

As predicted by the macro model, the sections of the rules dedicated to legislation were dramatically increased. Each stage of the legislative process was defined, and the powers and tasks of the EP were clearly delineated. But these were not by far the only, or even the most significant, revisions that occurred. The biggest structural revision was the replacement of the enlarged Bureau by the new Conference of Presidents (CoP). The new CoP no longer included the vice presidents (which now numbered fourteen). More importantly, voting in the new CoP was weighted based on the size of the party groups. Since the powers of the enlarged

Bureau had been steadily increasing since the first period, this gave the larger political groups additional powers in almost every aspect of internal EP life. The new CoP controlled everything from accounting and scheduling to allowing own initiative reports by committees. The result was an ability for the larger political groups to structure outcomes for their own benefit in all of these areas. At this point the Socialists (PES) and the People's Party of Europe (EPP) together accounted for over 70% of total EP membership. The other party groups ranged from a maximum of almost 9% (the Liberal group) to a minimum of under 3% (the Technical Group of the Right).

The creation of the CoP was not the only internal revision that increased the relative power of the larger political groups. At the same time, the minimum number of Members required to form a group was again increased (to twenty-six, twenty-one, sixteen, and thirteen if Members came from one, two, three, or four Member States, respectively). Additionally, however, the minimum number of Members required to perform the same task as a political group was increased from the smallest number required to form a political group to the largest (at the time from thirteen to twenty-six). In addition, in several key rules the words "or a political group" were deleted, therefore requiring at least twenty-six members to act.[8] This meant that the smaller groups could no longer perform all of the same tasks as the larger groups, who could easily muster twenty-six signatures from among their members [for example: Rule 112(2) request for quorum, and 137(2) amendments to committee assignments].

The macro model alone cannot adequately explain the overall trend during this period. There was a clear increase in the relative power of the larger political groups, primarily through the creation of the Conference of Presidents and the institution of weighted voting. This trend was intensified, however, through increases in the number of individual Members required to act and the deletion of political group rights in favor of numer-

---

[8] The 14th edition of the Rules adopted in May 1999 requires that Members come from at least two Member States. As a result, the largest minimum number required to form a group has been lowered to twenty-three (instead of twenty-six) because they must now come from two Member States instead of one (Rule 29). However, the minimum number of Members required to perform numerous tasks was raised to thirty-two, making it even less likely that the smaller groups would be able to muster enough signatures to meet the requirement.

ical requirements, which were larger than many groups.[9] Although the most important of these changes (the creation of the CoP) occurred during the rules revisions, which resulted from the adoption of the Maastricht Treaty, it was in no way a public good or specifically required by the Treaty itself.

At the same time the rules also became increasingly technical and complex, as the EP's new legislative and political powers were incorporated into them. In this way the macro model does accurately predict many of the internal revisions that occurred.[10] The adoption of new rules that allowed the EP to effectively respond to the new legislative demands of the cooperation and co-decision procedures was clearly a public good to the extent that it strengthened the institution as a whole. The ability of the EP to perform under an increasing legislative burden was a crucial element in convincing the other EU institutions and the public that the EP could function as an effective legislative body.

As the role of the Parliament changed within the broader European political context it was necessary for its internal organizational structure to adapt if the EP was to take advantage of its new powers. The technical changes in the rules and internal organization of the EP that were necessary to incorporate its new and increased role in the larger political environment are predicted by the macro model of legislative development. Throughout the twenty-seven years analyzed here, however, there were many other revisions to the Rules of Procedure that were not clearly predetermined by the character of exogenous increases in the European Parliament's institutional power. As a result we must turn to the micro theory of parliamentary evolution, which suggests that internal development is a result of individual Members acting rationally to pursue their goals. Thus, it predicts that changes to the internal structure of a parliament will be a function of the interests of those members capable of manipulating or controlling internal change.

---

[9] There were on average five groups (the Greens, the European Radical Alliance, Europe of Nations, the Rainbow Group and the Technical group of the Right) that had fewer than twenty-six members during this period. The high level of absenteeism prevalent in the EP made it highly improbable that another two or three groups (the European United Left, Forza Europa, and the European Democratic Alliance), who just cleared the threshold, would be able to achieve the numerical requirements.

[10] In fact, as we shall see in the next section, technical revisions were by far the most numerous type during this period, as a result of the massive revisions following the adoption of the Maastricht Treaty.

I have argued that, while the interests of MEPs might have always been the pursuit of policy objectives, the means to that end has varied depending on the political power of the EP as an institution. This has led me to predict that during the early part of the EP's history, when it had few powers and little potential to effect legislative outcomes, Members would join together to focus on increasing the power and efficiency of the EP relative to the other institutions of Europe. Once progress was made, however, and the power of the EP increased, Members and the party groups would begin to pursue their own policy objectives and manipulate the rules (if they could) to gain relative power within the EP.

The brief history given above supports these hypotheses. During the first period most reforms were focused on increasing efficiency (frequently through increasing the power of a single Member: the president). During the second period there was a shift toward increased political group power and some restrictions were placed on individual and nonaffiliated Members. The main tendency was to increase the power of the political groups relative to individual Members. Finally, during the third period a significant jump was made. Instead of all political groups benefiting, frequently only the two largest groups did. The most stunning example of this was the creation of the Conference of Presidents, but there were numerous others.

The general descriptions of the types of rules revisions proposed during the various periods largely support both the macro and micro models. They also emphasize the need to incorporate both models to gain a more complete understanding of not only *when* internal changes will occur, but also what the *character* of these changes will be. In the following section I will test the micro model more rigorously through a statistical analysis of all of the changes to the rules proposed between 1970 and 1996.[11]

The Micro Model Applied

To test my hypotheses about the impact of increased EP power on the type of internal revisions proposed and adopted more rigorously, I created a data-base of all of the rule changes proposed by the Committee on Rules

---

[11] The previous qualitative discussion included only those revisions that were adopted; the following statistical analysis will include all changes *proposed* by the rules committee.

of Procedure between 1970 and 1994.[12] The "general revision" to the rules of 1981 is not included in the database, but will be included where possible qualitatively.[13] The 1993 general revisions that resulted from the Maastricht Treaty are included in the database but will be discussed separately because of their overwhelming number and somewhat unique nature. Between March 1970 and March 1994 there were 576 changes proposed to the Rules of Procedure (not including the two general revisions mentioned above). The final outcome of the amendment (adopted, referred back to committee, or not adopted) of fifty-nine proposals could not be determined, and as a result these were not included in the analysis.

Proposed rules changes were divided into two general categories – adopted and not adopted – and then into several subcategories based on the purpose(s) of the proposed change.[14] Each amendment could be counted in more than one subcategory. The categorization of the different amendments into subcategories was based on three complementary sources. The actual textual change proposed was examined to determine what technically would change. In addition, the explanations given by the *Rapporteur* at the end of the committee rapport, as well as minority reports where these were issued, were studied to determine what the official purposes of the change were according to the committee (and the interpretations of the minority in the committee). Finally, the verbatim record of the debates on the proposed changes in plenary were used to determine the position of the various groups and independent Members as well as their interpretations of the significance of the proposed changes.[15] If the *Rapporteur*

---

[12] Only reports by the Committee of Rules are considered. Individual motions for a resolution that attempted to change the rules but which were not incorporated into a committee report were not included. Neither were reports on waivers of Members' immunity, which are dealt with by the same committee.

[13] Rules revisions proposed and adopted during the "general revision" of the rules in 1981 were not included in the database because there was no way to compare the new rules to the old. Instead of changing individual rules, a whole new set of rules was adopted with an entirely different organizational setup and little or no resemblance to the previous rules. As a result it was impossible to single out specific changes and classify them in a fashion similar to the other proposed changes.

[14] Any proposed changes that were referred back to committee were scored as not having been adopted since this generally occurs when it becomes evident that the report in its current form cannot garner the support of the required absolute majority.

[15] The Committee Reports are "session documents" and can be found in the *Official Journal of the European Communities (OJC)*, series A. The explanatory statements of the *Rapporteur* are given at the end of the report (although occasionally for long reports they are given

claimed that a change was being proposed to increase efficiency, but during the debates small parties or individual members decried the action for giving too much power to political groups, then the proposed change was scored as both increasing efficiency and increasing the power of the political groups. Many of the proposed changes were complex, requiring that they be scored in numerous categories.

Proposed alterations to the Rules of Procedure of the European Parliament were divided up among the following nine, nonmutually exclusive, categories based on what it was claimed that they were supposed to or could be interpreted as achieving:

Increase Efficiency: If the reasons behind the amendment were to improve the efficiency of the EP either in dealing with its legislative load or in its internal organization. It should be noted that this was the most frequently cited reason for adopting a change, and often controversial changes were proposed in the name of greater efficiency.

(De)Centralize Power: Amendments that gave more power either to the president and/or the enlarged Bureau, or those that gave more power to the committees. In effect, any change that would move power away from the full plenary.

Increase EP Power: These were amendments that sought to increase the power of the EP without an official legal grounding. These amendments frequently accompanied official increases to EP power and merely extended them to areas not specifically covered.

Increase Political Group Power: Any amendment that gave a specific role or power to the political groups, or increased the role of the groups in the internal organization of the EP as a whole (frequently the ability to act/perform tasks that individual Members could not).

Increase Large Political Group Power: Amendments that gave additional powers to large numbers of members. Requirements that required a large number of members to act (more than the minimum number required to form a political group). Changes that actually deleted

orally). Debates on the proposed changes to the Rules are printed in an annex to the *OJC* and are organized according to the plenary sitting. Detailed information on the outcomes of the debate (including votes on amendments and roll-call votes, if there were any) are given in the minutes of the plenary session, which are given in the *OJC*, series C). Thus for every proposed rules change three documents were used: the report itself (*OJC*, series A), the minutes of the plenary session where the changes was debated (*OJC*, series C), and the verbatim debates (annex to the *OJC*, series C).

previous provisions allowing political groups to participate in certain activities and instead required a specific number of members larger than that of many small political groups.

Increase Small Political Group Power: The opposite of the above. These were rare and usually consisted of lowering numeric barriers to action or in giving specific rights to individual members.

Increase Nonaffiliated Power: Amendments that helped to alleviate the burdens of being a nonaffiliated or independent member, usually bureaucratic but occasionally significant politically. These frequently accompanied amendments that boosted the power of the political groups, although they were far less numerous.

Address New EP Power: Amendments that dealt specifically with changes that were the result of an official new power granted by the other institutions of the European Union.

Technical: Any change that was the result of another proposed change (such as the deletion of a paragraph or rule that would be supplanted by a proposed amendment), semantical changes, clarificatory changes, as well as changes that did not appear to have any potential political effect and were not controversial.

Note was also taken of whether or not the committee was unified in support of its report. Where there were one or fewer votes opposed (and less than half abstaining) the committee was considered to be unified. Examples of each category of change are given in Appendix C.

There were some general trends and strategies that were consistent throughout the twenty-five years covered in this study which it will be useful to specify before we examine the individual periods. The first is that the majority of amendments included more than one type of change. The most consistent pattern was for revisions to be accompanied by a technical change. This means that the number of technical changes was consistently high (an average of 62% of all amendments included some technical revision). A second trend was for revisions that benefited some subsection of the Parliament to be justified by claims of greater efficiency. The result was that a high percent of all amendments (approximately 40%) were justified by an increase in EP efficiency.

For the purposes of this study, the most interesting categories are the first five (efficiency, centralization, EP power, political group power, and large group power) since these directly speak to the hypotheses outlined above by addressing the nature of EP internal developments and their relationship to individual Member preferences. Reforms that increased the power of small groups and the nonaffiliated Members were so few that they disappeared statistically. Both were generally included with revisions that resulted in the increase of political group, or large group, power to offset the potential negative effects of these changes.[16]

If Hypothesis 2 is correct, then in the period before direct elections (and even between direct elections and the introduction of the SEA) we should expect to see a large percentage of proposed changes to the rules that attempted to increase the power and efficiency of the EP as an institution. We should also expect them to receive broad support, as demonstrated through unanimity in committee. In the absence of roll-call votes it is impossible to tell whether there was broad consensus for adopting or rejecting an amendment in the EP as a whole. The simple passage of a proposed revision is not a sufficient measure since the two largest political groups, if they formed a coalition, could have passed any changes against the will of all of the other groups. Since the final votes in the committees were almost always given in the reports issued by the committee, and most groups were represented in the committee (proportionately), these votes are used as a proxy for general consensus. Hypothesis 2 predicts that, prior to direct elections, there should have been little attempt to structure the EP to benefit some members over others (changes should have been generally egalitarian in as much as they served to improve the efficiency of the EP overall).

Hypothesis 2a predicts that, after direct elections, and even more so after the SEA and Maastricht (which increased the political and legislative powers of the EP dramatically), we should see a change in the character of amendments to the rules. Instead of being primarily collective goods, internal reforms should frequently be concerted attempts to bias the organization of the EP in favor of specific groups (large political groups in particular) over others (small groups and nonaffiliated members). As a result, we should expect to see an increasing percentage of proposed changes, which expanded the powers of the larger political groups since these were the groups that could manipulate voting outcomes if they worked together.

The picture presented by the data supports these hypotheses, albeit with some exceptions and not as clearly as might be desired. Part of the

---

[16] There is only one exception to this: a successfully proposed change in November 1979 that doubled the speaking time of the nonaffiliated members due to their diverse political backgrounds. This was deleted during the 1993 Maastricht revisions.

Table 5.1. *All Revisions*

Period	Majority Power (%)	Minority Power (%)	Increase EP Power (%)	New EP Power (%)	Unified in Comm. (%)
Period I (188 total)	7 (4)	5 (3)	19 (10)	16 (9)	184 (98)
Period II (91 total)	12 (13)	10 (11)	2 (2)	12 (13)	40 (44)
Period III (661 total)	90 (14)	17 (3)	44 (7)	232 (35)	490 (74)

Period	Increased Efficiency (%)	Centralize Power (%)	Technical (%)	PG power (%)	NA power (%)
Period I (188 total)	100 (53)	28 (15)	71 (38)	23 (12)	1 (1)
Period II (91 total)	37 (41)	16 (18)	27 (30)	13 (14)	7 (8)
Period III (661 total)	141 (21)	56 (8)	337 (51)	38 (6)	6 (1)

lack of clarity is due to the complexity of the amendments themselves. Many amendments attempted to accomplish several things. As was mentioned above, most changes required complementary technical revisions and frequently attempts to benefit one group of members were offset by provisions to protect some other group. As a result, the significance of amendments varied notably, and a simple classification can only give an approximation of the general patterns. The patterns of changes are demonstrated graphically in Figures 5.1–5.8. The data analyzed in the following discussion are given in Table 5.1.

Period I (1970–1979) In accordance with Hypothesis 2, the highest number of amendments that attempted to increase the efficiency of the EP occurred during the first period. Out of a total of 182 rule changes, there were 100 attempts to increase the efficiency of the EP (over 53%). Other than technical revisions (which consistently made up a high proportion of total amendments), no other category even came close. Only 15% of the proposed changes attempted to centralize power and 12% strove to increase the role of the political groups. There were additionally nineteen (10%) attempts to increase the power of the EP artificially

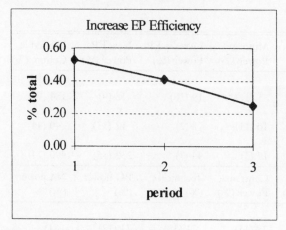

Figure 5.1 Increase EP Efficiency

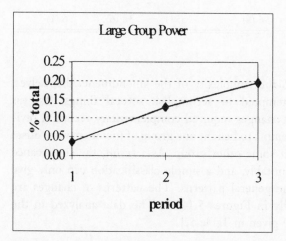

Figure 5.2 Large Group Power

(without treaty revisions). Despite the addition of budgetary power in 1970, its revision in 1975, and the introduction of direct elections agreed to in 1976, there were only sixteen (9%) proposed changes that specifically attempted to incorporate the new powers of the EP into the Rules of Procedure.

Also as predicted by Hypothesis 2, during this period there were very few proposals that increased the power of the larger political groups at the

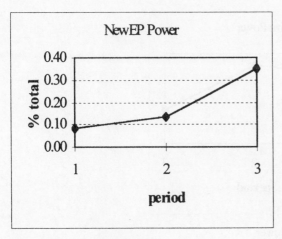

Figure 5.3 New EP Power

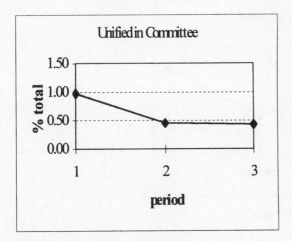

Figure 5.4 Unified in Committee

expense of the small groups or individual Members (only seven attempts, or less than 4% of all amendments). Almost 60% of these were justified by increased efficiency. There were similar patterns for amendments that granted additional powers to the political groups in general. Of the twenty-three proposed rules revisions that would have increased the role of the political groups, fourteen (or 61%) were justified by increased efficiency. This trend was even more remarkable for amendments that

109

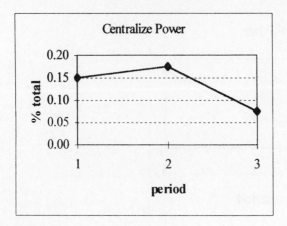

Figure 5.5 Centralize Power

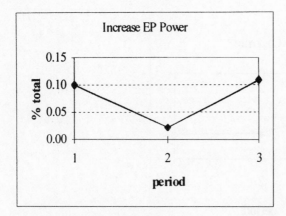

Figure 5.6 Increase EP Power

centralized power – twenty-two of the twenty-eight amendments proposed (almost 80%) were suggested to increase efficiency. Thus, the general push toward efficiency as well as the largely egalitarian nature of most proposed amendments predicted by Hypothesis 2 appears to be borne out by the data analyzed here.

However, these hypotheses also suggest that there should be a broad consensus within the Parliament, which would suggest a high passage rate and little controversy. The results of the data analysis show that in the case of the EP this does not appear to be entirely true. The rate of internal

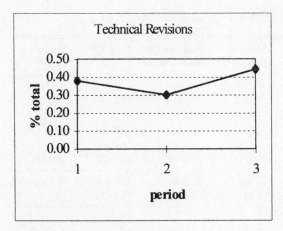

Figure 5.7   Technical Revisions

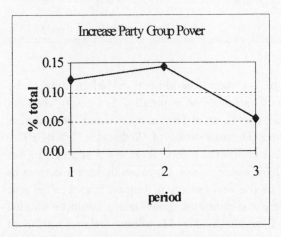

Figure 5.8   Increase Party Group Power

committee consensus (as defined earlier) was extremely high during the first period. Of the 182 changes proposed by the committee, there was general agreement on 178 of them (98%). However, the overall rate of success during the first period was only 61%, which seems low if amendments were primarily egalitarian and noncontroversial in nature. This low rate is largely due to the re-introduction of two major reports (197/76 and 198/76). These reports were sent back to committee when it became apparent that both of the largest groups (Socialists and Christian

111

Table 5.2. *All Revisions Except Docs. 197/76 and 198/76*

Period	Majority Power (%)	Minority Power (%)	Increase EP Power (%)	New EP Power (%)	Unified in Comm. (%)
Period I (115 total)	2 (2)	11 (10)	16 (14)	112 (97)	6 (5)
Period II (91 total)	10 (11)	2 (2)	12 (13)	40 (44)	12 (13)
Period III (661 total)	17 (3)	44 (7)	232 (35)	490 (74)	90 (14)

Period	Increased Efficiency (%)	Centralize Power (%)	Technical (%)	PG power (%)	NA power (%)
Period I (115 total)	64 (56)	17 (15)	40 (35)	15 (13)	1 (1)
Period II (91 total)	37 (41)	16 (18)	27 (30)	13 (14)	7 (8)
Period III (661 total)	141 (21)	56 (8)	337 (51)	38 (6)	6 (1)

Democrats) had failed to get their amendments tabled in time to be considered, either by the Committee or in plenary. As a result, they did not want to vote on the reports, or at least not on those sections that they felt needed amending (Debates sitting of Wednesday, 7 July, 1976: 103–106). It is impossible to tell if the technical error was strategic or not based on the debates. There was, however, a general desire for consensus that led the *Rapporteurs* of the two reports to request that they be sent back to committee so that the proposed amendments could be studied and incorporated (see statement by Mr. Hamilton, Debates sitting of Wednesday, 7 July, 1976: 103).[17] If only the second reports (335/76 and 336/76), which were near replicas of their predecessors, are counted, then the overall adoption rate for the first period increases significantly to 80% (see Table 5.2).

Period II (1979–1986) The results of the second period are more difficult to interpret for two reasons. First, a comparatively small number

[17] The rules stipulate that when the committee responsible requests referral back to the committee for further study, this request must be granted [rule 26(2), RoP, 1976].

of amendments were proposed (only 91) because the general revision of the rules, which was an ongoing project from 1979 to 1981, is not included in this data-set for the reasons described above. In addition, the second period was really a time of transition for the EP. It was neither the completely noninfluential body that it had been in 1970, nor the potentially powerful legislative actor that it became after the implementation of the SEA and the Maastricht Treaty. It is therefore difficult to predict based on Hypotheses 2 and 2a exactly what the behavior of the MEPs should be. It is most likely that during this transitory stage we will see actions of both an egalitarian and a self-interested nature.

While 53% of the proposed changes during the first period were aimed at increasing the efficiency of the EP, during the second period this number dropped to only 41%. At the same time, the percentage of proposed changes that gave additional powers to the larger political groups increased from only 4% to 14% (the actual number of amendments nearly doubling, from seven to thirteen). Surprisingly, the number of proposals that would have increased the role of the political groups (usually at the expense of the nonaffiliated Members) dropped from twenty-three to thirteen (although as a percentage of all amendments they remained almost the same at 14% as opposed to 13% during the previous period). The previous trend toward centralization continued with 18% of all amendments proposing changes that removed powers from the plenary to either the committees or the Bureau (president) and the enlarged Bureau. Although numerically the number of amendments proposed that increased the role of the political groups or led to centralized authority (both of which detract from the power of an individual Member) decreased during the second period, they increased as a percentage of all changes proposed. It is therefore logical to expect that, had it been possible to include the changes created by the general revision of the rules (adopted in 1981), there would have been a numerical increase as well.

There were few attempts to artificially increase the power of the European Parliament itself through manipulation of the rules during the second period, but again this does not include any attempts that were incorporated into the general revision. This is significant because of the 1980 Isoglucose decision by the European Court of Justice. The Parliament interpreted this decision to mean that it had the right, as well as the power, to delay its decision making in an attempt to force concessions from the Council. In response to this ruling, the general rules revision of 1981 included an elaborate procedure for referring a report back to committee before the final vote on the resolution if the Council refused to accept the EP's amendments [particularly if it did so without explanation (Rules, 35–39, RoP 1981)].[18] While the Court did decide that the Council had to wait for an EP opinion where so stipulated by the Treaties, it in no way stated that this gave the EP the right to delay legislation on purpose in order to extract compromises from the Council. This was the EP's interpretation, which it then used to increase its own powers through the manipulation of its Rules of Procedure.

While the addition of the new delaying procedure was well-received by the majority of the EP, the debates surrounding the general revision were extremely contentious, at one time inspiring over 5,000 amendments. The 1981 revisions made two fundamental changes: They greatly improved the clarity and schematization of the rules and they significantly expanded the role of the political groups within the internal structures of the Parliament. The former was accomplished through a complete reorganization of the rules and the addition of over sixty new rules, which formalized and clarified previous norms. The latter was realized by greatly increasing the ability of the political groups to act in ways that individual Members could not. This meant that the most controversial issue surrounding the revisions was the perceived reduction in the rights of small groups and individual Members (Debates, March 10, 1981: 14, 16–18, and 23–24).

An attempt by the EP to change its rules prior to the first direct elections, but in light of the impending doubling of its membership (from 198 to over 400), failed (Doc. 178/79). As a result, it was still possible in the newly elected Parliament to form a political group with only ten Members (provided that they came from three different Member States). Since such a group did form (The Technical Group for the Coordination of Independent Members), any attempt to increase the minimum threshold was hotly contested. The debate over increasing the minimum requirements for political group formation was exacerbated by the fact that a number of the other changes being proposed gave more power to political groups. Many of the nonaffiliated Members (whose numbers swelled from between three and five before direct elections to twenty after the accession of Greece in 1981) claimed that the changes proposed in the general revision would result in the practical requirement that Members join political

---

[18] See also the debates of March 10, 1981: 3 for the *Rapporteur's* explanation of the new rules.

groups to function effectively. They therefore insisted that the minimum requirements not be increased (Debates, 10 March, 1981: 28).

The initial report was referred back to committee twice, resulting in three different documents (1-193/79, 1-148/80/corr., and 1-926/80), although only the last report suggested the complete re-organization of the rules. The final agreement maintained the previous rule, which allowed political groups of only ten members if three Member States were represented, but increased the requirement if Members came from only one or two Member States. In addition, the role of the political groups within the EP was dramatically increased. While the political groups were mentioned in only six rules in 1972, in 1981 they were mentioned thirty-four times in twenty-two different rules. More significantly, they were specifically granted powers not available to individual Members in nineteen different rules.

The confrontation and disputes over the rules changes that resulted from the 1981 general revision suggest that, as predicted by Hypothesis 2a, there was much less consensus than had previously been the case. This conclusion is supported by the fact that only 44% of the proposed changes (not counting the 1981 revision) were adopted by a consensus in committee. Additionally, the percent of amendments adopted by the full plenary dropped from almost 80% in the first period to just over 60% in the second. At the same time, there was significant movement toward an increase in the powers of the political groups. This frequently occurred at the expense of the nonaffiliated members, who now had to band together (in groups of five, ten, or twenty-one, depending on the rule) to achieve the same powers as a single political group. When combined with the statistical results discussed earlier, this suggests that by the second period the previous attitude of consensus had, to some extent, broken down. The general focus of the Parliament (at least as far as changes to its internal structures were concerned) had shifted from primarily egalitarian attempts to increase efficiency to more confrontational political manipulations aimed at increasing relative power.

For those amendments for which we have a statistical summary, however, efficiency was still an important aspect. In addition, although the increased role of political groups had a negative impact on the non-affiliated members, there was little attempt to discriminate amongst the political groups themselves. While the number of nonaffiliated Members had increased since direct elections, they still accounted for less than 5% of the total membership of the Parliament. In this sense the second period does appear to be a kind of transitional phase, no longer primarily egalitarian, but not yet thoroughly confrontational. The benefits that were not distributed to all members, in fact, excluded very few.

Period III (1987–1994) In the third period, after the signing of the Single European Act, the situation changed considerably. It was only after the implementation of the SEA, and later the Maastricht Treaty, that the EP began to truly acquire legislative influence. The Single European Act, through the introduction of the cooperation procedure, gave the EP the power of conditional agenda-setting, allowing it to make strategic amendments that were more easily adopted than changed by the Council (Tsebelis, 1994). With Maastricht and the co-decision procedure, the EP gained the right to definitively veto legislation if it felt that the Council had not adequately incorporated its views into the final decision. Both of these changes resulted in a much more influential Parliament equipped with effective legislative tools, and the impact on its internal development was significant.

Once again there are some problems in attempting a statistical analysis of the changes to the rules that occurred during this period. While it is possible to include the rules revisions that took place in 1993 as a result of the Maastricht Treaty into the general database, the overwhelming number of changes (over 350) bury the results from other changes proposed during this period. In addition, many of the changes proposed in response to the Maastricht Treaty were largely technical in nature, or addressed only increases in EP power.[19] As a result, the changes made during the 1993 general revision will be analyzed separately from the rest of the amendments that occurred during this period (see Table 5.3).

Looking first at all revisions except those included in the Maastricht revision, there are several notable changes from the previous two periods. Hypothesis 2a predicts that as a parliament gains power majorities within it will attempt to manipulate the internal structures (via the rules) to benefit themselves. In the EP this suggests that during the third period we should expect to see a shift in power toward the largest political groups. In fact, there were fifty-two amendments (over 21%) that proposed to increase the power of the largest political groups to the detriment of the

---

[19] There were 206 changes that included technical revisions and 129 that incorporated new powers into the rules.

Table 5.3. *All Revisions Except Maastricht*

Period	Majority Power (%)	Minority Power (%)	Increase EP Power (%)	New EP Power (%)	Unified in Comm. (%)
Period I (188 total)	7 (4)	5 (3)	19 (10)	16 (9)	184 (98)
Period II (91 total)	12 (13)	10 (11)	2 (2)	12 (13)	40 (44)
Period III (296 total)	58 (20)	10 (3)	32 (11)	103 (35)	125 (42)

Period	Increased Efficiency (%)	Centralize Power (%)	Technical (%)	PG power (%)	NA power (%)
Period I (188 total)	100 (53)	28 (15)	71 (38)	23 (12)	1 (1)
Period II (91 total)	37 (41)	16 (18)	27 (30)	13 (14)	7 (8)
Period III (296 total)	74 (25)	22 (07)	131 (44)	16 (05)	4 (1)

smaller groups and independent Members. As discussed above, this was achieved primarily by canceling many of the powers given to political groups during the second period and instead requiring a large number of Members to accomplish the same thing. For example, if a previous rule allowed a political group or twelve members to call for an urgent debate, the new rule required twenty-three Members with no mention of political groups. Since the minimum number of Members required to form a political group was twelve, this change effectively restricted the powers of the smaller political groups only.

At the same time attempts to increase the efficiency of the EP fell from 55% in the first period and 41% in the second period to only 27% of all amendments (except Maastricht revisions) during the third period. Increases in centralization and, more importantly, the power of the political groups fell to 8% and 6% of the proposed changes, respectively. In both cases there were fewer changes proposed numerically than during the first period, despite the total number of proposals having risen from 182 to 244. Thus, during the third period the trend was overwhelmingly toward an increase in the power of the larger groups and away from the previous focus on the political groups in general.

There is also significant support for the hypothesis that changes to the rules become more contentious as the power of the institution increases. The rate of consensus within the committee on rules was 42% (down slightly from the second period, but a significant decrease from the first period). Despite the low rate of consensus, changes that increased the power of the larger groups were quite successful. Of the fifty-two changes proposed, forty-eight were adopted (over 92%). This suggests that there was a high level of collaboration between the larger groups to increase their own relative power.

The changes that came about as a result of the signing of the Maastricht Treaty were nearly as complete as the 1981 revisions. Over 350 changes were made in a general report, which included three smaller reports on different aspects of the revisions. The reports were presented to the full plenary after eighteen months of meetings between political group leaders as well as national parliamentary experts. There were three *Rapporteurs*, two from the Socialist group (PES) and one from the Christian Democratic (EPP) group. It should be noted once again that these were also the two largest groups in the EP, comprising between them almost 70% of the total membership of the EP.[20]

The large number of revisions inspired by the Maastricht Treaty can be misleading. A problem with quantitative analysis of this type is that it assumes that all changes are of equal significance. This is clearly not true in the case of the Maastricht revisions. Most of the changes proposed were aimed toward incorporating the new powers or making subsequent technical changes (40% and 56%, respectively).[21] In fact, less than 10% of all proposed modifications directly increased the power of the larger groups. However, these were extremely significant. The replacement of the enlarged Bureau by the Conference of Presidents and the addition of weighted voting substantially affected the balance of power between the large political groups and everyone else. In almost all areas of internal administration and organization, where decisions had previously been made either through consensus or with equal representation for all political groups via the enlarged Bureau, the larger political groups were now easily able to dominate if they worked together. This meant that it was no

[20] In 1993, the Socialists had 198 members and the EPP had 163, and the total membership of the EP was 518.
[21] Just over 50% of the revisions made to incorporate new powers also required technical revisions (68 out of 129).

longer necessary for all of the political groups to join together and seek compromises on potentially divisive issues.

Despite the overwhelming significance of this change, there was very little attention given to it in the debates during the full plenary session, in which the proposed changes were adopted. Both the PES and the EPP supported the general report, although there were differences of opinion between them on some particulars.[22] Some of the smaller groups, as well as the nonaffiliated Members, protested the general trend toward increased powers for the larger groups (in particular Members of the political groups of the extreme right), but not the creation of the Conference of Presidents in particular (debates No. 3-434, 1993: 44–47 and especially the explanations of vote, pages 141–143). In fact, the creation of the Conference of Presidents was mentioned only once, by a member of the Socialist group who hailed it, unsurprisingly, as a step forward. (Ibid., page 142).

An overwhelming majority (311 votes for, 18 against, and 31 abstentions) adopted the report on revision of the rules resulting from the Maastricht Treaty. The only party group to actively oppose it was the Rainbow group; the nonaffiliated Members also voted against. Thus, despite the significant shift of powers toward the two largest groups, the general level of consensus on the Maastricht revisions was actually higher than during the first period (over 86%).

The results for the third period are, therefore, somewhat mixed. There was clearly a general shift toward increased power for the largest groups. This is evident both quantitatively (all revisions except Maastricht) and qualitatively (Maastricht). In addition, the general trend toward changes focused on increasing internal efficiency continued to decrease (from 41% in the second period to just 27% in the third), as did consensus in committee on revisions *not* included in the Maastricht revisions (down to just 42%). However, the changes adopted as a result of the Maastricht Treaty remain something of a problem for Hypothesis 2a. Instead of a decrease in consensus it actually reached an all-time high (figures for specific items in committee are not available, but the proposal as a whole was adopted unanimously by the committee). Despite extremely important changes to the internal organizational structures of the EP that clearly meant a

---

[22] In particular, the two groups disagreed over when explanations of the vote should occur (an ongoing debate in the EP). The PES felt that it should remain before the final vote while the EPP pushed (successfully) for a more ambiguous language that allowed explanations only after the final vote.

significant increase in the powers of the two largest groups, the smaller groups (in particular, the Liberals and the Greens) did not rebel, or even complain. The bulk of the smaller political groups actually supported the revisions that would reduce their relative powers. Clearly this does not follow from the assumption that individual Members will want to increase their relative power as the potential of the EP to impact legislation increases. Perhaps the smaller groups knew that they could not block the changes and therefore bargained for other benefits, or perhaps they believed that the creation of the Conference of Presidents would be so beneficial in terms of efficiency that it was worth the loss of power. Unfortunately, alternate theories are hard to prove or disprove since the vast majority of discussions between the group leaders occurred behind closed doors and strictly off the record.

Conclusions

The general pattern of internal EP reforms roughly follows that predicted by the macro model of legislative development (Hypotheses 1 and 1a). The two most substantial rules revisions occurred as a result of large exogenous changes. The introduction of direct elections in 1979 was the obvious inspiration behind the 1981 general revision, and the adoption of the Maastricht Treaty led to almost equally broad revisions in 1993. Although the two other "critical moments" also led to rules revisions, they were on the whole less substantial. In particular, the 1970 Budget Act (and 1975 revision) led to only minimal changes to the rules and no thorough reform.

Also supporting the macro model is the fact that many of the reforms that occurred as a result of exogenous increases in the role or powers of the EP were collective goods in that they insured the continued relevance of the EP as an institution. Without substantial reforms to incorporate directly elected Members or new legislative procedures, the EP would have been unable to perform its prescribed tasks and eventually would have been marginalized. By demonstrating that it could function with an increased legislative load after the SEA, the EP furthered its crusade for legislative influence and convinced the other EU institutions that it should be taken seriously (Westlake, 1995: 138).

On the other hand, there were numerous reforms that cannot be directly tied to the need to incorporate new powers into the EP's internal organizational structures. Many of the reforms that were proposed in the name of "increased efficiency" were clearly not egalitarian. The most notable exceptions were the introduction of the Conference of Presidents and the effective block against numerous actions by small party groups on the floor of the plenary. These reforms cannot be fully explained by the macro model, which accurately predicts only their timing, not their character. To understand why these reforms were selected over others it is necessary to invoke the micro model of legislative behavior.

In applying the micro model to the European Parliament it was necessary to make several assumptions, based on the changing character of the EP as an institution. Since it seemed likely that in a lame duck legislature it would be in the interests of all Members to increase the power of the institution, I assumed that during the early years of the EP (prior to 1979) there would be a general consensus amongst MEPs. This would result in internal revisions that focused primarily on increasing the efficiency and, as a consequence, the power(s) of the EP.

Once the potential to have an impact on the legislative outcomes of the EU as whole was achieved, I predicted that internal consensus would begin to break down. In the absence of an electoral connection, I assumed that ideal policy outcomes would be the goals of Members. As a result, I predicted that certain segments of the EP would attempt to make internal revisions that benefited themselves so that they would have a higher probability of achieving their goals (policy objectives). This process would persist as long as the EP continued to gain more and more power in relation to the other institutions of the union. Internal revisions would begin to benefit a more and more restricted class of members (those who were powerful enough to successfully push for change in their favor). In the case of the European Parliament, I predicted that the larger groups (as opposed to the more typical ideological majority of the left or right) would be able to manipulate the rules to their benefit, and would increasingly do so as the powers of the EP grew.

The quantitative analysis of the changes to the Rules of Procedure proposed by the rules committee also largely support these hypotheses, although not without some significant exceptions. As predicted by the micro model, there was a generally decreasing focus on changes that increased the efficiency of the EP as a percentage of all changes. At the same time, changes that benefited the political groups, and later only the larger groups, became an increasing share of all proposed revisions. Also as predicted, consensus in the committee decreased, with the important exception of the revisions implemented as a result of the Maastricht Treaty.

Despite significant changes that dramatically increased the potential role of the two largest groups, the Maastricht revisions were adopted by a large majority with little dissent. There was no mention in the debates of the replacement of the enlarged Bureau by the Conference of Presidents and the change to weighted voting. While the fact that these changes occurred is predicted by Hypothesis 2a, the concurrence of the smaller parties is not. An explanation for why smaller political groups would willingly devolve their power to the larger groups is not immediately clear.

In addition to the puzzle of the Maastricht revisions, the inability to include the 1981 general revisions into the general database leaves us with some questions. While the new rules created by the 1981 general revision can be qualitatively discussed, it is not possible to take them apart and study individual changes to particular rules. It is therefore impossible to determine whether the revisions of 1981 wholly support the hypotheses or follow the trends of the other changes. As a result, the conclusions of the second period must be looked upon as somewhat tentative, although they do support the predicted hypotheses. On the whole, however, the results of this analysis largely support both the macro and micro hypotheses. This analysis has underlined the need to apply both models for a full understanding of the timing and nature of internal legislative development and the role of increased legislative power in shaping the character of internal institutional development.

This application of the macro and micro models has increased our understanding of the impact of external increases in the legislative power and political authority of the EP on the development of its internal organizational structures. In particular, the steadily increasing role of the party groups and particularly the two largest groups has been highlighted. Next we will examine how the same exogenous increases in EP power affected the interactions between party groups and the development of the party group system as a whole.

6

The Development of the Supranational Party Group System: Conflict and Cooperation in the Coalition Formation Process

As Chapter 5 demonstrated, the party groups have been fundamental in determining the internal organization of the EP as a whole. Just as the relative power of the groups vis-à-vis individual Members has varied over time, so have their relationships with each other. The purpose of this chapter is to trace the development of the party group system through an examination of the interactions between the party groups in the coalition formation process. This will help to determine the impact of increases in the legislative authority of the European Parliament on the character and evolution of the party system. The analysis will also serve as a test of the usefulness of the macro and micro models in predicting the course of party system, as opposed to parliamentary development.

Past studies of the European Union have generally concluded that the party groups, like the EP itself, are incidental to the functioning of the EU as a whole. The perceived absence of party discipline and leadership (a point that will be discussed further in Chapter 8) combined with their perceived frequent recourse to cooperation across ideological boundaries has led most scholars of the European Union to conclude that the party group system is either nonexistent or unimportant. While the role of the EP has recently begun to be re-appraised in the literature, the significance of the party groups and their interactions have not (Peters, 1992; Nugent, 1994; Corbett et al., 1995).[1]

---

[1] It is interesting to note that for the first time studies on power indices and interinstitutional power games have begun to incorporate the EP into their calculations (Colomer and Hosli, 1997; Laruelle and Widgrén, 1997; Steunenberg, Schmidtchen and Koboldt, 1997).

The growing importance of the party groups in the internal functioning of the European Parliament has already been demonstrated in Chapter 5. Here I examine the history and evolution of their relationships with one another. Through a statistical analysis of voting behavior I test the hypotheses about the changing nature of interparty group coalitions suggested by the macro and micro models and outlined in Chapter 3. By examining voting behavior I demonstrate that the nature of the party group system has, in fact, changed over time and that this change corresponds to external increases in the legislative authority of the EP as predicted by the macro and micro models. In the next chapter I respond to those who claim that interparty cooperation across ideological boundaries is pervasive and a sign of party group weakness. I demonstrate that cross-party cooperation is largely a function of the institutional design of the European Union. As a result, bipartisanship is a sign of the party groups' continued desire to participate effectively in the legislative process of the EU (i.e., pursue their policy goals) rather than their weakness or insignificance.

Applying the Macro and Micro Models

The decision to organize the internal structure of the European Parliament on the basis of ideological affinity rather than national identity or regional similarities was a crucial element in differentiating the EP from the other international assemblies of the time. The creation of political party groups helped to determine the developmental path of the EP, assisting in the eventual transition from international chamber of debate to politically influential legislature. The pattern and character of political party group interactions were not, however, pre-determined. Precisely because there had never been meaningful political parties within an international assembly, there was no developmental model for the party system of the European Parliament. Each Member State had different norms of political party interaction; thus, there was no standard of behavior shared by all Members of the EP. The lack of a pre-existing set of norms for interparty group relations at the international level led to the creation of a variable party system within the European Parliament. This flexibility allowed the party system of the EP to evolve and change in reaction to developments in the larger political environment of the European Union. The variability and evolution of the EP party system can be seen in the changes that have occurred in the working relationships between the political groups due to the shifting legislative potential and responsibilities of the European Parliament. Just as the European Parliament is still in the process of developing, the political groups are still testing and restructuring the character of their interactions.

The adapted macro model presented in Chapter 3 predicted that the party groups within the EP would modify their behavior and interactions in response to changes in the broader political environment. The micro model predicted that modifications would be initiated by, and to the benefit of, those who are able to implement change. Taken together, these models suggest that the relationships between political parties will be integrally connected to the role of the Parliament within the larger political system (Hypothesis 3) and the relative balance of power between the party groups within the EP (Hypotheses 3 and 4). The application of these models requires that we understand both the changing role of the EP in the larger political environment and the impact that this has had on the goals of the party groups, as well as their relative ability to achieve them.

Hypothesis 4 suggested that in a parliament, which has no legislative role to play, political parties have little use for interparty compromise or cooperation as far as legislative proposals are concerned.[2] This is because a party that is unable to affect policy outcomes is likely to be less cautious or moderate in its political rhetoric since it will not be forced to substantiate or initiate its plans and proposals.[3] Political parties with no real legislative responsibilities will frequently attempt to increase public support for their programs and policy objectives by making sweeping promises and attempting to clearly differentiate themselves from the opposition.[4] This forces the parties away from each other and towards the ideological extremes causing the polarization of the party system as a whole. The likely result is little or no compromise between ideologically opposed party groups or coalitions.

[2] As we have seen, this is not necessarily so for other aspects of parliamentary action, such as internal revisions or interinstitutional battles, where common goals are shared by all or some parties regardless of ideological differences.

[3] The same might also be true of a parliament with hegemonic legislative powers if there was a single party with an absolute majority (and thus no need for any interparty compromise).

[4] Sartori (1976) labels this type of political party "irresponsible," in reference largely to the old Italian Communist Party (PCI) in Italy.

Aslo, according to Hypothesis 4, however, once legislative power is attained the level of interparty cooperation is liable to increase significantly, *assuming that the legislature does not gain absolute control of the legislative process* and no single party controls an absolute majority. Once a parliament becomes an effective legislative actor parties are forced to moderate their positions for two reasons. First, without hegemonic control of the legislative process some compromise is necessary to coordinate and work effectively with the other actors involved. Second, extreme ideological positions, while a potentially effective electoral tool, rarely lead to viable policy outcomes. As a result, most parties begin to moderate their political objectives once they attain power and have the opportunity to effectively pursue their proposed objectives.[5] The breadth and depth of cooperation will depend on many factors, such as: the extent of the Parliament's autonomy; the relative division of power between parties; and the potential public backlash in response to the policies pursued (Sartori, 1976; Panebianco, 1982). If the hypotheses suggested by the macro and micro models are applicable to the EP, the level of party group polarization within the EP should decrease and intergroup cooperation increase, as the legislative powers of the EP grow.

To understand this relationship it is necessary to recall two things: that policy outcomes are the primary goals of both individual MEPs and the party groups (as discussed in Chapter 2), and that the European Union is a political system of checks and balances. The potential of the EP to impact EU policy, despite increases in its legislative authority, would be nullified if its proposals were too ideologically extreme to be adopted by the other institutional actors.[6] EP influence on the policy process of the European Union requires moderation and cooperation *between* political groups. If MEPs and party groups are rational actors in pursuit of their policy objectives, we should expect to see a general shift toward the center within the party system as a whole as the legislative powers of the EP increase.[7] In this sense, increased cooperation between party groups is a sign of political maturity, not party group irrelevance.

---

[5] This is a common trend even in established political systems, for example, the frequent phenomenon of campaign promises that fade or disappear once office is achieved.

[6] This is especially true of the Council, where national differing interests and a preference for national sovereignty have led to a general rule of consensus decision making (Hayes-Renshaw and Wallace, 1997).

[7] We should expect interparty cooperation only so long as the EP does not gain unilateral legislative power *and* a single dominant party.

Methodology

The best method for measuring the level of political polarization within a system will vary depending on the system itself. The party system of the European Parliament is unique in that it is almost nonexistent outside of the EP itself. The party groups do not organize mass memberships, they have only very tenuous international electoral platforms, and, most importantly, they do not create enduring coalitions in support of a particular government. Freedom from supporting a government means that coalition formation within the EP can be extremely variable, potentially shifting from one vote to the next without destabilizing the political system as a whole. Subject matter, legislative procedure, and historical period are all likely to have some influence on the type of coalition formed between party groups.

The membership of the coalitions that form between the groups, their relative strength, and durability are all important characteristics of the party system. To get an accurate picture of the nature of the party system of the EP and changes that may have occurred across time or legislative procedure, I examine the voting behavior of the party groups during roll-call votes. The bulk of all votes (roughly 75%) in the EP are taken visually (usually by raised hands, but occasionally by sitting and standing). Approximately another 10% of votes are registered electronically, but with no public record of whom supported which position. Generally, electronic votes are used to establish exact numbers when the vote is perceived to be close and a visual determination of victory unreliable (Guéguen, 1992). The remaining 15% of votes in the European Parliament are taken by roll-call vote (RCV).[8] Only votes taken by this last method provide the necessary information about the voting behavior of individuals, national delegations, and party groups to allow a statistical analysis of coalition formation behavior and patterns.

I examine roll-call votes that occurred between 1980 and 1996. I begin my analysis in 1980 for two reasons. First, the Members of the European Parliament were not directly elected until 1979. An independent party system could not fully develop as long as individual Members were still appointed by their national legislatures. Second, and more pragmatically,

---

[8] To be more precise, about 15% of the votes since 1980 have been roll-call votes. Prior to 1980 there was no electronic voting system and roll-call votes were much less frequent because of the incredible amount of time that they took to register.

roll-call votes were taken orally until 1980, when a new electronic registration system was installed. The amount of time required for an RCV dropped from upward of an hour per vote to less than a minute. The increased ease of roll-call voting led almost immediately to a huge increase in its usage. Before 1980 there were an average of fewer than four roll-call votes per monthly plenary session. This number has increased steadily over time. In extreme cases, like the annual draft budget, there can now be as many as 300 roll-call votes on a single proposal.

By reducing the time necessary to tabulate results, the installation of the electronic voting system significantly lowered the costs involved in calling for an RCV. While electronic votes are almost exclusively used for technical reasons, roll-call votes have largely become a political tool. There are three primary strategic goals of roll-call votes: control, information, and publicity, the first two being the most common.[9] Party group leaders frequently use roll-call votes to assess the internal cohesion of their group as a whole and, in particular, the influence of regional and/or national deviations.[10] Roll-call votes can also be used by the party group hierarchies as a means of enforcing or at least measuring the effectiveness of party discipline and the attendance rates of Members.[11] The importance of this use of the roll-call vote can be seen in the rapid and extensive development of internal party group whipping procedures. Special "sessions units" have been created to ensure that every MEP in the group has a copy of the group's positions and measure the extent to which these are followed.[12]

Party groups also frequently call for a roll-call vote to clearly, and publicly, differentiate themselves from other groups. In these cases the primary

---

[9] According to interviews with forty-seven MEPs from the PES, EPP, and ELDR groups held between January 1996 and May 1996.

[10] The use and potential expansion of sanctions against members of a group that are consistently absent or vote against the party line on important matters is being considered by both the European People's Party Group and the Party of European Socialists Group. Currently, reduced allocation of speaking time and a failure to be assigned to particularly interesting tasks (usually involving travel) are all potential sanctions against members who consistently fail to vote the political group line. The potential for party group elite to effectively use benefits and sanctions against Members of their groups is discussed in depth in Chapter 8.

[11] Member attendance was of primary importance to party group leaders and absenteeism was described as a significant problem for the EP by all interviewed.

[12] The use of whips is most developed in the PES, followed closely by the EPP. The development of whipping procedures within the party groups is discussed further in Chapter 8.

motivation is to make a public statement; measurement or control of internal group cohesion is secondary. More generally, this type of roll-call voting is used to highlight the activities and behavior of other groups, rather than investigate behavior in one's own group. The goal is to draw public attention to the activities of other groups that are objectionable to those calling for a roll-call vote.[13] A roll-call vote might also be called to draw attention to actions of the individuals calling for the vote (as opposed to the actions of others). For instance, prior to a national election, MEPs of the same member state might request a roll-call vote to demonstrate that they were voting in their home state's interests despite their own party group's stance on an issue. This often is the case when RCVs are called, despite an overwhelming majority on one side or the other.

Because there are numerous strategic reasons for calling roll-call votes, in most cases it is impossible to know why any individual RCV was called without an in-depth analysis of the particular circumstances. As a result it is extremely difficult to infer, based on the results of an analysis of roll-call voting, what occurs the rest of the time in terms of voting cohesion and coalition formation. This is an objective limitation of analyses of roll-call votes not only inside the EP, but in any context where the decision to have a roll-call vote is left to the strategic calculations of the actors instead of specific rules. Despite this limitation, an analysis of voting behavior during roll-call votes will increase our understanding of the party system of the EP, and how it has evolved over the last two decades.

Roll-call votes can occur on any subject and under any legislative procedure, although the strategic significance of RCVs may vary by procedure. When the European Parliament was created the only legislative procedure involving the EP stipulated by the Treaties was the consultation procedure. The European Parliament, through its own Rules of Procedure, gave the EP the right to create "own initiative" reports, which are known as resolutions (Rule 29 in the original Rules of Procedure in 1958, Rule 48 in the 14th edition, 1999). In 1987 the Single European Act (SEA) created the cooperation procedure, and in 1994 the Maastricht Treaty added the co-decision procedure (reformed by the Amsterdam

---

[13] This type of strategic roll-call vote is frequently used by the ELDR to protest what it perceives as the development of a PES/EPP oligarchy. The relationship between the EPP and the PES is discussed in depth later.

Treaty).[14] Each of these procedures granted the EP a different amount of direct legislative influence. Resolutions have no direct influence over legislative outcomes, and they are not acted on by any other institution, but they are the only type of proposal that can be initiated independently by the EP. Historically resolutions have been influential in motivating the other institutions of the EU to act on certain issues.[15] The consultation, cooperation, and co-decision procedures each give the EP increasingly more direct influence over legislative outcomes.[16]

In this chapter I examine one-hundred roll-call votes on resolutions occurring between 1980 and 1996. In the next chapter I expand the analysis to include an additional 200 votes, 100 each under the cooperation and co-decision procedures.[17] The focus in this chapter is longitudinal change in coalition formation patterns between 1980 and 1996, and in particular the impact that increased legislative authority has had on the process. In the next chapter I am more limited temporally due to the recent implementation of the new procedures (third and fourth legislatures only), and the focus of the analysis is a more in-depth understanding of the influence of institutional structure of the EU on patterns of coalition formation.

Correspondence analysis is the primary statistical tool used in both chapters to establish and analyze the patterns of coalition formation in the European Parliament.[18] The underlying data-sets consist of a table with the rows consisting of member state delegations to the party groups (i.e., French, Socialist) and columns consisting of the votes of these delegations (every MEP could vote "yes," "no," or be "absent").[19] The data-sets can

---

[14] There is additionally an "assent" procedure used, for example, during the accession of a new Member State. This was introduced by the Single European Act but is used infrequently.

[15] Examples include sanctions on South Africa under Apartheid and boycotts on animal products resulting from inhumane hunting practices.

[16] Each of these procedures is discussed in Chapter 4. The relative power of the EP under the cooperation and co-decision procedures is still somewhat unclear. For a discussion of the cooperation procedure, see Tsebelis (1994, 1996) and Moser (1996). For a discussion of the co-decision procedure, see Scully (1997) and Tsebelis and Garrett (1997).

[17] Votes under the consultation procedure were not included because of the relatively small influence of the EP under this procedure and the changing role of the consultation procedure across time.

[18] A logistic analysis is also used in the next chapter to evaluate the impact of subject area on coalition formation.

[19] Abstentions were not used in the statistical analyses because of their comparatively small number and statistical insignificance.

be understood as contingency tables where $X*Y$ votes (the number of votes analyzed $*$ the number of MEPs voting) are distributed to different vote positions and different delegations.

There are two properties of this technique that are necessary to understand the analysis that follows. The first is that if two columns or two rows are represented close to each other in the graphics, their profiles are similar (have low χ^2 distance). For example, if two delegations fall close to each other, their voting patterns are similar (i.e., their members vote in similar ways, in terms of percentages, across the whole set of bills). With respect to vote positions, if two of them are close to each other, it means that they have been supported by the same constellation of forces. For example, if the same coalition supported bill x and opposed bill y, the projection of "yes" for bill x will be identical with the projection of "no" for bill y.

The second property is termed the "barycentric principle" and permits inferences to be made from the association (correspondence) between columns and rows. Correspondence analysis projects rows into the center of gravity of the columns that produce them. Consequently, rows are projected into the area of columns with which they are associated (the corresponding numbers are high). Correspondence analysis is unique in this respect, because it permits inferences concerning rows to be drawn from the observation of the projections of columns, and vice versa. Thus, if some delegations are projected close to a cluster of votes, they are the ones casting those particular votes.

The inferences drawn from the distances between two columns or two rows are significantly different than the inferences drawn from the distance between a column and a row. Distances between two columns or two rows are chi-squared distances and have a direct substantive interpretation. Distances between the representation of a column and a row cannot be interpreted directly but have an indirect relation. Distances between rows are interpreted as differences in voting patterns of two groups, and distances between columns as differences in the composition of coalitions that supported or opposed the legislation.[20] The relationships between

---

[20] For more information on this procedure as it relates to coalition formation in the European Parliament, see Kreppel and Tsebelis (1999). For an extended discussion of the statistical method itself, see Benjecri (1973). For a discussion in English, see Greenacre (1984). I owe George Tsebelis a debt of thanks for patiently and repeatedly explaining this procedure to me.

party groups established by the correspondence analysis are checked through the use of correlation coefficients.

The period analyzed here covers the better part of the first four legislative periods after direct elections.[21] During this period the number and size of the party groups within the European Parliament have changed significantly. In the period immediately following direct election, the number of party groups quickly expanded from four to seven, reaching an all-time high of ten during the early 1990s. Only the Socialists (PES), Christian Democrats (EPP), and Liberal (ELDR) groups survived the entire period analyzed without major internal schisms and/or name changes. The EPP merged with the European Democratic Group (ED) (mostly British Conservatives) in 1992, but the two groups had an informal association since Britain's accession in 1973. The Communist and Neo-Gaullist groups have remained present throughout the period in one form or another, but both have suffered internal schisms and membership instability. The other groups, most of which are comparatively small, have been on the whole short-lived and unstable.[22] The majority of this analysis will focus on the three major party groups (PES, EPP, and ELDR) since their interactions can be charted across time. The behavior of the other groups will be examined primarily in terms of broad right–left coalition behavior rather than individually. A list of all of the party groups in the EP since 1979, their membership, and ideological location is given in Appendix D.

Individual roll-call votes were selected randomly. A month was chosen at random for each legislative procedure. A list of all roll-call votes under a given procedure occurring during the selected month for each year analyzed were collected into a single database and numbered chronologically. One hundred random numbers were generated for each legislative procedure, and the votes corresponding to these numbers were used for the analyses.[23] Votes selected were not restricted by the level of

---

[21] Elections to the EP are in June, so legislatures run July 1979–June 1984, July 1984–June 1989, July 1989–June 1994, and July 1994–June 1999.

[22] An exception is the Green group, which has been in existence since 1989. It is still too soon to judge the future durability of this group, although it appears promising since the group increased its seat share in the 1999 election significantly.

[23] For resolutions all votes were used for the years 1980, 1981, and 1983 because of the small number of total roll-call votes occurring during the selected month during these years.

participation, content (amendment or final proposal), or size of majority coalition.[24]

I examine several aspects of EP voting behavior, including changes that have occurred across time, differences between party groups and national delegations, and patterns and changes in the rate of absenteeism since not voting is, in effect, a kind of voting behavior. In addition, the extremely high rate of absenteeism in the EP is likely to have had an important influence on coalition behavior in general.[25]

Patterns of Coalition Formation: Resolutions (1980–1996)

During the first and second legislative periods the majority of EP roll-call votes were on resolutions. Although the consultation procedure existed, it does not appear to have inspired recourse to strategic use of roll-call voting to the extent that resolutions did.[26] During the latter two legislatures roll-call voting on resolutions dropped off significantly, probably because of a decrease in the raw number of resolutions presented as a result of the addition of the cooperation and co-decision procedures.[27] Unlike the other legislative procedures, resolutions are not limited to specific policy areas. As a result, resolutions vary widely in topic, relative importance, and level of participation.

I Legislature: 1979–1983[28]

The variable nature of resolutions might logically lead to incoherent voting patterns, if coalitions in the EP vary primarily by policy area. This

---

[24] Numerous previous studies of roll-call voting have limited their analysis to specific types of votes (final proposals), set participation thresholds, or required a specific distribution of votes between the majority and the minority. See in particular the works by Attina' (1990, 1992) and Brzinski (1995).

[25] This will be more important in the next chapter, since the impact is likely to be higher under the cooperation and co-decision procedures during the second round, when there are absolute majority requirements.

[26] Since data were drawn only from the November or December plenary sessions, this may be due to timing. It is possible that roll-call votes under the consultation procedure occurred more frequently in other months.

[27] During the second and third legislatures there were changes to the rules of procedure that limited the ease and ability of individual Members or small groups to present "own initiative" resolutions independent of a committee proposal.

[28] The first legislature ran from July 1979 to June 1984. No votes from 1979 are included here for the reasons outlined previously.

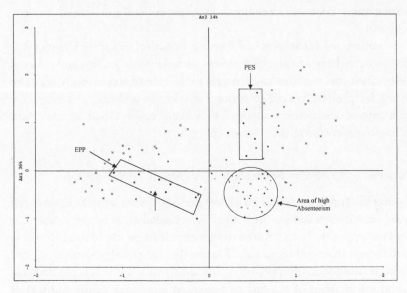

Figure 6.1 Ideology and Participation – Resolutions I Legislature

does not seem to be the case. During the first legislature there are two clear patterns in the data: Voting coalitions are divided between the left and right, and absenteeism is nearly universally high, although there are also significant variations between party groups. The clear left–right ideological split and the importance of participation in the EP during the first legislature are demonstrated in Figure 6.1.

In the figure each "x" represents a vote position ("yes" or "no") on a particular resolution; an absent "position" is represented by a period. The squares are national delegations that belong to the Christian Democratic Group (EPP), the diamonds are delegations that belong to the Socialist Group (PES), and the "+" are delegations belonging to the Liberal-Democratic Group (ELDR). The first axis (horizontal) accounts for 36% of the total variation in voting behavior, and the second axis accounts for 14%.

The majority of the EPP delegations fall to the left of the vertical axis while all of the PES delegations fall to the right. This clear division between members of the EPP and members of the PES along the

134

horizontal axis indicates that this axis represents ideology. This means that delegations that fall near the vertical axis are ideologically centrist, delegations to the left agree more with the EPP, and those to the right are more likely to agree with the Socialist group. The comparatively centrist role of the ELDR can be seen by the location of these delegations between the EPP and PES (though closer to the former). The other party group delegations conform to this general pattern, with groups on the ideological left primarily to the right near the Socialists and groups on the ideological right closer to the EPP in the left half of the figure.[29]

The vertical axis is slightly more difficult to interpret, but it can be generally understood as a combination of numerical support (for vote positions) and participation (for party groups). Vote positions close to the horizontal axis received a large percentage of the vote relative to other vote positions for the same resolution. As vote positions move farther away from the horizontal axis they have comparatively fewer supporters. As they move to the left their supporters are members of the ideological right, and as they move toward the right the ideological left supports them more. The high level of absenteeism can be seen by the position of the "."'s close to the horizontal axis. These are clustered slightly to the right, suggesting that the party groups of the ideological left have a slightly lower rate of participation than the party groups of the right (i.e., more absences).

The spatial distance between delegations belonging to the PES and EPP is a graphic representation of the large proportion of the variation in voting behavior explained by ideology (36%). The clear division between the groups of the right and left suggests a high level of ideological dogmatism and relatively little cooperation between the Socialists and Christian Democrats. There are, in fact, very few vote positions ("x"s) that fall between the two party group clusters. The lack of cooperation between the EPP and PES is supported by the correlation coefficients of the different party groups (Table 6.1). While the correlation coefficients between the EPP and the European Democratic Group (.93) and the Socialists and Communists (.55) are both high, the coefficient between the EPP and PES

---

[29] Any symbol not an "x" or a "." is a delegation to a party group. Only the delegations to the EPP and the PES were highlighted to help make the figure more easily interpreted. The other delegations and party groups follow the same pattern, with the exception of the Technical Group of Independent Members, which cannot be located on the traditional left–right ideological spectrum.

Table 6.1. *Correlation Coefficients – Resolutions I Legislature*

	COM	EPD	EDG	ELDR	NA	EPP	PES	TECH
COM	1							
EPD	0.18	1						
EDG	−0.36	−0.17	1					
ELDR	−0.03	0.12	0.54	1				
NA	0.02	0.14	0.20	0.20	1			
EPP	−0.32	−0.09	0.93	0.58	0.20	1		
PES	0.55	0.04	0.13	0.36	0.37	**0.15**	1	
TECH	0.39	0.25	−0.18	−0.03	0.44	−0.19	0.21	1

COM = Communist group, EPD = European Progressive Democrats, EDG = European Democratic group, ELDR = European Liberal and Democratic and Reform group, NA = nonaffiliated, EPP = European Peoples' Party group, PES = Party of European Socialists group, TECH = group of Technical Coordination.

is extremely low (.15). The Liberal Group votes with both the EPP and the PES, though more frequently with the former.

Another important aspect of coalition formation and party system behavior is success, since policy is the final goal of the legislative process. This is true even when the ability to impact final legislative outcomes is extremely small and indirect. The success of the different voting coalitions can be seen in Figure 6.2. Here only vote positions that won are "X"s while those that lost are represented by wedges. The proximity of almost all of the winning vote positions to delegations belonging to the EPP demonstrates the dominance of the ideological right over resolutions during the first legislature. The supremacy of the right is not, however, clearly linked to a numerical advantage. The Socialist group was actually larger than the EPP, with an average membership of 119 compared to 111. The right wing coalition of the EPP and the EDG had only a small numerical advantage over the PES and the Communist coalition (174 versus 165). The real strength of the right lies in its higher level of internal cohesion (both within and between the party groups) and a higher rate of participation (see Table 6.2).

While the EPP and EDG each had an internal cohesion rating of 98%, the PES and Communist group had cohesion scores of only 89% and 88%, respectively.[30] The right wing coalition's advantage was compounded by

---

[30] Cohesion scores were tabulated on the basis of "yes" and "no" votes only with the function: $(Y + N)/N$; if $<.5$, $= 1 - ((Y + N)/N)$, if $>.5 = (Y + N)/N$.

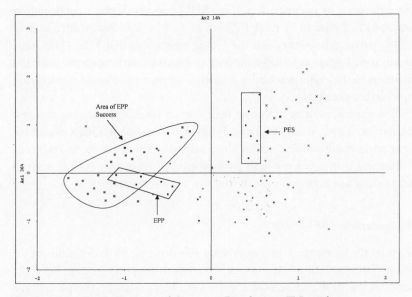

Figure 6.2 Party Groups and Success – Resolutions II Legislature

Table 6.2. *Party Group Cohesion and Participation – Resolutions I Legislature*

Party Group	Avg. Percent Voting	Internal Cohesion	Avg. # Members
COM	37	0.88	46
EPD	35	0.97	22
EDG	63	0.98	63
ELDR	41	0.95	39
NA	34	0.85	13
EPP	53	0.98	111
PES	44	0.89	119
TECH	30	0.91	11
Total	47	n/a	424

COM = Communist group, EPD = European Progressive Democrats, EDG = European Democratic group, ELDR = European Liberal and Democratic and Reform group, NA = nonaffiliated, EPP = European Peoples' Party group, PES = Party of European Socialists group, TECH = group of Technical Coordination.

the difference in participation. The EDG had the highest participation rate at 63%, followed by the EPP with 53%. The Socialist group had only a 44% participation rate, and the Communists a dismal 37%. The combination of higher internal cohesion and higher participation made the coalition of the right practically invincible against the almost numerically equal leftist coalition.

The general picture of voting behavior on resolutions during the first legislature is one of an ideologically divided parliament with a dominant right wing coalition due not to electoral success, but to the internal cohesion and comparatively high participation of its members. The overall image does not change much during the second legislature.

II Legislature: 1984–1988

Despite the continued predominance of ideology as a determinant of voting patterns, there are some differences in party group behavior between the first and second legislatures. Most notably, the percentage of variation explained by ideology alone dropped from 36% to only 25% (see Figure 6.3). This decrease is due in part to a general increase in

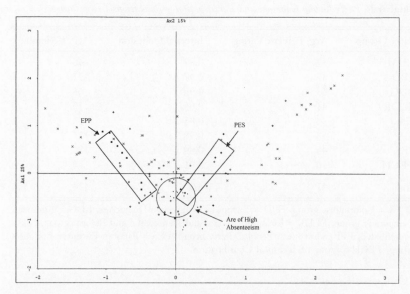

Figure 6.3   Ideology and Participation – Resolutions II Legislature

138

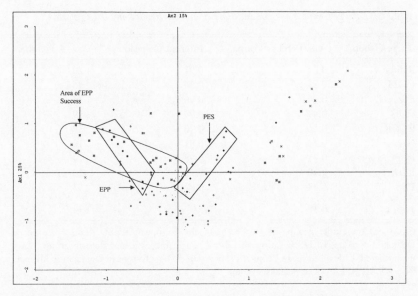

Figure 6.4 Party Groups and Success – Resolutions II Legislature

absenteeism. While total average participation for the first legislature was 47%, it was only 38% during the second legislature. This increase in overall absenteeism is demonstrated in Figure 6.3 by the large cluster of group delegations and voting positions located just below the intersection of the x and y axes. The centrality of this cluster means that participation fell relatively equally across the ideological spectrum.

Another difference between the first and second legislatures is the relative success of the left and right wing coalitions. While the right still won more votes than the left, it no longer had the near complete control over resolutions that it did during the first legislature (Figure 6.4). The number of successful vote positions ("x"s) in the right half of the figure increased from only 4% in the first legislature to 24% in the second. There was also an increase in the number of successful vote positions falling in the center of the figure, and supported predominantly by the Socialist and Liberal Groups, but with some scattered support from members of the EPP. The appearance of vote positions supported in all or part by the three major party groups marks the beginning of a significant trend of "grand coalition" votes.

The increased success of the PES-led left wing coalition had two main causes. The most obvious was the electoral success experienced by the

Table 6.3. *Party Group Cohesion and Participation – Resolutions II Legislature*

Party Group	Avg. Percent Voting	Internal Cohesion	Avg. # Members
Rainbow	0.27	0.91	20
COM	0.33	0.94	46
ER	0.54	0.90	16
EDG	0.43	0.99	59
ELDR	0.26	0.90	38
NA	0.20	0.81	10
EPP	0.41	0.98	114
EDA	0.10	0.98	30
PES	0.44	0.89	152
TOTAL	0.38	n/a	484

COM = Communist group, ER = Group of the European Right, EDG = European Democratic group, ELDR = European Liberal and Democratic and Reform group, NA = nonaffiliated, EPP = European Peoples' Party group, EDA = European Democratic Alliance, PES = Party of European Socialists group.

groups of the left, and the PES in particular, in 1984. The Socialist–Communist coalition jumped from 165 members to 198, while the EPP–EDG coalition actually lost one member and fell to 173. The PES on its own had 152 members, significantly more than the EPP's 114. The Liberal group remained nearly the same with 38 (as opposed to 39) members. An increase in MEPs belonging to the extreme right from 22 to 36 and the creation of a new "Group of the Right" (ER) were not enough to offset the success of the PES.[31]

The strong numerical superiority of the PES was made more significant by the large decrease in the participation of the other party groups. The average rate of participation for the EP as a whole fell from 47% to 38%. The rates of the EPP and EDG fell from 63% to 43% and 53% to 41%, respectively. The PES was the only group that did not suffer an increase in member absenteeism (see Table 6.3). In fact, only the small extremist Group of the Right had a higher average rate of participation than the PES during the second legislature.

Another difference between the first and second legislatures was the decrease in cohesion within the left and right coalitions, although internal party group cohesion remained nearly constant (Table 6.3). The

[31] This is due, in particular, to the reluctance of the center-right to work with the groups of the extreme right.

Table 6.4. *Correlation Coefficients – Resolutions II Legislature*

Party Group	Rainbow	COM	ER	EDG	ELDR	NA	EPP	EDA	PES
Rainbow	1								
COM	0.42	1							
ER	0.24	−0.25	1						
EDG	−0.25	0.19	0.12	1					
ELDR	−0.03	0.32	0.16	0.70	1				
NA	0.33	0.18	0.21	0.38	0.29	1			
EPP	0.05	0.19	0.37	0.67	0.73	0.43	1		
EDA	−0.04	−0.19	0.48	0.17	0.33	−0.02	0.47	1	
PES	0.51	0.46	0.21	0.02	0.10	0.39	**0.12**	−0.12	1

COM = Communist group, ER = Group of the European Right, EDG = European Democratic group, ELDR = European Liberal and Democratic and Reform group, NA = nonaffiliated, EPP = European Peoples' Party group, EDA = European Democratic Alliance, PES = Party of European Socialists group.

previous lack of cooperation between the EPP and PES was maintained, but the close relationships between these two groups and their perspective coalition partners diminished. The most striking example of this is the decrease in the correlation coefficient of the EPP and EDG (Table 6.4). While in the first legislature the two had been nearly unanimous, they had a correlation coefficient of only .67 in the second legislature. Cooperation between the PES and the Communist group also decreased, although not as dramatically, falling from .55 to .46. Interestingly, the Liberal group made a decided move toward the right, with a correlation coefficient of .73 with the EPP and only .38 with the Socialists.[32]

On the whole, the party system of the EP was fundamentally the same during the first and second legislatures. The shifts that occurred in the relative strength and participation rates of the various party groups were changes that occurred within the same general party system structure. The dominant role of ideology and the existence of clear and stable coalitions of the moderate right and moderate left were consistent throughout the period. The role of the European Parliament in the broader political environment also remained largely unchanged during most of this period. There were several ineffective attempts to increase the legislative and

[32] This is still a marginal increase over the first legislature, where the coefficient was .36.

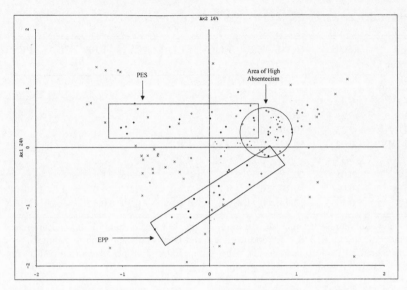

Figure 6.5   Ideology and Participation – Resolutions III Legislature

political authority of the EP throughout the decade, including the Stuttgart Solemn Declaration (1983) and the EP's own Draft Treaty on European Union (1984). It was not until the Single European Act was implemented in 1987 that a new phase in the development of the European Parliament was initiated. The new legislative powers granted to the EP by the SEA had a huge impact on interparty group relations, ultimately altering the character of the party system itself.[33]

III Legislature: 1989–1993

The clearest indication of the shift in the party system of the EP is the dramatic reduction in the role of ideology as a determinant of voting behavior. While in both of the previous legislatures ideology had explained at least 25% of the voting behavior, more than any other single variable, in the third legislature the role of ideology slipped to second place, explaining only 16% of the total variation (Figure 6.5). Previously the party

---

[33] See Chapter 4 for a more in-depth discussion of the Single European Act and its impact on the institutional role and legislative authority of the European Parliament.

groups had been divided between left and right along the horizontal axis; this division occurs along the secondary vertical axis in the third legislature. The division between party groups of the ideological left and right is still significant, but it is no longer the primary defining characteristic of the EP party system. In the third legislature the varying rates of participation separate the party groups more than ideology (explaining 24% of the variation). Groups to the right of the figure have a lower participation rate than those to the left. This is demonstrated by their graphical proximity to the "absent" vote positions (represented by "."s) in Figure 6.5.[34] There does not appear to be a significant difference between the participation rates of the party groups on the ideological left and those on the right.

The increase in the cooperation of the ideological left and right can be seen not only in the decreased role of ideology shown in Figure 6.5, but also in the huge increase in the correlation coefficients of the EPP and PES (Table 6.5). While the coefficient had been at just .12 during the second legislature, it jumped to .33 in the third. It is important to note that the tendency to cooperate occurred primarily between the PES and EPP; most of the other party groups of the left and right continued to vote with their ideological allies. One significant difference is the EDG, which voted with the PES more often than the EPP did. Between 1984 and 1988 the PES and EDG had a correlation coefficient of just .02; between 1989 and 1993 that number jumped to .47.[35] The increase in cooperation between the EPP and the PES had a tremendous impact on the party system as a whole because of their numerical dominance within the EP.[36]

Increased cooperation between the EPP and PES resulted in a kind of oligarchy within the EP. Because of the high proportion of total seats controlled by these two groups, anything they could agree on was guaranteed to pass. Their success, as well as the extent of their cooperation, is demonstrated by the location of the vast majority of vote positions during

[34] Remember that vote positions closest to the horizontal axis are those with the most votes. The farther away from the horizontal axis a vote position is, the less support it received from MEPs.

[35] The extremely close organizational and working relationship between the EPP and the EDG should be kept in mind. In fact, in 1992 the two officially merged and the European Democratic Group was dissolved.

[36] The EPP and the PES have been the two largest groups throughout the history of the EP, although their combined strength has varied from a low of just over 50% to a high of nearly 70% of the total EP membership. After the 1999 elections they controlled approximately 66% of the total seats.

Table 6.5. Correlation Coefficients – Resolutions III Legislature

Party Group	Rainbow	COM–LU	ER	EDG	EUL	ELDR	NA	EPP	EDA	PES	Green
Rainbow	1										
COM–LU	0.12	1									
ER	0.09	0.01	1								
EDG	0.11	−0.16	0.30	1							
EUL	0.09	0.09	−0.22	0.29	1						
ELDR	0.19	−0.01	0.25	0.65	0.30	1					
NA	0.57	−0.02	0.14	0.34	0.11	0.41	1				
EPP	0.12	0.22	0.22	0.57	0.21	0.87	0.48	1			
EDA	0.08	0.43	0.62	0.17	−0.25	0.32	0.26	0.50	1		
PES	0.13	0.08	0.02	0.47	0.81	0.34	0.19	0.33	−0.05	1	
Green	0.53	0.31	−0.29	−0.11	0.14	0.17	0.18	0.16	−0.09	0.00	1

COM–UL = Communist–United Left group, ER = Group of the European Right, EDG = European Democratic group, EUL = European United Left, ELDR = European Liberal and Democratic group, NA = nonaffiliated, EPP = European Peoples' Party group, EDA = European Democratic Alliance, PES = Party of European Socialists group.

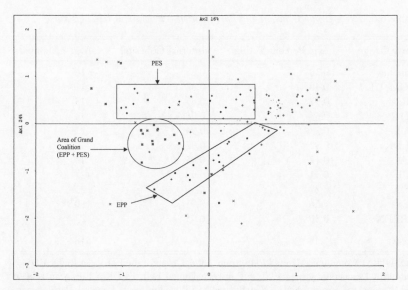

Figure 6.6   Party Groups and Success – Resolutions III Legislature

the third legislature *between* the clusters of delegations belonging to the EPP and those of the PES (Figure 6.6). Once again diamonds mark delegations to the PES and those belonging to the EPP are labeled with squares. Successful vote positions are X's while wedges mark unsuccessful vote positions. The vast majority of successful vote positions were those supported by *both* the EPP and the PES.[37] It is this increase in cooperation that resulted in the extraordinary decrease in the role of ideology within the European Parliament.

There were few other significant shifts in the behavior of MEPs between the second and third legislatures. Participation did increase overall to 48%, thus returning to its 1980–1983 level. On the whole, however, this marked simply a return to the situation during the first legislature (Table 6.6). The EDG regained its superiority, with only a 32% absentee rate, with the EPP at 49%. The Socialist group managed to slightly surpass the EPP with only 44% of its members absent on average. As in the first legislature, these three groups had the highest rate of participation amongst their members, with the other groups dropping off

---

[37] There were only two complete exceptions to this, where the EPP and PES clearly and wholly opposed each other.

Table 6.6. *Party Group Cohesion and Participation – Resolutions III Legislature*

Party Group	Avg. Percent Voting	Internal Cohesion	Avg. # Members
Rainbow	0.30	0.88	16
COM–UL	0.40	0.82	11
ER	0.37	0.87	15
EDG	0.68	0.98	34
EUL	0.33	0.94	27
ELDR	0.32	0.92	47
NA	0.12	0.95	14
EPP	0.51	0.98	127
EDA	0.27	0.90	23
PES	0.56	0.91	180
GREEN	0.50	0.95	23
TOTAL	0.48	n/a	518

COM–UL = Communist–United Left group, ER = Group of the European Right, EDG = European Democratic group, EUL = European United Left, ELDR = European Liberal and Democratic group, NA = nonaffiliated, EPP = European Peoples' Party group, EDA = European Democratic Alliance, PES = Party of European Socialists group.

quickly to a low of 27% (or 73% absent on average). For the most part, other aspects of the previous party system structure remained unchanged. The relative balance of power between the ideological left and right remained largely the same, with a slight overall increase in the membership of party groups on the right.[38]

The PES actually increased its percentage of total EP membership from 31% to 35%, while the EPP remained nearly constant until the 1992 merger with the EDG, which increased its share of EP seats from 25% to 31% (Table 6.6). Surprisingly, there was also little change in the internal cohesion of the major party groups. The previously high levels of group solidarity continued throughout the third legislature despite the clear move away from ideology. It might have been expected that there would be some increase in internal dissension as cooperation with a previous ideological foe increased. Dissent could have been displayed either by an increase in absenteeism or increased voting defections, but neither occurred (Table 6.6).

[38] Because of a major re-shuffling of the party groups it is difficult to make precise comparisons. This is compounded by the existence of groups on the ideological extremes that cannot usually be considered as useful coalition partners.

The differences between the second and third legislatures are few, but they are extremely important. While participation rates, internal party group cohesion, and the relative size of the left and right coalitions all remained largely unchanged, the importance of ideology as a determinant of voting behavior fell dramatically. Increased compromise between the two largest groups most likely led to the creation of more moderate legislative proposals for two reasons. First, the numerical superiority the EPP and PES when working together meant that they had no need for additional allies from the ideological extremes. This could easily lead to the marginalization of the other party groups of the far left and right, decreasing their impact on successful legislative proposals. Second, given the near numerical equality of the PES and EPP, it is unlikely that either was frequently able to enforce its will on the other. Moderation and compromise seem a much more likely outcome of EPP–PES cooperation than extremism. It should be noted that there were no procedural reasons for increased EPP–PES cooperation. The only change was the increased role of the EP as a whole in the EU legislative process as a result of the SEA and the addition of the cooperation procedure; the resolution procedure remained wholly unchanged.

IV Legislature: 1994–1996

The clear move away from ideology toward cooperation by the two largest party groups continued in the fourth legislature despite a slight increase in the overall importance of ideology. The percent of voting behavior determined by ideology grew from 16% in the third legislature to 20% in the fourth (see Figure 6.7). The growing division between the PES and the other groups of the left appears to have caused this increase. Unlike the previous case, however, there appear to be three clear clusters of party groups. Just above the horizontal axis are the groups of the right and the Liberals, closest to the horizontal axis are the Socialists, and below them, *in a separate cluster*, are the other party groups of the left. Participation is once again the primary axis, explaining 25% of the total variance. As in the previous legislature, there do not appear to be any significant differences in the rates of absenteeism between the left and right wing party groups.

Although there is a clear separation between the EPP and PES in Figure 6.7, the distance between the two is smaller than in the previous legislature. The implication that cooperation between the two groups increased

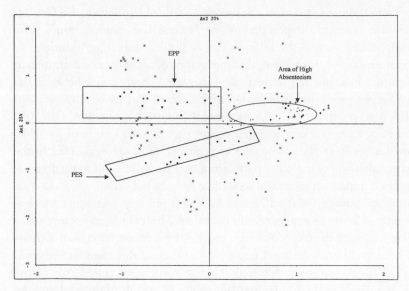

Figure 6.7 Ideology and Participation – Resolutions IV Legislature

during the fourth legislature is supported by their correlation coefficient, which reached an all-time high of .45 (Table 6.7). The increased dissension between the PES and its previous allies on the left suggested by Figure 6.7 is substantiated by the correlation coefficients in Table 6.7. The PES's highest coefficient is with the EPP. Its traditional partners, the Group of the European Left and the Greens, fall to third and fourth place, respectively, with correlation coefficients of .38 and .34. Disagreement between the EPP and its traditional coalition partners was apparently lower since the EDG had already merged with the EPP and cooperation with the Liberal group continued to be relatively high (though much lower than during the third legislature).

The majority of successful vote positions fell between the EPP and PES, once again suggesting frequent recourse to the "grand coalition" and a high level of cooperation between these two groups. There were some successful vote positions that fell outside of the area of the EPP–PES coalition, the majority of which were clearly supported by the EPP and its traditional allies to the right (Figure 6.8). The ability of the right to pass its proposals in spite of PES opposition is probably due to the internal division of the left wing coalition discussed above. Also evident in Figure 6.8

Table 6.7. *Correlation Coefficients – Resolutions IV Legislature*

Party Group	ERA	EN	EUL–NGL	ELDR	NA	EPP	PES	UfE	Green
ERA	1								
EN	−0.09	1							
EUL–NGL	0.72	−0.18	1						
ELDR	0.00	0.37	−0.23	1					
NA	−0.24	0.49	−0.34	0.65	1				
EPP	0.10	0.27	−0.17	0.53	0.62	1			
PES	0.42	−0.07	0.38	0.11	0.10	**0.45**	1		
UfE	0.05	0.30	−0.20	0.71	0.52	0.67	0.14	1	
GREEN	0.67	−0.09	0.69	−0.06	−0.18	−0.04	0.34	−0.19	1

ERA = European Radical Alliance, EN = Europe of Nations, UEL–NGL = European United Left-Nordic Green Left, ELDR = European Liberal and Democratic and Reform group, NA = nonaffiliated, EPP = European Peoples' Party group, PES = Party of European Socialists group, UfE = Union for Europe.

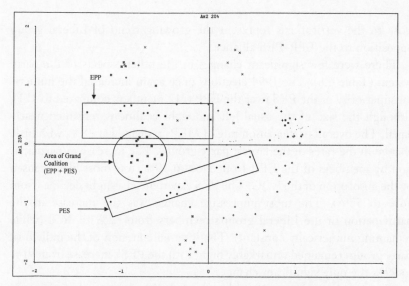

Figure 6.8 Party Groups and Success – Resolutions IV Legislature

is an increase in the number of extremist vote positions of both the right and left, which receive very little support. These are almost universally the result of small groups on the right and the left opposing the grand coalition of the EPP and PES. The small cluster of unsuccessful vote positions

Table 6.8. *Party Group Cohesion and Participation – Resolutions IV Legislature*

Party Group	Avg. Percent Voting	Internal Cohesion	Avg. # Members
ERA	0.28	1	20
EN	0.38	0.86	19
EUL–NGL	0.34	0.99	32
ELDR	0.46	0.96	47
NA	0.22	0.94	31
EPP	0.59	0.98	171
PES	0.52	0.99	212
UfE	0.39	0.91	48
GREEN	0.44	0.99	26
TOTAL	0.48	n/a	614

ERA = European Radical Alliance, EN = Europe of Nations, EUL–NGL = European United Left–Nordic Green Left, ELDR = European Liberal and Democratic and Reform group, NA = nonaffiliated, EPP = European Peoples' Party group, PES = Party of European Socialists group, UfE = Union for Europe.

close to the vertical axis represent the growing trend of Liberal group opposition to the EPP–PES alliance.[39]

There were few significant changes in the other aspects of the party system (Table 6.8). The 1994 elections once again increased the numerical superiority of the PES over the EPP (212 members compared to 171), although the size of the usual left and right coalitions remained nearly equal. The overall participation rate of MEPs remained at 48%, with little change in the rates of the largest party groups. The increase in participation by members of the EPP, from 51% to 59%, was most likely caused by the absorption of the EDG. The PES experienced a slight decline (from 56% to 52%). The most impressive change was the increase in the participation of the Liberal group's members from 32% to 46% (while remaining numerically constant). The internal cohesion of the individual party groups remained remarkably high, with the PES's increase from 91% to 99% the only significant change.

The most notable aspect of the fourth legislature was the continued increase in PES–EPP cooperation and the comparative weakness of the left wing coalition. It is probable that the two are integrally connected.

[39] The existence and importance of this trend was suggested to me during interviews with several members of the Liberal Group conducted in February–May and November–December 1996.

The difficulty of the left in passing proposals against strong right wing opposition was not caused by a numerical disadvantage, a lack of group participation, or diminished internal group cohesion. Numerically the left actually had a slight advantage, and the increase in PES cohesion should have roughly balanced the decreased participation of its members, leaving the left as a whole no worse off. Instead, it appears that the groups of the far left began to distance themselves from the growing tendency of the PES toward compromise and cooperation with the right and the EPP in particular. This internal division amongst the groups of the ideological left allowed for some victories of the right when the EPP and PES opposed each other.

Conclusions

This analysis suggests that the party system that existed in 1996 looked significantly different than it did just fifteen years earlier. The defining characteristic of voting behavior on resolutions in the first legislature was ideological polarization and clear coalitions of the left and right. Cooperation between the PES and EPP was almost nonexistent. The two major groups were closely allied with the smaller party groups to their left and right. In the late 1980s a fundamental shift in coalition building between the EPP and PES began. Instead of looking to their right and left for political allies who would support them, perhaps moving their positions more toward the ideological extremes, they began to look to each other. The rapid increase in cooperation and compromise between the two largest groups, at the cost of losing support from its traditional allies for the PES, redefined the character of the EP party system. In the place of the previous polarized system based on ideological extremism, a new moderate party system founded on bipartisan cooperation evolved.

This new-found moderate bipartisanship during votes on resolutions was not the result of any changes to the resolution procedure itself, which remained unmodified. It did, however, coincide with other changes to the legislative process in the EU, most notably the introduction of the cooperation procedure by the Single European Act. I argue that this was not coincidence. Rather, the change in coalition patterns was a direct result of the institutional transformation of the European Parliament from a chamber of debate to a legislative body. As predicted by Hypotheses 3 and 4, the party groups within the EP changed their strategies as a result of the changing institutional structure of the EU. When the EP was powerless the party groups could best achieve their policy goals by motivating others (the public and the other institutions). This was often better accomplished through conflict than compromise.

Once the EP gained some direct access to the legislative process (through the cooperation, and later the codecision procedures), however, this tactic was no longer the best. The acquisition of even limited legislative power meant that the EP as a whole and the party groups individually now had to work with the other institutions to have any effect. This required compromise and moderate positions, given the ideological diversity present in both the Commission and the Council. It is certainly true that the voting requirements of the later stages of the new procedures forced cooperation in some cases by requiring an absolute majority of component members to pass amendments, but this cannot explain the movement toward bipartisan compromise on resolutions (where there is no voting requirement). To examine the increasing frequency of the grand coalition more closely (and in particular the role of ideology and rules in its formation), the next chapter examines voting behavior and coalition formation since 1987 under the cooperation and co-decision procedures.

7

Cooperation and Co-Decision:
The Role of Ideology and Rules[1]

The previous examination of coalition formation across time focused exclusively on behavior during votes on resolutions. As the only form of decision making in the EP that has remained constant across time (in terms of both existence and relative importance) resolutions were an obvious choice to trace change in the patterns of coalition formation. Here, however, the focus will shift to examining patterns of coalition formation when, presumably, it matters most. That is when the EP can directly impact legislative outcomes. The cooperation and co-decision procedures grant the EP real legislative influence through amendment and veto powers. How the EP and the party groups behave under these procedures is of the utmost importance. If the party groups can effectively use the new powers granted to the EP, the possibility to effect legislative outcomes and achieve policy goals becomes a reality; if they cannot, the EP risks once again being relegated to observer status within the EU legislative process.

Therefore we must understand the extent to which the EP has been able to surmount the procedural challenges of the new procedures *and* come up with compromise proposals that are acceptable to the other EU institutions. In other words, we must find out if the party groups have been able to adapt not just to their new legislative role, but also to the restrictions placed upon their actions by the majority requirements of the second and third rounds and the institutional organization of the EU as a whole.

[1] Parts of this chapter were previously presented at the 1999 annual meeting of the American Political Science Association and published by *European Union Politics* (Kreppel, 2000b). In addition, the data on the cooperation procedure used in this section were originally analyzed in Kreppel and Tsebelis (1999).

As a result, it is important to understand the role of ideology in the EP since the Single European Act. If the frequent recourse to the grand coalition witnessed under resolutions exists under the cooperation and co-decision procedures as well, what does this mean in terms of the ideological differences between the party groups? Has the acquisition of legislative power under the current set of voting and institutional restrictions led to the abandonment of ideology to achieve EP influence? Has the EP, in fact, evolved from a chamber of debate into a legislative body, or has pragmatism forced the EP to evolve into something wholly different? To what extent is the evolution of interparty group relations predictable based on the hypotheses presented in Chapter 3?

In this chapter I examine these questions in two ways. First, I look at voting behavior and character of coalition formation under the cooperation and co-decision procedures. I use the same statistical techniques employed in the previous chapter to facilitate comparisons to the patterns witnessed for resolutions. In the second section I examine the role of ideology in the coalition formation process through the creation of a formal model of cooperation between the EPP and PES. This is supported empirically in the third section through a logistic analysis of the impact of legislative subject on patterns of coalition formation. The data used for this chapter consist of 200 roll-call votes under the cooperation and co-decision procedures between 1989 and 1996 (100 votes under each procedure). The votes were selected randomly using the same procedure described earlier for resolutions.[2]

Coalition Formation Under the New Procedures

Since the cooperation and co-decision procedures were not implemented until 1987 and 1994, respectively, it is not possible to verify a similar transition in party group behavior after the SEA as occurred in voting on resolutions. It is possible, however, to see if the general trends of low participation, high internal party cohesion, and cooperation between the two major parties witnessed during the third and fourth legislatures for resolutions also existed during the same time period under these new procedures.

An important difference that is immediately obvious between the various procedures is the much higher rate of participation among the

---

[2] See Chapter 6 for a full description of the random selection process.

Table 7.1. *Party Group Participation and Cohesion – by Procedure*

Party Group	Avg. Percent Voting Cooperation	Internal Cohesion Cooperation	Avg. # Members Cooperation	Avg. Percent Voting Co-Decision	Internal Cohesion Co-Decision	Avg. # Members Co-Decision
ELDR	40%	0.90	47	71%	0.87	47
EUL–NGL	40%	0.98	27	35%	0.95	32
NA	10%	0.97	14	37%	0.88	31
EPP	54%	0.95	127	76%	0.94	171
PES	65%	0.97	180	74%	0.96	212
EDA–UfE	24%	0.94	23	48%	0.91	48
Green	56%	0.98	23	61%	0.98	26
TOTAL	53%	N/A	518	65%	N/A	614

EUL–NGL = European United Left–Nordic Green Left, ELDR = European Liberal and Democratic and Reform group, NA = nonaffiliated, EPP = European Peoples' Party group, PES = Party of European Socialists group, UfE = Union for Europe.

larger groups for votes under co-decision and to some extent cooperation. Overall participation during votes on resolutions never averaged more than 48%. There was some improvement for votes under the cooperation procedure, but still nearly 50% of the MEPs failed to participate on average. The overall rate of participation under co-decision, on the other hand, averaged 65%, with the EPP and PES averaging 75% (Table 7.1). This tremendous increase in participation suggests that both the MEPs and the party groups believed that the co-decision procedure offered the EP additional legislative influence. It should be noted that the increase in participation for co-decision votes was not just a by-product of the special majority requirements of the second round. There was almost no difference in participation rates between the two rounds of the procedure, while there is a significant difference between the cooperation and co-decision procedures (which both have the same vote restrictions in the second round).

Internal party group cohesion under the cooperation and co-decision procedures was, once again, extremely high (Table 7.1). The only partial exception was the Liberal group, which dropped to an 87% cohesion score under co-decision compared to 96% for resolutions during the same period, and 90% under the cooperation procedure.[3] Given the dramatic

[3] Internal party cohesion is computed using the same equation as in Chapter 6.

increase in participation throughout the EP, it is surprising that more groups did not experience a decrease in internal cohesion. The continuation of high internal party group cohesion across procedures despite the large increase in participation under co-decision suggests that absenteeism is not primarily used to express political opposition.

With the exception of increased participation, voting behavior under the cooperation and co-decision procedures appears to be similar to what we have seen for resolutions. But what about the patterns of coalition formation? Leaving aside for the moment the predictions of the micro and macro models discussed in Chapter 3, a high level of cooperation between the EPP and PES should not necessarily be expected a priori. The cooperation and co-decision procedures greatly enhanced the legislative authority of the EP, and in the process rekindled public interest in its activities, both of which could have worked counter to PES–EPP cooperation (Eurobarometer, 1994, in particular, questions B8–B10). The potential to have a significant impact on the policy of the EU might have brought to the fore underlying ideological differences between these two groups that could be neither ignored nor reconciled. In addition, increased public awareness of EP activities might have made it difficult for diverse political families, generally in opposition to one another nationally, to cooperate extensively at the supranational level.

Other aspects of the cooperation and co-decision procedures as well as the institutional structure of the EU, however, potentially re-enforced the new trend of compromise and moderation discussed above. The underlying goal of most MEPs throughout the history of the EU has been to increase the legislative powers of the European Parliament as a whole and eventually achieve policy goals. It is possible, and even probable, that the major party groups tried to overcome the ideological divisions between them so that the Parliament's new powers would not be diminished by an inability to reach cohesive, broadly acceptable (to the other EU institutions) decisions quickly. This is in line with the predictions of Hypothesis 4. The cooperation and co-decision procedures add new tools to the legislative arsenal of the EP and offer new opportunities to the party groups to obtain their goals, but only if they can work within the constraints of the rules and the institutional structures of the EU as a whole.

The existence of these countervailing pressures of conflict and compromise is evident in the results of the statistical analyses, which are much more complex than was the case for coalitions during votes on resolutions. In fact, the patterns of coalition formation for roll-call votes under the

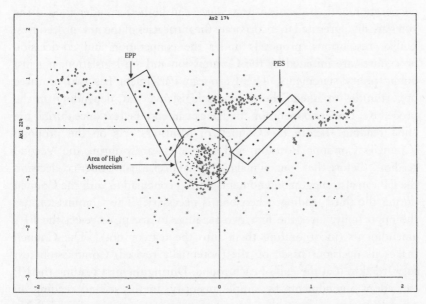

Figure 7.1 Ideology and Participation – Cooperation and Co-Decision Procedures

cooperation and co-decision procedures during the third and fourth legislatures differ significantly from those witnessed for votes on resolutions during the same period.

At first glance, party group interaction appears to revert to the patterns witnessed in the first and second legislatures for resolutions (Figure 7.1). Ideology was once again the primary axis for votes under the cooperation and co-decision procedures, explaining 21% of the total variation. Although the position of ideology as the primary axis for cooperation and co-decision votes is significant, the actual percentage of the variation explained by ideology is only marginally larger than it was for resolutions during the same period (average 18%). The more significant difference is the amount of variation explained by participation. Under co-decision and cooperation participation accounted for only 17% of the variance, compared to an average of 25% for resolutions during the same period. This is probably due to the generally higher level of participation under the new procedures.

The apparent difference between a comparatively high level of cooperation for resolutions and the obvious importance of ideology under the cooperation and co-decision procedures can be better understood if the votes are disaggregated to incorporate the intricacies of the new procedures. Unlike resolutions, proposals under the cooperation and co-decision procedures are initiated by the Commission and are legislation, not just public policy statements. The European Parliament has two or three opportunities to amend the proposed legislative text, depending on the procedure. Under cooperation the EP can amend the text once during the "first reading" before the Council of Ministers acts on the proposal (Council's Common Position) and once afterwards, during the "second reading" (before the Council makes its final decisions). Under co-decision the EP can also suggest amendments during conciliation with the Council during the third reading, when one is necessary.[4] The Commission has the opportunity after the first two readings to accept or reject the EP's amendments (incorporating them into the text or not).[5] The Council makes its decisions based on the (potentially revised) Commission text forwarded to it at the end of each round. During the first reading the EP can adopt amendments by simple majority; in the second reading an amendment must garner the support of an *absolute majority* of the EP. No amendments are allowed from the floor during the third reading.[6] The effect of the two-stage procedure on the voting behavior of MEPs and the party groups in the EP is demonstrated by the difference in the voting behavior of the EPP and PES during the first and second rounds (Figures 7.2 and 7.3).

During the first round there is less cooperation between the two major parties (Figure 7.2). The overall pattern of coalition formation is similar to that observed for resolutions during the first and second legislatures. The standard party group alliances of the right and left regain much of their previous strength. The EP as a whole appears, once again, to be more ideologically divided (Table 7.2). As previously, ideology is the primary axis, explaining 23% of the variation in voting behavior, and participation is the second axis, explaining 17%.

The special majority requirements and the institutional arrangements of the EU mitigate the influence of ideology during the second round.

---

[4] For a more complete description of these procedures see Chapter 4 and Corbett et al. (1995).

[5] Under co-decision the Commission plays only an advisory role during conciliation.

[6] EP amendments must be proposed by the EP's delegation meeting with the Council Members in conciliation. The EP as a whole then must either accept or reject the joint proposal.

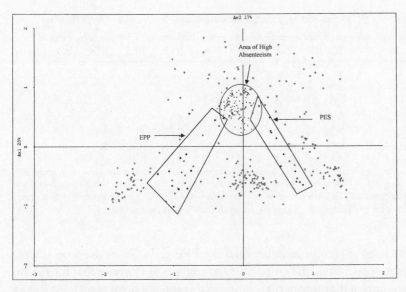

Figure 7.2   Ideology in the First Round – Cooperation and Co-Decision Procedures

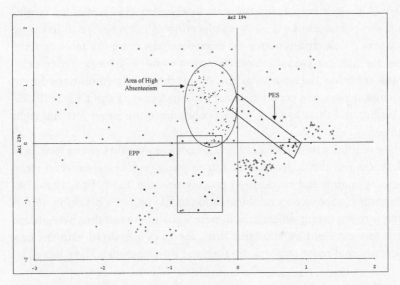

Figure 7.3   Ideology in the Second Round – Cooperation and Co-Decision Procedures

Table 7.2. *Correlation Coefficients Cooperation and Co-Decision – First Reading*

	ELDR	EUL–NGL	NA	EPP	PES	EDA–UfE	Green
ELDR	1						
EUL–NGL	0.39	1					
NA	0.56	0.56	1				
EPP	0.65	0.09	0.30	1			
PES	0.30	0.59	0.14	**0.27**	1		
EDA–UfE	0.55	0.64	0.73	0.41	0.37	1	
Green	0.52	0.63	0.33	0.14	0.45	0.35	1

EUL–NGL = European United Left–Nordic Green Left, ELDR = European Liberal and Democratic and Reform group, NA = nonaffiliated, EPP = European Peoples' Party group, PES = Party of European Socialists group, UfE = Union for Europe.

The level of compromise between the EPP and PES in the second stage of the cooperation and co-decision procedures is closer to that for resolutions during the same period, although it is still not quite as high. As Figure 7.3 demonstrates, the axes are shifting, but the shift is not as complete as it appeared to be for resolutions during the same time period. Statistically, the axes do switch, with participation becoming the first axis (explaining 23% of the variation) while ideology becomes the second (explaining 19%).[7] Although graphically the shift is less clear than it was for resolutions, the switch can be seen by the location of the majority of left wing party group delegations above the horizontal axis (with the most extreme being the furthest away). In contrast, most of the right wing group delegations are below the horizontal axis. As was the case for resolutions during the same period, the correlation coefficients between the EPP and PES are higher and there is some loss of cohesion in the larger left and right coalitions (Table 7.3).

The tension within the party groups between conflict over ideological differences and the desire to have some impact on EU legislation is clear. The cooperation and co-decision procedures offer the EP the chance to have a substantive impact on the creation of EU policy. This ability brings to the fore important differences in policy goals between the party groups of the left and right. At the same time, the rules associated with the new procedure, and more importantly the need for proposals to be adopted by

[7] This is very similar to the results for resolutions where participation accounted for 25% of the variation and ideology accounted for 18%.

Table 7.3. *Correlation Coefficients Cooperation and Co-Decision – Second Reading*

Merged Second	ELDR	EUL–NGL	NA	EPP	PES	EDA–UfE	Green
ELDR	1						
EUL–NGL	0.18	1					
NA	0.24	0.68	1				
EPP	0.54	0.10	0.04	1			
PES	0.58	0.21	0.10	**0.39**	1		
EDA–UfE	0.22	0.26	0.57	0.23	0.22	1	
Green	0.37	0.42	0.07	0.10	0.55	−0.14	1

EUL–NGL = European United Left–Nordic Green Left, ELDR = European Liberal and Democratic and Reform group, NA = nonaffiliated, EPP = European Peoples' Party group, PES = Party of European Socialists group, UfE = Union for Europe.

Table 7.4. *EPP–PES Coalitions by Procedure and Reading*[1]

	Total # Votes	# Split Votes	% Split Votes	# Coalitions	% Coalitions
First Cod	47	17	36%	30	64%
First Coop	60	25	42%	35	58%
Second Cod	53	15	28%	38	72%
Second Coop	40	14	35%	26	65%
First Total	107	42	39%	65	61%
Second Total	93	29	31%	64	69%
Resolutions pre-1987	47	23	49%	24	51%
Resolutions post-1987	53	16	30%	37	70%

[1] The Grand Coalition was considered to have formed when a majority from the two groups voted together.

the Council and Commission, requires some level of cooperation between the PES and EPP if the Parliament as a whole is to have any impact on EU legislative decision making.

It is interesting that cooperation between the PES and EPP was easier during this period for resolutions than it was for legislation decided under the cooperation and co-decision procedures, suggesting that voting requirements alone cannot explain the increased tendency toward cooperation during the second round of the cooperation procedure. This is supported by the absence of cooperation in nearly one-third of the second reading votes and the existence of cooperation in roughly 60% of the votes during the first round (Table 7.4). In fact, in strict numerical terms the frequency of the grand coalition does not appear to vary that much regardless of legislative procedure or stage (first or second reading). In fact, it varies as much or more *across time* as it does across procedure or reading. On average, the grand coalition was formed 68% of the time under co-decision, 61% of the time under cooperation, 70% of the time for resolutions post-SEA, 61% during the first round, and 69% of the time during the second round. In other words, in all cases after the implementation of the SEA the coalition was formed on average 61%–70% of the time while before the SEA (during resolutions) the grand coalition was formed only roughly 51% of the time.

The Role of Ideology in the European Parliament

Clearly voting restrictions alone cannot explain all of the patterns of coalition formation between the EPP and the PES witnessed above. One possible alternative explanation for the variation in voting behavior that does exist between the two rounds is that that the first round of the procedure is used by the party groups as a bargaining round, not between the EP and the other EU institutions, but between the groups themselves *when there is a significant ideological conflict*. Both the EPP and the PES might be tempted to fight for their most preferred policy outcome during the first round in the hopes that it would be adopted by the Commission and Council. What happens when this approach fails and the preferences of the EP majority are ignored in the first round by the other institutions? It seems likely that the groups would try to compromise during the second round (to avoid negating the potential power of the EP as a whole) *unless either or both prefers no action to anything that they can mutually agree upon*. Increased cooperation between party groups in the second stage is likely even without the existence of special majority requirements, since it is the last chance for the EP as a whole (and the EPP and PES in particular) to impact final EU policy outcomes.

The potential for bargaining or battling back and forth between both the party groups (EPP and PES) as well as the EP as a whole and the other EU institutions is the key to understanding the role and function of ideology in the EP. The party groups are forced to fight two battles: the first against each other to determine what the position of the EP will be, and a second against the other EU institutions to determine the extent to which the position of the EP will be adopted. This can be better understood in terms of the preferences of the party groups, which will determine whether the grand coalition is formed and when (first, second, or both rounds).

To model the behavior of the party groups it is necessary to make some general assumptions about our actors. First, all actors are assumed to be rational with transitive Euclidean preferences. Information is perfect and complete (to simplify the model). Also, for simplicity's sake I will model the two party groups as individual actors.[8] Given these restrictions it is possible to create a set of potential outcomes to the bargaining process based on the following preference orderings. There are fundamentally five possible outcomes for each party group.[9]

1. **GEP**: The EP makes the strategic proposal that is closest to one party group's ideal point yet still acceptable to the Commission and the pivotal member of the Council. That is both the specific group and the EP "win."

2. **CEP**: A compromise between the EPP and PES that is acceptable to the Commission and the pivotal member of the Council. The EP "wins" but the party groups must compromise.

3. **OEP**: The strategic proposal closest to the ideal point of the other party group is selected by the EP and is acceptable to the Commission and the pivotal member of the Council. The EP and the other party group "win" (situation 1 in reverse).

4. **CL**: The party groups compromise but the amendment is not acceptable to the Commission and/or the pivotal member of the Council. The EP loses despite group compromise.

5. **NCL**: The groups do not compromise and the EP adopts no proposal, or the adopted proposal is not acceptable to the Commission and/or the pivotal member of the Council.

The outcomes of the votes depend on the preferences of each of the two groups. In some cases cooperation in both rounds will be the best strategy. In other cases cooperation in only one or neither of the rounds will make more sense. What determines the best strategy of the party groups is the *position of their preferred outcomes* relative to each other, the other EU institutions, and the status quo. For each group

---

[8] Although, given the amazingly high rates of voting cohesion on roll-call votes of these two parties (over 90%), this is not a very large exaggeration of the actual situation.

[9] This section borrows the interpretation of Council, Commission, and EP bargaining outlined by Tsebelis (1994).

there are three possible preference orderings, depending on the location of their ideal point vis-à-vis the other group and the status quo. The primary determinant of behavior is the level of disagreement between the two groups, particularly the preference of one group for the unmodified proposal or status quo rather than the ideal "winning" position of the other group. The possible preference orderings for the party groups are

(1) If GEP = CEP = OEP > CL ≥ NCL, *then* compromise in *both* the first and the second rounds.
(2) If GEP > CEP > OEP > CL > NCL, *then* in the first round no compromise, in the second round compromise.
(3) If GEP > NCL > CEP ≥ OEP > CL, *then* compromise in *neither* the first nor the second round.

Once again the fundamental difference between (2) and (3) is that in the third ordering one (or both) of the groups prefers to have the Parliament do nothing (accept the status quo or proposal) rather than accept the position (amendment) of the other group. In this situation there is no mutually acceptable compromise between groups. A visual representation of the different possible outcomes is given in Figures 7.4–7.7.

These figures are one-dimensional models of the bargaining process between the Council, the Commission, and the EP. The Council is represented as a seven-member body (labeled 1–7) because the true qualified majority requirement in the current fifteen-member Council is roughly equal to 5/7. The Commission is represented as a single body, and the EPP and PES represent the Parliament. The best position that the Parliament as a whole can make is represented by X* when there is agreement between the two groups and by X* and X' when there is not. The status quo is SQ, and a P marks the pivotal member of the Council (i.e., the member whose vote is necessary to achieve or block a qualified majority decision).

The EP must make a proposal (amendment) that makes the pivotal member of the Council marginally better off than the current status quo (SQ) to win his/her vote. In the first example (Figure 7.4) the EPP and PES are quite close to each other and can easily agree to the proposal X*, which is the best that they can propose that both the Commission and the pivotal Member of the Council will prefer to the status quo. In this case, the EPP and the PES will agree and their amended proposal will be adopted by the other institutions in the first round. If the EP has mis-

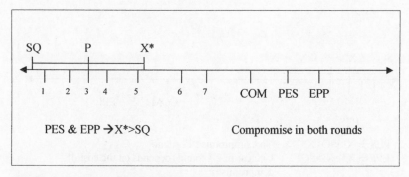

Figure 7.4   GEP = CEP = OEP > NCL = CL

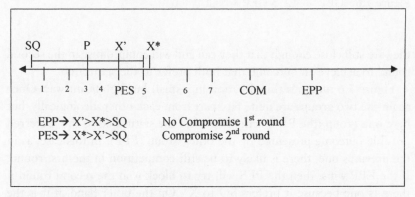

Figure 7.5   GEP > CEP > OEP > NCL > CL

calculated its proposal and a second round amendment is necessary, the two groups will agree once again.

In Figure 7.5 the situation is somewhat different. In this case the EPP and the PES are deeply divided. As a result they each have different preferred outcomes that are possible given the location of the Council and the Commission. The EPP prefers the X* proposal while the PES prefers the X' proposal, which is their own ideal point in this case. Thus, in the first round of the procedure both party groups will support different possible proposals (X* and X'). One of these will win in the EP. Regardless of which initial proposal is successful, the two will join forces in the second round to achieve the EP-endorsed proposal if necessary because both prefer either proposal to the status quo. Clearly there is a significant amount of ideological differences between the two groups in this case, but

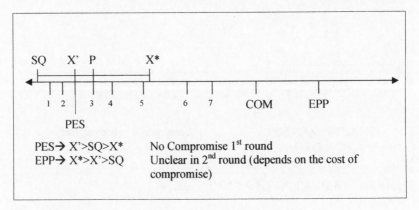

Figure 7.6 GEP > CEP > OEP > NCL > CL

they are still close enough that they can and will compromise in the second round to achieve an outcome that both prefer to the status quo.

Figure 7.6 modifies this situation in a small but significant way. Once again the two groups are quite far apart from each other ideologically, but here one group (the PES) actually prefers the status quo to the preferred possible outcome presented by the other group (EPP). In this case, as in the previous one, there is likely to be stiff competition in the first round. If the EPP wins, then the PES will try to block it in the second round if there is one because it prefers SQ to X*. On the other hand, if it is the PES that wins in the first round and it is up to the EPP to attempt to block in the second round, the action becomes less clear.

Clearly the EPP prefers X' to the status quo, but the difference is marginal and the cost of agreement might be high. In this case the actions of the group may well be determined by the perceived costs of too much compromise for too little gain. The PES will get their ideal point (X') and the EPP will get an outcome only marginally better than the status quo. In other words, if decisions are made only on the basis of strict spatial preferences, then the EPP will support the PES position. If the decision-making process is more complex (as it surely is), then the actions of the EPP in this case become less predictable.

In the final example demonstrated, illustrated in Figure 7.7, the two groups have irreconcilable differences and will be unable to work together in either round if action is determined solely by policy preferences. Once

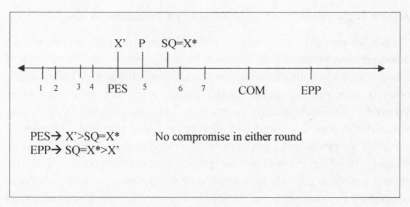

Figure 7.7   GEP > NCL > CEP > OEP > CL

the status quo lies between the ideal positions of the two groups it is almost impossible that they will be able to reach a compromise other than the status quo (or no action) since both will prefer the current situation to anything that the other party group prefers more. In this case the EP will become an extremely contentious body. If the PES is successful at getting its amendments adopted by the EP in the first round, they are still unlikely to be adopted by the Commission, Thus requiring unanimity in the Council for adoption, which is unlikely given that Members 6 and 7 will prefer the status quo. By the same token, if the EPP is successful in the first round, the best that it can do is nothing (by adopting the SQ position). In this situation the EP is marginalized in the legislative process. Thus, we can see that the proximity of the two groups to each other and in relation to the status quo is essential for compromise to be achieved. The closer the ideal points are to each other, at least relative to the positions of the Council, Commission, and status quo, the more likely it is that compromise will be achieved between the two groups in the EP, regardless of the round of the procedure.

We already know from the previous discussion that agreement is not always achieved in the EP under any procedure and that the grand coalition fails to be created on average 34% of the time. The above models help us to understand theoretically the underlying preferences that form the basis for this coalition behavior. Now we will turn our attention to the empirical reality of when such coalitions form and fail to form.

Where Is the Ideology Hiding? Areas of Contention in the EP

To gain a better understanding of when the two groups are unable to find a compromise position it is necessary to disaggregate the data to try and find patterns of coalition formation. To accomplish this task I use logistic analysis with the formation of the grand coalition as the dependent variable.[10] The independent variables include the committee of origin, whether the vote was on an amendment or a final proposal, and control variables for procedure (cooperation or co-decision) and reading (first or second). In addition, because the committees are very broad, I isolate several specific legislative topics, some of which cross committee borders (workplace environment) and some of which were largely subsumed within a single committee (public health).

This additional disaggregation was done for two reasons. The first was to try to make distinctions between diverse legislative subjects that are covered by one committee, for example, the Environment Committee, which includes bills on public health and consumer protection as well as the environment. The second reason was that some topics, such as worker's rights and safety, appeared to be divided amongst the committees and disagreements between parties would then also be dispersed and not immediately obvious if we looked only at the committee of origin. By codifying the legislation in this way we can capture more of the true impact that subject matter has on coalition formation.

The data used for this analysis are the same as were presented above for the cooperation and co-decision procedure. There were a total of 200 votes included in the sample, three of which were dropped from the sample because they were statistically identical for all variables. Two logistic analyses were completed – the first with Committees only and the second with legislative topics only because of the high correlation (collinearity) between some topics and some committees.[11] The results of the logistic analyses are given in Tables 7.5 and 7.6.

---

[10] As before, the grand coalition was considered formed when a majority from both groups voted together.

[11] It should be noted that it was necessary to exclude one of the committees and one of the topics from the analysis to avoid perfect linear correlation. I selected to exclude the Women's Affairs committee because it was the smallest, with only three roll-call votes, and the "other" topic committee since this had no empirical value. The excluded committee and topic can be understood to have taken on the value of "other" representing all committees and topics not included in the data-set but they are not analyzed independently.

Table 7.5. *Logistic Analysis for Significance of Committee of Origin*

Logit Estimates	Number of Observations = 197		
	LR chi^2 (8)		= 38
	Probablity > chi^2		= 0.0000
	Pseudo R^2		= 0.1504
	Coefficient	Standard Error	Z-Score	P > /Z/
---	---	---	---	---
Reading	−.6690	.4251	−1.574	0.116
Final	**1.144**	**.6269**	**1.825**	**0.068***
Cooperation	.0878	.4372	0.201	0.841
Transportation	1.266	1.506	0.841	0.400
Social	−2.216	1.423	−1.557	0.119
Legal	−1.750	1.375	−1.272	0.203
Environment	.2376	1.290	0.184	0.854
Energy	−.7953	1.354	−0.587	0.557
Economic	.3848	1.502	0.256	0.798
Culture	**−2.546**	**1.508**	**−1.688**	**0.091***
Constant	*1.274*	*1.383*	*0.921*	*0.357*

* = P > 90%, ** = P > 95%, *** = P > 99%. All tests are two-tailed.

Table 7.6. *Logistic Analysis for Significance of Legislative Topic*

Logit Estimates	Number of Observations = 197		
	LR chi^2 (8)		= 8
	Probablity > chi^2		= 0.000
	Pseudo R^2		= 0.133
	Coefficient	Standard Error	Z-Score	P > /Z/
---	---	---	---	---
Reading	−.1067	.4768	−.224	.823
Final	**1.4294**	**.6932**	**2.062**	**.039****
Cooperation	.6304	.4113	1.533	.125
Consumer Protection	−.3473	.4616	−.752	.452
Environmental	**1.8783**	**.8238**	**2.280**	**.023****
Economic	.9655	.6447	1.498	.134
Workplace Safety	**−1.4788**	**.5916**	**2.499**	**.012****
Public Health	**1.3018**	**.5337**	**2.439**	**.015****
Constant	*−.2235*	*.3804*	*−.588*	*.557*

* = P > 90%, ** = P > 95%, *** = P > 99%. All tests are two-tailed.

Table 7.5 examines the influence of committee of origin and Table 7.6 looks at the same recurring legislative topics. Both tables include the additional dummy variables for procedure (cooperation or co-decision), reading (first or second), and type (amendment or final). Of these three dichotomous variables only type is significant. The positive coefficient tells us that there is a significantly greater chance that the grand coalition (GC) will form when the vote is on the resolution as a whole than when it is on a particular amendment. On the other hand, there is no apparent statistically significant relationship between either the procedure (cooperation or co-decision) or the reading (first or second) and the formation of the grand coalition. This again goes against popular wisdom, which holds that the grand coalition is more likely to form in the second round, given the absolute majority requirement.

The impact of the committee of origin appears to be extremely weak, with the surprising exception of the Cultural Affairs Committee. This significant negative relationship between grand coalition formation and the culture committee is most likely spurious, however, since fifteen of the sixteen votes from the Cultural Affairs Committee were on a single, clearly contentious legislative proposal (COD 95/074-Pursuit of Television Broadcasting Activities). Without a larger data sample it is impossible to know if other proposals in this committee are as polemical. The other committees are all far from being of statistical significance in terms of explaining the formation of the grand coalition. This is probably because of the broad range of issues covered within most committees, which potentially serves to hide those issues that are contentious.

Dividing the legislative proposals by topic rather than committee of origin avoids this pitfall and allows us to also look at topics that appear to cut across committees. The results of the logistic analysis by topic are given in Table 7.6. There are three different topics that are statistically significant in the determination of the grand coalition – environmental issues, worker and work place issues, and public health issues. For environmental and public health issues the coefficients are positive, suggesting that in these areas the two groups are very likely to form a grand coalition, regardless of procedure or reading. The third statistically significant topic is worker and workplace issues. Here the coefficient is negative, suggesting that for proposals within this topic there is a much higher level of disagreement between the EPP and the PES and as a result considerably less recourse to the grand coalition.

The usefulness of examining votes by topic as opposed to just committee of origin becomes even clearer when we look at the dispersion of these three topics. Both public health and environment proposals come primarily, and not unsurprisingly, from the Committee on the Environment, Public Health and Consumer Policy. But so do the bulk of the proposals labeled as consumer protection, which were not significant in determining the formation of the grand coalition. This helps to explain why the Environment Committee as a whole was not significant in Table 7.5.[12] In contrast, the proposals dealing with worker and workplace issues came from five different committees.[13] Their dispersion across committees made it impossible to see the conflict between the two groups on these sorts of issues as long as we focused only on the committees.

This analysis demonstrates the significance of a second round of legislative bargaining. The addition of a second stage into the legislative procedure appears to have created an opportunity for the party groups to fight their ideological battles against each other in the first round without diminishing the potential of the EP as a whole to impact legislation in the second round. Impasses occur only when the preferences of the two groups are so distant that one or both would prefer to have the EP do nothing rather than compromise with the other group. This is a very different situation than that created when voting on resolutions, where the EP as a whole has only one chance to make a public statement. In other words, the higher level of cooperation witnessed during resolution votes may be due to the fact that the EP has only one shot at making a public statement. In this way the double round procedure (even with the special majority requirements) may actually add to the possibility of ideological dissention within the EP, despite the eventual need to compromise with the other legislative institutions of the EU.

---

[12] There were thirty-nine votes on public health issues, twenty-one on environmental issues, and forty-five on consumer protection issues. All of the environmental, all but two of the public health, and thirty-nine of the consumer protection votes were from the Environmental Committee.

[13] There were twenty-eight votes on worker and workplace issues coming out of the Economic (2), Environment (2), Legal Affairs (5), Social Affairs (16), and Women's Affairs (3) committees.

Conclusions

The analysis in this chapter of voting behavior in the EP leads to several very interesting conclusions about both the party groups in general and the formation of the grand coalition between the EPP and the PES. One of the most important is the remarkably high level of internal group cohesion regardless of time or legislative procedure. This once again calls into question the common perception of the party groups as weak and undisciplined. Although there are numerous examples of national delegations defecting from their party groups on a specific vote, the overall trend is extremely positive. This is particularly true of the two largest groups.

Another interesting and certainly less positive discovery of these analyses is the extremely high level of absenteeism across time and all three legislative procedures. There does appear to be some correlation between perceived EP legislative influence and attendance. While participation averaged just over 45% for resolutions, it jumped to 52% for votes under the cooperation procedure and 65% for votes under co-decision. These data are particularly alarming if we consider that roll-call votes (only 15% of all votes in the EP) often have comparatively high attendance rates because they are called on important or contentious issues. It should be stressed that there was very little variation in attendance between the first and second rounds under the cooperation and co-decision procedures. Thus, the special majority requirement does not appear to have a significant impact on individual Member participation. This is clearly something that must be considered when the EPP and the PES are trying to influence legislative outcomes during the second round under cooperation and co-decision; but as the analysis made clear, voting rules alone cannot explain the formation of the grand coalition.

It is also interesting that, despite the increases in participation under the cooperation, and especially the co-decision procedure, the level of internal party group cohesion remained universally high, with the sole exception of the Liberal group (which still maintained a respectable 87% internal cohesion score). This suggests that high absenteeism is not usually a sign of internal party group dissension. On the whole Members do not appear to be opposing the position of their party group by not voting. At the same time, the level of absenteeism is still high compared to many national parliaments and continues to hamper the activities of the EP.

Although informative, these conclusions do not directly address the predictions of the micro and macro models about coalition formation and the development of the EP party system as a whole. To test the micro model, and make predictions about the character of party system evolution in the European Parliament, we must know, or make assumptions about, the goals of the party groups. This includes an understanding of the ability of the party groups to achieve their goals and how this has evolved as a result of the changing role of the EP within the larger political environment.[14] In Chapter 3 I suggested that the primary objectives of the Members and party groups, from the outset, has been the achievement of their various policy goals.

In the early years of the EP, when there was little potential for effective legislative participation by the EP, this could rarely be achieved through direct action. The Parliament's institutional weakness meant that there was little need for the party groups to cooperate where strong ideological differences existed. Since the opinions and proposals of the EP were largely ignored by the other EU institutions, it was not necessary for the groups to formulate broadly acceptable compromise positions. I concluded that in the absence of an ability to directly affect legislation party groups would be forced to resort primarily to active, public, position-taking. For this to be effective, it was necessary for the various groups of the left and right to differentiate themselves and extol clear political and policy goals. The result predicted by Hypothesis 4 was that there would be a behavioral norm of ideological dogmatism and political polarization within EP. As a result, the EP would serve as a chamber of debate where issues important to Members could be discussed but no solutions effectively pursued.

As the role of the EP within the broader political environment evolved, from largely insignificant to potentially influential, the constraints placed on party group activity changed significantly. The polarization of the left and right on questions of EU policy served the Members of the EP only as long as the Parliament remained relatively powerless and largely ignored by the other EU institutions. Once the potential to have a direct influence over legislative outcomes was realized ideological, rigidity was no longer

---

[14] A simplification is made here to include the goals of the individual MEPs within those of the party groups. This is possible because of the extremely high rates of internal group cohesion, but there are obviously times when the goals of the groups and Members conflict.

in the interests of the political groups, or the EP as a whole. This is particularly true because the legislative powers eventually granted to the Parliament by the SEA, the Maastricht Treaty, and most recently the Amsterdam Treaty are not unilateral.

The assent and cooperation of the Commission and the Council are still necessary for legislation to be adopted. This means that the party groups can no longer afford the previous level of ideological dogmatism if their proposals are to be acceptable to the other institutions. The rules and norms governing interactions with the Council and the Commission require legislative proposals to be compromises generally acceptable to the ideological right and left as well as to the individual Member States. Hypothesis 4 says that the actions of the parties will reflect their goals and the tools at their disposition to achieve those goals. This suggests that, to make the most of the EP's newly acquired legislative potential and realize their policy goals within the restrictions of both the new procedures and the broader institutional environment, the political groups would cooperate across ideological boundaries. This requires creating compromise proposals moderate enough to be acceptable to a wide range of political and national interests.

The majority requirements of the new procedures are extremely restrictive because of the consistently high level of absenteeism within the EP. It is important to stress, however, that neither the institutional setting nor the voting restrictions are strong enough to force cooperation between the EPP and the PES when there are significant differences between them in terms of their preferred policy outcomes. Frequent recourse to compromise and moderation between the EPP and the PES has not led to the extinction of ideology in the European Parliament. As the logistic analysis made clear, there are policy areas where the two groups have a difficult time agreeing and frequently prefer no action to compromise and cooperation across ideological borders.

The fact that compromise between the EPP and the PES is not universal does not mitigate the significance of the grand coalition in terms of both the influence and evolution of the EP and this analysis. The results of the statistical analyses here and in Chapter 6 strongly support the predictions of both the macro and micro models. The data discussed above suggest that the addition of the cooperation and co-decision procedures had a significant impact on the character of the party group system. The potential to directly affect legislative outcomes led to a reduction in the role of ideological dogmatism within the coalition formation process for both resolutions and the cooperation and co-decision procedures. In effect, the development of the party groups system generally follows the predictions of Hypotheses 3 and 4.

The existence of the special majority requirements in the second round are important and the need for interinstitutional collaboration is even more important, but the real key to understanding party group behavior in the EP is the shift in the legislative power of the EP. Once the EP was given the potential to influence legislative outcomes *in a nonhegemonic way* it became necessary for the underlying character of the party group system to shift from dogmatic to pragmatic. Only this explanation can account for the shift in voting behavior witnessed under resolutions after the SEA. Neither the majority restrictions nor the need for Commission and Council agreement were required for resolutions during the third and fourth legislatures. In fact, the only thing that changed between the first two and the last two legislatures for resolutions was the increase in EP legislative authority under *other* procedures.

Although the legal authority of EP resolutions did not change after the Single European Act, the general perception of the EP and its legislative role within the European Union did. The probability that the other institutions of the EU would act on, or at least consider, EP resolutions most likely grew as a result. This type of increased compromise and cooperation between party groups as the realization of parliamentary proposals became more likely is explained by Hypothesis 4, which predicts that the actions of the parties will reflect the tools and opportunities at their disposal. Can the macro and micro models also explain the differences in voting behavior between the first and second rounds under the new procedures?

I suggested above that this could be understood if we think of the new legislative procedures as two-stage games. The EP has two opportunities to convince the other institutions to adopt its amendments. Where significant differences exist between the EPP and the PES, the two-stage procedure allows them to fight for their relative ideal positions during the first round and compromise to maximize EP influence during the second round. Thus, the first round is an ideological battle while the second is an interinstitutional one. This explanation is useful because it accounts for the variation in coalition behavior between the two rounds while still permitting grand coalitions in the first round if there is broad ideological consensus and the absence of grand coalitions in the second round if ideological barriers cannot be overcome. This pattern of conflict and compromise can easily be compared to primaries in the United States and the French double-ballot electoral system. Both systems initially pit individuals or parties against each other in a first round, only to then require that they work together in a second round to achieve their mutual best outcome.

The party system of the European Parliament, like the Parliament itself, is clearly still in the process of developing. Effective legislative strategies are still being tested. At the same time, the legislative process itself is frequently being revised.[15] The result is a party system with only partially established behavioral norms that will continue to develop as the role of the EP in the broader political environment changes. Thus far, the capacity of the EP, and especially the party groups, to adapt to its expanding legislative role has allowed it to evolve from a polarized chamber of debate into an effective legislative body. The ability of the party groups, and in particular the EPP and the PES, to use cooperation and compromise as strategic tools in the interinstitutional struggle for power was a crucial part of this transformation.

The cooperation and co-decision procedures differ significantly from EP resolutions. Proposals under these procedures are created outside the EP, which can only offer amendments, while resolutions are created and passed wholly within the EP.[16] The legislative process is far more complicated and time-consuming for cooperation, and especially co-decision proposals. Both incorporate multiple readings and complex bargaining between and, it appears, within institutions. Finally, the potential of the EP to have a *direct* impact on final EU legislation exists only under the cooperation and co-decision procedures. Despite these differences, the patterns of voting behavior in each of the legislative procedures and across time suggest a definite transformation in the character of coalition formation as a result of the EP's acquisition of legislative authority.

Having examined both the role of the party groups in the institutional evolution of the EP and the development of the party system, the next step is to look more closely at the internal development of the groups themselves.

---

[15] The Amsterdam Treaty has greatly reduced the use of the cooperation procedure, replacing it with a modified version of the co-decision procedure in most cases. For more information see Jacobs (1997).

[16] There is no limit, however, to the scope of their powers of amendment beyond the desire to have these amendments adopted by the Commission and the Council. The EP can, and frequently does, add new policy dimensions to legislative proposals through the amendment process (Kreppel, 1999b).

8

The Internal Development of the Supranational Party Groups: An Elusive Goal

The internal development of the party groups is perhaps the least studied aspect of the European Parliament. Although there are numerous books written on the party groups before (Van Oudenhove, 1965; Fitzmaurice, 1975) and immediately following direct elections (Pridham and Pridham, 1979, 1980; Henig, 1979, 1980; Guidi, 1983), almost nothing has been written since that specifically focuses on the internal organization of the groups.[1] There is an emerging body of work that examines the voting cohesion of the party groups but fails to examine their internal organization beyond that (Attinà, 1990, 1992, 1993; Brzinski, 1995). Even the best attempt to discover the role of the party groups within the EP thus far (Raunio, 1996) still largely ignores the *internal* development of the groups themselves.

The reason for this lacuna is simple: There is very little available information on the internal development of the groups. For example, even the largest and most stable groups rarely keep organized records of their previous internal rules.[2] Beyond the dearth of historical documents, and probably more important, is the informal nature of much of the internal organization of the party groups. As we shall see in this chapter, one of the most important aspects of internal party group organization is given only passing mention in the rules of both of the two largest groups (the EPP and the PES). In effect, there are very little quantitative or consistent data on the internal development of the groups available. The most

---

[1] Even these early works spend very little time discussing the internal organization of the groups beyond which national parties were represented.

[2] I am indebted to Alain Santiago from the PES and Ingetraut Kotzhk from the EPP for those historical versions of the party group internal rules that I do have.

common methods of examining the internal evolution of political parties and elite control over individual Members are therefore either inappropriate or impossible to apply within the party groups of the EP. As a result, much of this chapter is based on a series of interviews with both Members of the EP and officials in the party group secretariats, as well as numerous historical documents that have been provided by the party group secretariats in Brussels.[3]

Despite the difficulty of gauging internal change over time within the groups, it might be expected that the rapid and dramatic evolution of the party group *system* within the European Parliament after 1987 would have inspired a similarly rapid and expansive evolution within the party groups themselves. In fact, a synthesis of the macro and micro models of institutional development led to the prediction that party group elite would attempt to influence the actions of individual Members through the manipulation of the internal structures of the groups when external events supplied an effective excuse.[4]

An application of the macro model suggested that the rapid increase in total EP membership and Member diversity that resulted from the introduction of direct election in 1979, and the increases in EP power after 1986, would lead to significant internal reform within the groups. In particular, it was predicted that the groups would develop and/or formalize their internal hierarchical structures in response to increased membership and the concomitant organizational dilemmas that they faced. The macro model did not predict the precise nature of these internal reforms since this requires only that internal reforms follow external reforms and be logically connected. The micro model of development was used to more precisely predict the character of internal party reform.

The micro model of development, in conjunction with an examination of the development of political parties in other legislatures, suggested that the party group elite would use the introduction of direct elections and the increased powers of the EP (and the new majority requirements) as an excuse to solidify their control over rank-and-file members. I predicted,

---

[3] These interviews took place during three distinct periods: the first between February and May 1996, the second during November and December 1996, and the third during March 1998. A total of over sixty interviews were conducted.

[4] This hypothesis is developed in Chapter 3; see Chapters 2 and 5 for the application of the model to the EP as a whole.

based on the American literature, that this would occur through the increased use of benefits and sanctions against Members (Cox, 1987; Cox and McCubbins, 1993). As we shall see, however, this has not occurred, or at least not in the manner suggested by the predictions developed in Chapter 3. To understand why we must examine not only the origins and history of the party groups, but more importantly the development of informal norms that have come to decisively limit the authority of the group elite, much to the latter's chagrin.

My examination of the internal development of the party groups (or lack thereof) begins with a historical examination of the creation of the party groups. This includes some common, and conflicting, explanations of why ideologically based groups were created to begin with and the internal tension within the EP between national and ideological interests. In the second section I examine the distribution of power within the party groups according to the *formal* internal rules of the two largest groups. This is followed by an examination of the true allocation of power within the groups based on historical norms, or *informal* rather than official rules. This section focuses, in particular, on the role of the national delegations within the political groups and their control over the allocation of benefits and sanctions to rank-and-file members. In the third, and final, section I examine what the internal distribution of power within the groups means in terms of the effectiveness and evolution of the groups and the EP as a whole, looking in particular at the institutional impact of power disaggregation.

The Historical Development of the Party Groups

The creation of political groups within the EP was by no means pre-ordained. On the contrary, neither the original Treaties for the European Economic Community (EEC) nor its predecessor, the Common Assembly of the European Coal and Steel Community (ECSC), mentioned the creation of ideologically based associations. The Maastricht Treaty officially recognized the creation of the political groups only in 1992 (Article 138a). Other international assemblies created after World War II were organized primarily by national identity (the Council of Europe, the OECD, the United Nations, etc.). Yet, during the first meeting of the Common Assembly (CA), the election of its president was decided along ideological and not national lines.

When the Common Assembly of the European Coal and Steel Community was convened for the first time on September 10, 1952, there were no ideological associations within its membership. Members sat in alphabetical order.[5] Despite the overt political tone of the first presidential election, there were no further attempts to address or incorporate political tendencies into the internal organization of the new body during its constitutive meetings. In fact, there were significant examples of attempts to incorporate potential *national* differences. The most significant was the decision that there should be five vice presidents so that each Member State could potentially have a representative on the newly created executive bureau.[6] The first draft of the Common Assembly's rules did not include any mention of political organizations or even the existence of ideological diversity among the Members.

The potential significance of the diverse ideologies represented in the CA was first discussed in January 1953 in regards to a draft text of the definitive version of the Assembly's rules. It was proposed that the draft rules be revised to include more specific language on the appointment of Members to the various Committees (Mutter report on behalf of the Rules of Procedure and Accounts Committee, Doc. 1, January 1953: 5, 12). In particular, it was suggested that the following text be added to the provision regarding the nomination of Members to committees:

Nominations shall be forwarded to the Bureau (officers), which shall submit the necessary proposals to the Assembly, due consideration being given to an equitable representation of the participating States *and of the various political traditions*. (Emphasis added, author's translation)

The Assembly approved the proposed text without debate (*Common Assembly Proceedings*, January 10, 1953: 146). This was the first time that ideological differences between Members were officially recognized, and it marked the beginning of the creation of the first supranational parliamentary parties. After only four months of existence, the Common Assembly became the first international Assembly to consider the ideological

---

[5] This was also the case in the Consultative Assembly of the Council of Europe, but not in the General Assembly of the UN, where members were arranged by nationality.

[6] It should be noted that the *Rapporteur* was careful to insist that the candidates should be chosen on the basis of their skills and not their nationality. But, he also noted that since it was possible to select any number of vice presidents, it made sense to select a number that allowed for the possibility of complete national representation (*Common Assembly Debates* September 10, 1952).

variations among its members as a determining factor in its internal organization. The further consolidation of the political groups was not long in coming, despite several clear concessions to national identity.[7]

By March 1953, a de facto division into three distinct political groups had appeared: Christian Democrat, Socialist, and Liberal (in order of size). The official or de jure recognition of the groups would have to wait until June 1953, only ten months after the Common Assembly's constitutive meeting. The move to officially establish the emerging political groups was led by Mr. Mollet, leader of the proto-Socialist group (*Common Assembly Proceedings*, no 2, March 11, 1953: 12). Mr. Sassen, leader of the Christian Democratic Members, emphatically supported this position (*Common Assembly Proceedings*, no 2, March 11, 1953: 14). The de facto existence of the political groups led the rules committee to conduct a study on the implications of political party group formation and suggested courses of action. This report was discussed for the first time in March 1953. The final text of the report was drawn up in June of the same year. On June 16th the Assembly, without discussion, unanimously passed a resolution adopting the report (Resolution #13, *Journal Officiel*, July 21, 1953).

The report from the Rules Committee emphasized the crucial role of political parties in the internal organization of parliamentary action. The *Rapporteur*, Mr. Struye, noted that the groups had in essence already formed and all that was required was to give them official legal recognition (explanatory statement by Mr. Struye; *Common Assembly Proceedings*, no. 4, 1953: 47–51). This recognition took the form of a very simple addition to the rules regulating the formation of political groups. The new rule 33*bis* (later changed to rule 34) simply stated that Members could form groups according to *political persuasion*. All that was required to form a group was a declaration of formation including the name of the group, its executive, and the signatures of its members. The only restrictions were that groups be politically (not nationally) based, that they have at least nine members, and that no individual could belong to more than one group (Resolution 13, *Common Assembly Proceedings*, January 10, 1953).

From this point forward the political groups were both a factual and a legal reality. The internal organization of the Common Assembly, and later

---

[7] For example, the distribution of nationalities among the different committees was strictly regulated, with careful attention paid to an equitable balance and some consideration of relative size (resolution #9, January 10th, 1953, *Journal Officiel*, February 1953).

the European Parliament, was increasingly founded on their existence. The political groups were given financial support, determined in part by their relative size (with a base amount given to all groups and then an additional sum given per member). The groups each organized independent secretariats and were given office space within the Common Assembly's work places in Strasbourg. Debates in the CA were increasingly organized on the basis of official group positions instead of individual Member statements. The leaders of the political groups were soon invited to participate in the agenda-setting process within the Parliament's Bureau.[8] By the time the Common Assembly was disbanded to make way for the new European Parliament in 1957, the political groups had become a significant force in its internal organization.

This trend was if anything accelerated in the newly formed E.P. Whereas the party groups had not existed, and indeed were not expected to form at all, when the Common Assembly was created, they were already alive and healthy during the constitutive meeting of the European Parliament. In fact, the groups had done much of the preparatory work leading up to the first meeting of the new body, and the smooth transition between the Common Assembly and the European Parliament has been attributed to them (Van Oudenhove, 1965: 129). It had been decided ahead of time that the standing rules of the CA would function, temporarily, as the provisional rules for the new E.P. This meant that the political groups were automatically recognized since they had been awarded official standing in the previous Common Assembly.

The initial result was a kind of oligarchy of political group presidents. Together the three party group leaders nominated a single candidate for president of the E.P. (the well-known French federalist Robert Schuman) and made a successful joint proposal nominating the eight vice presidents and even designating their rankings.[9] They also forwarded successful proposals on the number and jurisdictions of the new committees as well as

---

[8] This was formalized by another rules revision in May 1954. This modified Rule 11 to officially allow the participation (without the right to vote) of the party group presidents in the meetings of the Committee of Presidents (the Bureau plus the committee chairmen), where the agenda was discussed and decided (*Common Assembly Proceedings*, no. 6, 1954: 27).

[9] The number of vice presidents was increased to eight in light of the increase in size of the E.P. (142 compared to the 78 members of the Common Assembly). The rank order of the vice presidents is significant because, according to the rules, the candidate with the most votes is ranked first, etc. The ranking then determines who takes over for the president if he is unable to perform his duties for any reason.

their membership, and the name of the new assembly.[10] Thus the trend of group dominance of the internal functioning of the EP was continued. Political groups became responsible for all nominations. Eventually, party group positions were officially given precedence in the ordering of statements during debates on the floor in the EP (*EP Proceedings*, no. 17, September 25, 1959: 221–222; *Journal Officiel*, October 10, 1959).

All of these actions demonstrate the extent to which the previous experience of political party groups in the Common Assembly was crucial to the development of the new European Parliament. As in the case of the Treaty of Paris, which established the Common Assembly of the ECSC, the Treaties of Rome made no reference to ideological associations or the potential role of supranational political parties. Yet, the Members of the EP decided to continue and expand the tradition of political groups.[11] The dominance of political groups continued to grow throughout the 1960s, although the number of political groups increased by only one (a Gaullist group made up primarily of French members was formed in 1965 after they split from the Liberal group in late 1963).

The 1973 expansion of the European Communities to include the United Kingdom, Denmark, and Ireland increased the total membership (from 142 to 198) and caused several key changes to the relative size and power of the political groups.[12] It did not, however, alter the position of the groups in the internal organization of the EP, which continued to be significant. The acceptance of the role of the party groups by the new members occurred without discussion. By this point the status of the groups within the EP was firmly established and nearly universally accepted.

---

[10] This last caused some conflict because of the linguistical variations among the various countries. The final agreement was for the new assembly to be called the European Parliamentary Assembly in French and Italian and the European Parliament in Dutch and German, because of ambiguities with the word "assembly" in these languages. In 1962 the Members decided to use the name European Parliament in all languages. This term was finally adopted by the other institutions of the European Community (who had continued to officially refer to the EP as the "Assembly") in 1987 as part of the Single European Act.

[11] The expansion of the roles and powers of the political groups is discussed in depth in Chapter 5 in relation to the revision of the EP's Rules of Procedure.

[12] The accession of the United Kingdom caused some initial confusion since the Labor party members did not take their seats until after the adhesion of the United Kingdom was accepted by a national referendum in 1975. The Conservative Members, on the other hand, participated but did not join any pre-existing group, deciding instead to form their own group, the European Democratic Group (EDG), with a few additional members from Denmark and France.

There were fundamental changes to the party groups' structure after the introduction of direct elections in 1979. The number and relative power of the political groups underwent a massive upheaval, as new parties were formed and old groups attempted to adapt to the doubling of EP's membership (from 198 to 404 Members). Despite the increase in the number of Members in the new directly elected EP, the minimum numbers required to form a group initially remained those of the old appointed EP.[13] This low threshold, combined with the greater ideological variation among Members, led to a significant increase in the number of party groups.[14] Despite these changes, the overall role of the groups in the internal organization and functioning of the EP was in no way diminished, if anything it was increased.[15]

After direct elections the number of party groups varied between seven and twelve, but the number of nonaffiliated members remained small (averaging less than 5%).[16] After every expansion new Members have either formed new groups or, more frequently, joined existing groups. The predominate role of the political groups in the EP as well as the financial benefits that now accrue to them (particularly the larger groups) helps to explain why new members might decide to join or create political groups rather than remain "unattached," but the fact remains that this was in no way preordained or even to be predicted based on the experience of other international assemblies.

The question of why the political groups initially formed has not been well-studied. Most discussions of the birth of the political groups within the EP attribute their formation to the cultural political traditions and/or the historical environment of the immediate postwar era. Both of these approaches attempt to explain why the "natural" tendency to form national

[13] Only ten members were required if they came from three or more Member States. For a discussion of the abortive attempts to revise the rules both before and after direct elections to reflect the increased size of the EP, see Chapter 5.

[14] Prior to direct elections both the extreme right and left had been significantly underrepresented since these were usually in opposition in the home parliaments and thus not generally appointed to the EP.

[15] See Chapter 5 for a discussion of the evolving role of the political groups in the internal organization of the EP after direct elections.

[16] There were some periods when the numbers of nonaffiliated members increased, such as immediately after Greek accession, when appointed members decided not to join any party groups until after their own direct election. Other instances of temporary increases in nonaffiliated members have occurred when groups lost a member and were thus no longer eligible for group status. These were usually temporary situations and do not demonstrate a desire by a large or cohesive group to not form or join a political group.

groups, or even no groups at all, was almost immediately superceded in favor of the creation of overtly supranational political organizations. I outline in the following the general cultural and historical approaches and examine their usefulness in explaining the initial formation of the party groups in the Common Assembly. This is important because it helps us to understand how the creation of overtly ideological party groups pushed the question of national influence into the internal functioning of the groups themselves, largely stagnating their internal development.

Cultural and Historical Explanations of Political Group Formation

Cultural accounts of EP development are based on the assumption that past political experience determines future actions. In such a case, the political structure of the new European institutions created by the Treaties of Paris and Rome was, to some extent, pre-determined by the political realities and practices of the six Member States who participated. Although not developed explicitly as a predictive theoretical argument, the cultural approach is implicit in many studies of the European Parliament (Henig, 1979; Pinder, 1991). The general thrust of the argument is that, since individual Members of the Common Assembly (and later the EP) were appointed by their national Assemblies, they were experienced politicians, usually with significant political party experience. As a result, when faced with the task of organizing themselves within the Common Assembly they naturally gravitated toward ideologically based political associations since these were familiar.

A more complicated theory of political group formation attempts to explain their creation in the Common Assembly (and the EP) in light of the historical context of the origin of the European Coal and Steel Community and later the European Economic Community (Van Ouden-houve, 1965). This explanation focuses on the extreme anti-nationalist sentiments that existed in the post–Word War II era. The Coal and Steel Community was originally conceived as a mechanism to tie the economies of France and Germany together. By unifying coal and steel production, Jean Monnet and other European leaders hoped to eliminate the possibility of another war on the Continent, while at the same time resolving the long-standing conflict between Germany and France over the Ruhr region (a major source of coal). The founding father of the European Union, Jean Monnet, was a staunch European federalist who believed that the nationalism which had led to the first and second world wars had to be overcome if Europe was to prosper and function effectively in the new global system of superpowers. This opposition to nationalism was fundamental to the creation of the ECSC and the EEC. According to this explanation, political groups were formed in the Common Assembly, and later the European Parliament, as a kind of symbolic stand against nationalism, a conscious effort to move away from the national representation of the Council of Europe and the OECD.

There is support for both the historical and cultural approaches in speeches made within the Common Assembly and studies written at the time. Within the Common Assembly there were strong arguments made against the creation of any type of national associations, and even against structuring the internal executive in a way to facilitate national representation (*CA Proceedings*, no 1, September 11, 1952: 8). Despite a natural respect for the need of an equitable distribution of posts by nationality (for example, committee assignments), there was a general agreement amongst Members that nationality should not be the primary basis of internal organization. Just a few years after the creation of the European Parliament, Guy Van Oudenhove explained the creation of political groups by stating that the grouping of delegates into national coalitions would have been "utterly 'un-European', and was therefore ruled out *a priori*." He continued, stating that "what was required was to find a formula whereby the individual Members could be grouped outside the national delegations provided for in the Treaties. Hence the idea of cutting across the national frontiers by means of a 'political' grouping process, in which membership was determined by ideological affinity" (Van Oudenhove, 1965: 236).

It can also be demonstrated that Members did feel that a greater level of internal organization was necessary to function successfully and efficiently (*CA Proceedings*, no 2, March 11, 1953: 8–14). This was in part due to the fact that the new Common Assembly was imbued with powers not available to the Consultative Assembly of the Council of Europe. The Common Assembly had the power to determine its own agenda, establish its own internal structure, and offer "own initiative" resolutions to the other institutions of the Coal and Steel Community. Above all, it could censure the executive, a power previously unheard of among international assemblies. These additional powers lent the Common Assembly a unique status, viewed at the time as "midway between a national parliament and the classic type of international assembly" (Van Oudenhove, 1965: 9; see also Lindsay, 1958).

186

The Internal Development of the Supranational Party Groups

If its Members viewed the Common Assembly as a Parliament instead of an international assembly *and* there was a strong sentiment against forming nationally based internal groups (and this is supported by the debates in the CA and EP), it could help to explain why political, ideologically based organizations were formed within the Common Assembly and continued in the EP but not the Consultative Assembly of the Council of Europe. But what happened to the national alliances that could be considered the more natural development given the common linguistical and cultural experiences of Members from the same country? The common assumption that the development of the supranational party groups effectively surmounted petty nationalism is perhaps too optimistic.[17] The role of national delegations that were formed *within* each of the party groups (frequently unofficially) has been largely ignored. This is a tremendous mistake if we want to understand the internal organization of the party groups and the impact that the character of their internal development has had on the evolution of the EP as a whole. In fact, the common view of the role of the party groups within the EP as a whole might be artificially inflated by an ignorance of the role of the national delegations within the groups themselves.

The Distribution of Positions of Authority Within the European Parliament

As the earliest debates demonstrate, the decision to organize the internal structures of the Common Assembly (and later the European Parliament) along ideological rather than national lines was controversial. In fact, within the EP's rules there were (and continue to be) several concessions to the need to respect nationality as much as ideological diversity.[18] On the whole, however, the European Parliament has maintained the reputation of a truly "supranational" institution in which petty national self-interest is secondary to the pursuit of broad "European" ideological goals. This image may be something of an exaggeration if the role of the national delegations within the party groups is examined more closely. Before we

---

[17] In the spate of recent analyses of voting behavior in the EP, the common conclusion is that ideology is more important than nationality in determining coalitions. On the whole this has led to the conclusion that national identities have by and large been superseded (Attinà, 1990, 1992; Brzinski, 1995; Raunio, 1996).

[18] This is true, for example, in the distribution of committee assignments and leadership positions in the enlarged bureau.

187

can examine the party groups themselves, it will be useful to understand a bit more about the internal functioning of the EP as a whole, in particular the methods used to determine who fills which position within both the hierarchy of the EP and the committees and delegations.

Officially, the posts within the EP hierarchy are distributed by free, competitive elections every two and a half years (once in July, just after the June elections, and once midway through the legislative term, in January).[19] In practice, all internal offices but the presidency are distributed proportionately (according to the d'Hondt method) amongst the party groups on the basis of their size. In effect the party groups establish lists of candidates, which are then voted on by the Parliament as a whole. Consensus regarding who will be elected is generally achieved ahead of time (at least between the largest groups), which facilitates the process (Westlake, 1994: 184–197; Corbett et al., 1995: 96–104).

In effect, only the office of president has ever been seriously contested, and this only until 1989, although the 1999 presidential election appeared to mark an end to the long-established EPP–PES coalition.[20] To win an election, a presidential candidate must receive the support of an absolute majority of EP Members during the first through the third rounds of balloting. If no candidate has achieved this, then during the fourth ballot the top two vote winners run again and only a simple majority is required for election. Until 1989 the elections for the EP presidency were frequently quite competitive, even requiring third and fourth ballots.[21] As the result of an infamous meeting between the leaders of the EPP and the PES groups (the so-called "meeting of the Giants") the presidency of the EP was shuttled between these two groups between 1989 and 1999, effectively excluding all other groups.[22]

---

[19] The election of EP officers is covered in Chapter III of the Rules of Procedure (Rules 13–18), 1999 (14th edition).

[20] There have been times when the election of some vice presidents has required a second or third ballot, but this is unusual and in the end the candidate supported by the party group leadership usually wins. During the 1999 election both the PES and the EPP presented candidates for the first time since 1989. As a result, a kind of informal coalition was formed between the ELDR and the EPP for the presidential election with the agreement that the EPP would control the presidency for the first term and the ELDR would control it for the second (Kreppel 1999a).

[21] The elections in 1982 went to a fourth ballot and in 1986 to a third ballot, where the British Conservative Member Lord Plumb won by a margin of only five votes.

[22] Before 1989 the Liberal group controlled the presidency three times (1962–1964, 1973–1975, and 1979–1981), and the European Democratic group (which later merged with the EPP) controlled it once (1987–1989).

Despite the official rules of the Parliament, the allocation of committee chairmanships and vice chairmanships is also generally based on a proportional distribution between the party groups. The Rules of the EP require only that:

At the first Committee meeting after the election of Committee Members pursuant to Rule 137, the committee shall elect a bureau consisting of a chairman and one, two or three vice chairmen who shall be elected in separate ballots. (Rule 142)

In practice, however, the party groups present their preferences within the Conference of Presidents (previously the Bureau) on the distribution of committee chairmanships, vice chairmanships, delegation chairmanships, and so on. The d'Hondt method has been used at least since 1979 to distribute these committee positions amongst the party groups on the basis of their relative size within the EP as a whole. In effect, each party group knows how many positions it can expect (i.e., how many chairmanships, vice chairmanships, etc.) and submits a list of its preferences to the Conference of Presidents (CoP). Since it is likely that more than one group will request the same thing (chair of the environment committee, for example), the lists created by the groups are ordered in terms of the group's priorities.

The allocation process begins with the group that has the most "points," which is based on size and the number of points already used up (for example, in the election of the president and vice presidents of the EP). This group selects its most preferred position (using up some pre-specified number of points). The choice continues to go to the group with the highest number of points. Usually this involves switching back and forth between the two largest groups a number of times until they have used up enough of their points to allow a different group (the third largest) to have the most points. The process continues until all of the positions have been allocated.

The actual membership of the Committees and Delegations is done on a purely proportional basis between the party groups, with attention paid to the equal distribution among the different nationalities. Rule 152 of the 1999 Rules of Procedure requires only that:

Members of committees and temporary committees of inquiry shall be elected after nominations have been submitted by the political groups and the non-attached Members. The Conference of Presidents shall submit to the Parliament. The composition of the committees shall, as far as possible, reflect the composition of the Parliament.

In practice, the lists created by the party groups are eventually adopted, with very little revision (Corbett et al., 1995).

This general understanding of how positions of authority and influence within the EP get distributed highlights the very crucial role of the party groups. At the plenary level it is the party groups and their leadership that make most of the decisions, but to focus only on the macrocosm of the EP as a whole ignores what occurs within the groups themselves. Because of the need to cater to national diversity as well as ideological affiliation, the general pattern within the EP has been to distribute positions proportionally first to the party groups (ideology), which then go through a similar process internally on the basis of nationality. Thus, after a group is allocated its share of key positions (committee chairs, etc.) it must then distribute these proportionately amongst its own membership on the basis of the size of the various national delegations within the group. This is done, with little variation between the groups, on the basis of a very similar point system as that used by the EP as a whole.

The distribution of authority positions within the EP is thus a very complicated procedure, and one in which the need for "fair" representation (i.e., proportional) is generally considered to be of primary importance. The rest of this chapter is aimed at looking at the process of distribution that occurs within the groups themselves and how this has affected the power of the group leaders and their ability to control or influence individual member actions.

The Distribution of Positions of Authority Within the Party Groups

Hypotheses 6 and 6a outlined in Chapter 3 predicted that as the EP gained in legislative power and authority the leaders of the party groups would exert more energy controlling their Members to ensure that group goals were not hindered by renegade Members. Hypotheses 5 and 5a suggested that large environmental changes offered group leaders an opportunity to make internal reforms that would give them greater control over individual Member activities. I predicted that this trend would increase as the powers of the EP expanded and the potential of the party groups to achieve stated policy goals grew. The analysis of roll-call votes discussed in Chapters 6 and 7 seem to support these hypotheses given the increasingly high level of internal group cohesion across both time and legislative procedure, particularly for the two largest groups. A detailed analysis of the internal organization of the groups points to a quite different conclusion.

In this section I analyze the development of the formal organization and rules of the two largest party groups, the Party of European Socialists group and the European People's Party.[23] In particular, I examine the impact that external shifts in the political authority and power of the EP have had on internal group organization and the extent to which the internal organization of the groups has evolved over the last quarter-century. In the next section I look at the distribution of benefits to Members to determine the extent to which the allocation of benefits (committee chairmanships and *Rapporteurships*) appears to be a reward for Members who both vote the group line and regularly participate in plenary.[24]

My analysis focuses on these two groups for three reasons. First, they have both existed consistently since the very first groups were formed in 1953, which permits a historical analysis.[25] Second, as the two largest groups they are not as constrained as the smaller groups by the limitations of the d'Hondt method of distribution among nationalities. Because the national delegations within the larger groups tend, not surprisingly, to be much larger than within the smaller groups, the constraint that a given position go to a German or a Spanish Member is not nearly as restrictive.[26] Finally, as we have seen throughout, it is primarily the two largest groups that have come to determine the course of the EP's internal development and the content of EP amendments and own initiative resolutions. The "hegemony" of the EPP and the PES within the Parliament has been

---

[23] The European People's Party group is commonly assumed to be Christian Democratic in orientation. While this was true historically, since the inclusion in 1986 of the Spanish Popular Party, the 1992 formal inclusion of the British Conservatives and the 1999 inclusion of the right wing Italian "*Forza Europa*," the group has become significantly less Christian Democratic. This ideological dispersion has been lamented by many within the group who feel that the full adhesion of groups that lack the basic Christian democratic ideology has cost the group its internal consensus and political compass. The change in the composition of the groups was reflected by a name change to the European Peoples Party and European Democrats (EPP–ED) in July 1999.

[24] Regular participation in committee, while important, is not officially monitored and therefore cannot be used as a measure of Member performance.

[25] The only other group with the same historical continuity is the European Liberal Democratic group.

[26] In other words, there are more German or Spanish Members to choose from and group leadership could, conceivably, select that Member which it most prefers.

frequently noted by scholars and much bemoaned by the smaller groups within the EP.[27] It is essential then that we understand how these two groups are themselves organized internally and the extent to which they are, in fact, able to control their Members. A more complete comprehension of the balance of power within the groups between the formal leaders and the national delegations may lead to a more complete understanding of the internal development of the EP as a whole, in particular the centralization of power within the executive (Conference of Presidents) and the increased role of the party group elite that has evolved within that body.

The Development of the Internal Rules of the EPP and the PES

Although both groups had formal internal rules as far back as 1955, the earliest version that I was able to obtain for either group dates from twenty years later, 1975. Despite this large lacuna in the available data, an examination of the rules, what they do and do not include, and how this has changed over time will still prove interesting.[28] The internal Rules of Procedure (RoP) of the party groups are not as extensive as those of the EP as a whole, but they do offer some insight into the extent to which the groups have evolved over time, and the intended direction of that evolution.

The Group of the Peoples' Party of Europe The 1975 version of the EPP's internal rules included a total of thirty-two rules divided into nine chapters.[29] The RoP required that Members be affiliated with a national "Christian Democratic" party or a kindred party (Rule 3, 1975). Other individuals could join the group if they agreed to the group's platform and if Members from the same nationality approved (Rule 4, 1975). There was also a provision for Members to be cast out if two-thirds of the Members agreed (Rule 6, 1975).

---

[27] The European Liberal Democratic group has lamented this in particular. For an example see the debates surrounding the election of the president of the EP in January 1997 in the Annex to the *OJC* Debates 4–493, January 1997: 4–7.

[28] I have all of the various versions of the rules for the EPP group dating from 1975 to the present. For the PES I have the 1977, 1986, 1989, 1991, and 1996. It is not clear how many other versions there may have been in between those that I have.

[29] Until 1979 the European Peoples' Party group was named the Christian Democratic group. To minimize confusion I use the EPP throughout this analysis.

The primary organs of the group in 1975 (four years before direct elections) were the Plenary Assembly, the Bureau, and the presidency. The most powerful of these, according to the Rules of Procedure, was the plenary. This body officially had the power to take decisions on all political questions occurring within the EP, as well as control over the designation of group representatives and speakers, the allocation of committee and subcommittee membership, and nominations to all EP hierarchy and committee chair positions allocated to the group (Rule 8, 1975). The full plenary also elected the group's Bureau and Presidency, nominated three group auditors, and had final control over the group's budget (Rule 8, 1975).

The Bureau was primarily the secretariat of the group. It consisted of both elected and "statutory" Members. The latter were any Members of the group who were Members of the EP Bureau, chairs of committees, or ex-presidents of Parliament. Elected members included the president, the vice presidents, and the leaders of the national delegations (Rule 9, 1975).[30] The Bureau was in charge of preparing the decisions of the group and overseeing their implementation. It was also in charge of all personnel decisions, as well as financial or administrative problems that were not expressly reserved for the other organs of the group (Rule 10, 1975). The presidency was selected from within the Bureau and had as its primary tasks the representation of the group externally, leadership of the group during the full plenary sessions of the EP, and leading the group's internal meetings (Rule 12, 1975).

Chapter 6 of the group's rules, "Interventions and Communications," is interesting in that it explicitly attempted to limit or control the actions of individual Members within the full plenary. In particular, Rule 21 (1975) required Members to inform the competent Member of the presidency (and provide a complete copy) prior to presenting a resolution, an amendment, or an order of the day to the full plenary. The same rule also permitted the presidency of the group to delay the actions of the individual up to ten days to allow for consultation with the full group. In addition, any Member who wished to pose a written question to the Commission or Council was required to give a copy to the presidency prior to submitting the question to the relevant institution. This is the only section of

---

[30] The 1975 version of the Rules does not make clear how many vice presidents there were, stating only that they should be elected. The leaders of the national delegation were, and still are, elected within the delegations themselves.

the Rules that attempted to directly hinder individual action, but the restrictions were significant, especially given the extremely limited powers of the Parliament as a whole during this period.

The general tenor of the group's Rules remained largely unchanged throughout the following twenty-two years. Additional positions of influence were added when committee "coordinators" and permanent working groups (which included more than one committee) were created and officially added to the Rules of Procedure in 1989 (Rules 15–17).[31] The exact date of their creation is something of a mystery. They had informally developed long before they were officially included in the group's rules. In the 1986 group handbook they were already treated as normal, but in the pre-existing rules (1979) they were not mentioned. In fact, the group's rules remained formally unchanged for ten years (between 1979 and 1989), despite several obvious internal developments. The most recent version of the rules remains surprisingly similar to the 1977 version, including only thirty-four rules in eight chapters. The most notable exception to this is the complete deletion of the previous Chapter 6 on interventions and communications. In the 1989 version of the Rules there are no restrictions on individual Member activities.[32] Another change was the formalization of decision making within the group with the addition of rules regarding the necessary majorities and quorums (Rules 19–20, 1989).

The extent to which the internal organization of the EPP group has remained the same over time is quite extraordinary given the dramatic changes that it underwent between 1975 and 1996. The increase in membership as a result of direct elections was not the only significant internal change experienced by the group. The addition in 1986 of the Spanish center-right Popular Party and the formal accession in 1992 of the British Conservatives, both of which were clearly not Christian Democrat parties, created a much more diverse group.[33] The group's Rules of Procedure became somewhat more technical over time. However, aside from the addition of specific voting requirements and the development of working groups to organize committee and legislative activity (which arose primarily from the extension of the EP's legislative powers), there

[31] There are five working groups that loosely follow the divisions: Foreign Affairs, Economic Affairs, Budget and Agricultural Affairs, Social Affairs, and Internal Affairs.

[32] Inserted into this section are instead Rules regulating the meetings of the group with regard to outside observers. In general, the meetings of the group are closed.

[33] This was exacerbated still further by the 1999 accession of the Italian *Forza Europa* party, but this lies outside the time period analyzed here.

was little internal reaction to the changing dimensions and diversity of the group.

The primary organs of the group remained the same and had, fundamentally, the same powers throughout the period covered here. Even changes in the internal organization were incorporated into the previous structures. The composition of the new working groups and committee coordinators (1989) were officially decided by the plenary, and new working group chairs became members of the Bureau (Rules 9 and 10, 1996). The number of vice presidents was fixed at five in 1989 and increased to six in 1996 (Rule 12).[34] Otherwise the official organs of the group remained largely the same. To this extent, the macro model is not a very effective predictor of internal party group change. There was some reaction to the addition of the cooperation and co-decision procedure because of the need to effectively cope with a significantly increased legislative load but surprisingly little reaction to the advent of direct elections. The disappearance of the previous restrictions of individual Member activities is an interesting development, but not one that can be directly connected to the expansion of the group.

The Group of the Socialist Party of Europe   The development of the Socialist group is significantly different from that of the EPP. The 1977 version of the PES's Rules of Procedure was superficially even more basic than those of the EPP, with only twenty-one rules in eight chapters. In many ways, however, they were already more well-developed. Adhesion to the group was based on an individual's membership in a Socialist party within his/her Member State. If someone who was not a Member of a Socialist party wished to join, the application was studied by the group Bureau and decided by the plenary based on the Bureau's suggestion (Rule 2, 1977).

The basic organizational structure of the PES was significantly different than that of the EPP. The organs of the group consisted of the full plenary (labeled simply as "the group"), a Bureau, and a treasurer, but no "presidency." The powers of the Bureau were similar to the combined powers of the EPP Bureau and presidency, with a few notable exceptions. The Socialist Bureau consisted of at least nine members with a minimum of one representative from each Member State represented within the group (Rule 10, 1977). The tasks of the Bureau included the coordination

---

[34] This was partially a result of the accession in 1995 of Austria, Finland, and Sweden.

of the activities of the group, control over the group's secretariat, creating and maintaining contacts with the Socialist parties of the European Community and the Socialist International, and the formulation and study of all questions and propositions to be presented in the name of the group (Rule 11, 1977). In addition, from as far back as 1977 the Bureau had the power to convene temporary working groups to study issues of particular concern to the group (Rule 12, 1977).

Like the EPP, the allocation of positions within the EP's hierarchy as well as committee and delegation membership were decided by the full plenary of the group. However, unlike the EPP, this decision was made based on a proposal from the Bureau (Rule 6, 1977). The Socialists also included a "morality clause" into their rules, allowing Members to vote against the group "for grave political motives" as early as 1977 and perhaps earlier (Rule 7). This clause was initially created to allow *individuals* to vote against the group; it has, however, come to be used primarily by the national delegations, particularly when national electoral interests are at stake (interviews February–May 1996 and March 1998).

There was less control over individual Member activities in the early versions of the PES Rules. These did not include any provisions requiring Members to report to the group prior to the introduction of oral or written questions. On the other hand, the active participation of Members both in committee and during the full plenary of the EP was required (Rule 17, 1977). In addition, any Member who wished to intervene in his own name during the debates of the full plenary had to inform the president of the group ahead of time (Rule 5, 1977). There were no explicit provisions regarding individual Member amendments, resolutions, or questions.

On the whole, the rules of the Socialist group have evolved much further than those of the EPP. By 1986 there were forty-eight individual rules in the same eight chapters and a subject index. Several previous rules and norms were made more explicit. The required attendance of Members at all meetings of the full EP plenary, the group, their committees and delegations was clarified in Rule 4. New rules governing the organization of group meetings, the election of officers, and the constitutive meeting of the group after general elections were added (Rules 6–12, 1986). The Bureau of the group was expanded and awarded additional powers. Each national delegation retained a seat in the Bureau, but those with more than eleven members were awarded an additional seat [Rule 14(2), 1986]. The

Bureau was given the power to decide who would replace Members on committees and delegations [Rule 13(5), 1986], and to appoint group representatives to attend outside events (Rule 15, 1986).

In addition, rules governing the internal organization and working methods of the Bureau and the full plenary were added, in particular the requirement that one-third of its members be present to take a decision and the official institution of simple majority decision making (Rule 19, 1986). Within the full plenary, official agendas were introduced as well as restrictions on individual Member's speaking time, specific rules on points of order, personal statements, and the disruption of meetings were added (Rules 21, 25–29, 1986). As in the EPP group, committee coordinators were added and broad working groups organized (Rule 35, 1986).

Interestingly, as in the case of the EPP, restrictions on the individual activities of Members were largely removed. Previous rules that required an individual to notify the chair prior to individual action were deleted. Instead, Rule 37 was added, which permits Members to table resolutions and written questions even if the group as a whole has not endorsed them. Furthermore, individual members who have invoked the "morality clause" within the group are free to propose their own amendments within the full plenary (Rule 38, 1986).

The level of specificity and technical organization within the PES group's rules greatly surpassed those of the EPP by 1986 and have continued to increase since then, although without any significant additions to the general internal structure of the group.[35] The transformation of the Rules after direct elections is impressive. The Rules of 1986 were clearly modeled after the Rules of Procedure of the EP as a whole, including several similar provisions.[36] The development of specific rules regulating the internal organization of group business and the activities of Members within the EP as a whole have largely followed the predictions of the macro model. Although a full set of all versions of the PES's internal Rules of Procedure is not available, the dramatic shift in the Rules before and after the introduction of direct elections suggests that this

---

[35] One interesting addition is the requirement throughout the rules that women receive adequate representation.

[36] For example, the oldest Member of the group convenes the constituent meeting without the right to conduct any official business beyond the election of the group chair (Rule 6, 1986). This is extremely similar to Rule 12, 1999 (14th edition) of the EP's Rules of Procedure.

change was extremely influential.[37] The addition of committee coordinators and working groups, as in the case of the EPP, suggests that the addition of the cooperation procedure also affected the internal development of the group.[38]

On the whole, the macro model is only a partially satisfactory predictor of internal group development. The reasons behind the significant variation between these two groups are not clear. The pattern is present in the informal evolution of the groups as well. For example, while the Socialist group has had an organized "whipping" or sessions unit at least since 1979, the EPP only formally created its whips office in 1995 (interviews, March 1998). Given that both groups have experienced the same pattern of environmental changes over the past twenty-five years, there is little in the macro model that can explain the significant differences between them in terms of their internal organizational development.

The Allocation of Benefits

The list of benefits that appear to be controlled by the party groups, and therefore the leaders of the groups, is substantial. The EP's Rules of Procedure, and most studies of the EP, suggest that the groups decide committee and delegation membership, the allocation of committee chairmanships, vice chairmanships, and the same for the various subcommittees, heads of delegations, and temporary committees. The positions within the EP hierarchy are also left to the domain of the party groups after the initial d'Hondt distribution according to party group size, although this is not officially sanctioned in the Rules of Procedure. Other potential benefits that the groups might use to reward Members include speaking time on the floor of the EP (also distributed amongst the groups by the d'Hondt method) and *Rapporteurships* within committees. These are officially decided by the committee chair in most cases but in fact are also distributed amongst the groups on the basis of a similar point system based on group size.

Thus the list of possible benefits at the disposal of the party elite is not negligible. In fact, they are very similar to, if not greater than, those

---

[37] The 1986 version of the Rules does not state the date of the previous version, so it is impossible to know how many intervening versions existed.

[38] The working groups were an unofficial addition that is still not fully recognized in the Rules.

available to party leaders in the U.S. Congress. In both cases the actual election of Members remains clearly outside the domain of the party leaders, but control over desirable positions within the legislature (which might enhance re-election prospects) appear to be under the control of the group leadership in both. In the American case, Gary Cox and Matthew McCubbins argue that these powers allow the party leadership to exert control over its Members when it is important (Cox and McCubbins, 1993).[39] Can the same be said of the party groups in the EP? Despite the fact that voting cohesion in the EP is actually higher on average than it is in the U.S. Congress, the answer is "no."

To examine the relationship between individual Member behavior (participation and voting the party line) and the allocation of benefits I examined the distribution of committee chairmanships between 1979 and 1997 and *Rapporteurships* both under the cooperation procedure between 1989 and 1994 and under the co-decision procedure between 1994 and 1996. In particular, I compared the voting behavior and participation of those MEPs in the EPP and the PES who received a disproportionate share of these benefits with the average levels of participation and cohesion of the same group.

Like most leadership posts within the EP, committee chairs are appointed twice during each legislature, once in July just after the June elections and again in January two and a half years later. There were a total of 127 committee chair positions available between the first direct elections in 1979 and the end of the first half of the fourth legislature (1997).[40] Between 1989 and 1994 a total of 345 different proposals were considered under the cooperation procedure, while there were only 52 proposals considered under co-decision between 1994 and 1996. As the small total number of positions available makes clear, competition is relatively high even for *Rapporteurships* within the EP. The distribution of these positions is given in Table 8.1.

The scarcity of these positions might result in their very even distribution between MEPs, as the table shows; however, there were clearly individuals who received far more than their "fair" share of benefits. The question is, was this overcompensation a reward from party group

---

[39] The idea is that Members are free to pursue individual goals when the vote is not considered to be a matter of importance by the party elite.

[40] The number of committees varied between sixteen and twenty. Subcommittees were not included.

Table 8.1. *Distribution of Benefits*

	Committee Chairs[1]	Rapporteurs[2]– Cooperation	Rapporteurs– Codecision
Total available	127	345	52
Availability per MEP	n/a	<1	<.5
Average per recipient	1	4	1
Maximum per recipient	4	24[3]	4

[1] Committee chairs are counted in 2 1/2 year "terms," despite the fact that occasionally a committee chair will leave in the middle of his/her term.

[2] *Rapporteurships* are counted for the whole bill for comparison's sake, although there are cases where there are separate *Rapporteurs* for the different readings.

[3] This unusually high number is due in large part to a series of proposals that were linked but broken down into a series of separate reports. The next highest number is 13.

leadership for their exemplary behavior in plenary? If not, how and why were these individuals selected to receive a high level of benefits? An analysis of the voting behavior and participation of those MEPs who received the lion's share of benefits suggests that it was not their behavior in the plenary that was the motivation. A comparison between the average behavior of MEPs and those who received a disproportionate portion of their group's benefits illustrates the inappropriateness of the "benefits for behavior" model suggested by the predictions of the micro model outlined in Hypotheses 6 and 6a.

Most individuals who have been chair of a committee have held that position for only one term (85%). Another 10% have served two terms, while only three individuals have served three or more terms. Since the overwhelming number of committee chairs serve only one term, any MEP who has served more than this is considered a "superchair." The definition of a "super-*Rapporteur*" is comparable. Of those MEPs who have been *Rapporteurs* under the cooperation procedure, most have held the position an average of four times (87%); the remaining 13% will be referred to as "super-*Rapporteurs*." In a similar way, those who have been *Rapporteur* under the co-decision procedure more than once (27%) will also be considered "super-*Rapporteurs*."[41]

The participation and voting behavior (voting against the "party line") of the superchairs and super-*Rapporteurs*, as well as the average behavior

[41] Of the thirty-seven individuals who have been *Rapporteurs* on a co-decision bill, only 8% have done so three or more times.

Table 8.2. *Behavior of EPP and PES "Superchairs"*

	Average Participation[1]	Frequency of Voting Against the Party Line
EPP Super Chairs 1979–1989	50%	3%
Average EPP 1979–1989	48%	2%
PES Super Chairs 1979–1989	47%	6%
Average PES 1979–1989	48%	10%
EPP Super Chairs 1989–1994	53%	4%
Average EPP 1989–1994	54%	5%
PES Super Chairs 1989–1994	62%	2%
Average PES 1989–1994	65%	3%
EPP Super Chairs 1994–1996	78%	3%
Average EPP 1994–1996	76%	6%
PES Super Chairs 1994–1996	82%	4%
Average PES 1994–1996	74%	4%

[1] Participation is determined using the roll-call votes described and analyzed in Chapter 5. For committee chairs between 1979 and 1989 participation in roll-call votes on resolutions are used. For committee chairs between 1989 and 1994 votes under the cooperation procedure are used, and between 1994 and 1996 votes under the co-decision procedure are used. This variation makes it difficult to compare the participation of chairs across time but does permit for a comparison between super-chairs and other MEPs.

Table 8.3. *Behavior of EPP and PES Super-Rapporteurs*

Super-*Rapporteurs*	Average Participation	Frequency of Voting Against the Party Line
Cooperation (EPP)	84%	4%
Average EPP Members	54%	5%
Cooperation (PES)	69%	3%
Average PES Members	65%	3%
Co-Decision (EPP)	80%	4%
Average EPP Members	76%	6%
Co-Decision (PES)	81%	5%
Average PES Members	74%	4%

of MEPs from the same group, are given in Tables 8.2 and 8.3. As these tables demonstrate, in most cases those who received numerous terms as committee chair or an unusually high number of *Rapporteurships* were neither particularly more active nor more supportive of the party line than the average for their party group. There were some cases where the performance of the super-*Rapporteurs* was significantly better than average in terms of participation. In particular, EPP *Rapporteurs* under the co-operation procedure participated 30% more frequently than the average EPP Member, but the pattern does not hold under co-decision and is not nearly as strong for Members of the PES. Because of the overall high level of internal party group cohesion, it is not surprising that the superchairs and super-*Rapporteurs* did not support the party line significantly more often than the average for their party group. In two cases support for the position of the party group was actually less, but only marginally so.

If an individual's performance in terms of participation and support of the group position is not the motivating force behind the allocation of benefits to group Members, what is? On what basis do group leaders decide how benefits will be distributed? The answer is quite simply that the group leadership does not decide. Although the Rules of Procedure of the EP, the Rules of Procedure of the two largest groups, and the bulk of the current literature suggest that the power to decide the allocation of such benefits as committee chairs and *Rapporteurships* lies with the group leaders, the fact is that it does not. The unwritten norms of both party groups delegate this authority to the national delegations in their midst.

The Informal Role of the National Delegations

The unwritten rules that function within both of the largest groups shift power away from the group elite to the national delegations. Because of their informal nature, it is very difficult to say precisely when, how, or even why these norms developed. The fact that they exist currently and that they severely hinder the ability of the group elite to control or sanction renegade Members is largely undisputed.[42] In neither the EPP nor the PES do the Rules of Procedure imply that the national delegations have a powerful, or even significant, role within the group.[43] In fact, until 1985

---

[42] This fact was noted to varying degrees in all of my interviews with group leaders, past and present (five interviews total), as well as interviews with various members of the groups' secretariats (over twenty interviews total).

[43] Within the thirty-four rules of the EPP the national delegations are mentioned just twice, Rules 9 and 14 (1996). In Rule 9 the presidents of the national delegations are included in the Group Bureau. The national delegations are not awarded any specific powers within the groups, although all members of the same nationality may together request a meeting

the delegations were not even officially recognized by the Socialist group.[44] Despite the minimal reference made to them in the official Rules of Procedure of either group, at least since 1979 the national delegations have been effectively in control of the allocation of group benefits to their Members (interviews February–May 1996 and March, 1998; Bataille, 1990).

This came about initially because of the need of the groups to respect national identities, particularly since the EP as a whole largely ignored them. It is likely that, before direct elections, when there were only three or four groups and less than 200 Members, much of the process was truly informal and occurred through consensus rather than a strict proportional division within the groups based on national origin (interviews February–May 1996 and March, 1998). However, as the size of the EP grew (to over 400 after 1979 and 626 today) and the number of nationalities continued to expand (from the original 6 to the current 15) the need to ensure fair representation amongst the Member States as well as the party groups appears to have become essential.

To this end, the groups employ the d'Hondt method to distribute everything from committee memberships to positions within the EP Bureau between the various national delegations within the group. This could be achieved, according to the Rules of either group, by the Bureau of the group selecting the appropriate individuals, with an eye toward the necessary national representation. This would leave control over the allocation of these benefits firmly within the hands of the group leadership, despite the need to distribute positions proportionally based on delegation size, allowing the group leadership to consolidate its power vis-à-vis individual Members. This is not what currently occurs. Instead, the decision of which individual is to fill a particular position is transferred to the

of the full group plenary (Rule 15, 1996). There is not even officially the possibility for the national delegations to make suggestions or proposals as to the allocation of committee and EP positions.

[44] *Nowhere* in the Rules of the PES were the national delegations mentioned until 1986. The only reference made to even national diversity was in Rule 10 (1979), which required that every Member State have at least one member on the Bureau. The 1986 Rules included an official and explicit recognition of the existence of national delegations. The new rule stated that "Members of the same nationality may organize themselves into a national delegation" (Rule 3, 1986). This addition was formally created in January 1985, but long before then Members of the same nationality were meeting informally (Bataille, 1990: 53). Despite their official creation, the national delegations were not formally given any power or organizational role within the group.

leaders of the national delegations, and has been at least since 1979 in both the EPP and the PES. It is this final aspect of the allocation process, and not the need to distribute positions by d'Hondt, that debilitates the group leadership and makes it all but impossible to control individual members through the effective use of benefits and sanctions.

In effect, the national delegations function within the groups in a manner similar to the way the groups function within the EP as a whole. Delegation leaders are aware ahead of time of the number of positions that will be allocated to their Members (based on relative size) and create lists of preferences. Once again, each position is worth a certain number of points and each delegation is allocated points based on its size within the group (Bataille, 1990; interviews March, 1998). This process is not limited to positions in the EP hierarchy and the committee and delegation chairs. All positions are allocated on this basis – vice chairs, appointment to delegations and committees, and even positions within the group such as working group chairs and committee coordinators. Only the distribution of speaking time on the floor of the EP has remained primarily in the control of the group Bureau, although here too national representation is taken into consideration (interviews March, 1998).

In this process it is clearly the largest delegations within each party group that benefit the most. Here again, there is a striking similarity with the EP as a whole. Within the two largest groups there tends to be two dominant national delegations. In both groups the two largest delegations consistently accounted for nearly 50% of the group's membership.[45] In the fourth legislature (1994–1999) the two largest national delegations account for 47% and 45% percent of the PES and EPP membership, respectively, despite the fact that there were fifteen national delegations in each group. Thus, we see a re-creation of the EPP–PES hegemony within the EP at the micro level of the party groups.[46] The German and British national delegations have consistently been the two largest within the Socialist group, with a brief interruption between 1991 and 1993, when the Italian delegation was substantial. In the EPP there has been more variation. Although the German delegation has remained significant throughout, the

---

[45] This was less true after the last enlargement and the 1999 elections. In the fifth legislature the German and UK delegations account for just under 40% of both the PES and the EPP.

[46] The importance of the largest delegations within each of the largest groups has been noted and decried within the EP. During the 1997 presidential elections numerous MEPs officially objected to this trend. Annex to the *OJC* Debates 4–493, January 1997: 4–7.

Table 8.4. *The Five Largest National Delegations in the PES (1979–1999)*

PES	France	Germany	Italy	Spain	UK	Total Group
1979	22	35	18	n/a	18	112
1984	20	33	12	n/a	33	130
1989	22	31	14	27	46	180
1994	15	40	18	22	63	198
1999	22	32	16	24	30	180

Table 8.5. *The Five Largest National Delegations in the EPP (1979–1999)*

	France	Germany	Italy	Spain	UK	Total Group
1979	6	42	30	n/a	n/a	105
1984	9	41	27	n/a	n/a	110
1989	6	32	27	16	n/a	121
1994	13	47	12	30	19	157
1999	21	53	34	28	37	233

Italian delegation was substantial until 1994 and again after 1999 (falling dramatically in size in-between due to changing political situations at home). The Spanish delegation was the third largest delegation until 1994, when an electoral victory by the Partido Popular increased its size and made it the second largest until the 1999 elections. Between 1992 and 1994 and again after 1999, the UK delegation has been significant (Tables 8.4 and 8.5).[47]

The shift of power away from the group leaders and toward the national delegations and, in particular, the largest delegations is re-enforced by the slender, but growing, connection that exists between the national delegations within the groups and the national parties in the Member States that create the final lists for EP elections. The absence of a traditional "electoral connection" between Members of the EP and their electorate has already been discussed (see Chapter 2), but there is a growing link between MEPs and their national parties.

---

[47] It is important to note that the British Conservatives did not officially join the EPP until 1992. Before then they formed the basis of the European Democratic Group (EDG), which frequently voted with the EPP but was officially quite separate.

Since direct elections, the common view has been that the national parties have cared little about the activities of the EP and the MEPs since the EP was viewed as a largely impotent institution. What the MEPs did was of little import since they acted within a powerless body (Robinson and Bray, 1986; Westlake, 1994: 98–114). As the role of the EP has increased, however, the activities of the MEPs have come under increasing scrutiny by their national parties, particularly if those parties are in power at home (Hix and Lord, 1997b).[48] Since the leader of the national delegation is frequently the first person on the national party's electoral list, he or she is likely to have strong connections with the national party, and perhaps even some influence over future electoral lists.[49]

This potential connection between the leadership of the national delegations and the national parties who create the electoral lists adds still another power to the delegations not available to the group elite: effective sanctions. While the group leadership can verbally chastise Members, there is little that they can actually do. If the group leadership did, in fact, control the allocation of the benefits described above, they could simply withhold them from Members who did not perform adequately.[50] The fact that they do not, together with the growing interest of the national parties in the activities of the EP and the impotence of the group elite to control Member re-election, leads to a palpable inequality between the leaders of the national delegations and the leaders of the party groups. The latter find themselves inexorably in second place.

The Impact of National Delegation Power

The ability of the national delegations to control the distribution of benefits within the groups means that there has been very little development

---

[48] A recent example includes the expulsion of two UK Labour Members from their national party after they ignored the explicit directions of the national party. The two Members were then forced to leave the PES group as well, joining the Green Group (PES press release, January 7, 1998).

[49] This applies to all Member States except the United Kingdom, where single-member districts were used instead of electoral lists and proportional representation until 1999.

[50] It should be noted that throughout my interviews the biggest complaint of group leaders was not Members who voted against the party line, but rather Members who simply did not show up, or, if they did, refrained from voting. As has been mentioned, absenteeism remains one of the EP's biggest problems, especially during votes on those legislative procedures that require the approval of an absolute majority of the EP's membership to be valid.

of the groups' internal hierarchy. This does *not* mean that there has been no attempt by the group leadership to influence Member activities. The older versions of the rules of both groups required individual Members to inform the group Bureau if they intended to act independently at the plenary meeting through the proposal of amendments, questions, own initiative reports, and so on. (Rule 21, EPP *Reglement*, 1979; Rule 19, PES *Reglement*, 1977). Since the 1989 revisions this has been taken out of the Rules of the EPP, however, it remains partially in the Rules of the Socialist group (Rules 37 and 38, PES Rules of Procedure, 1996). In addition, the Socialist group also includes a provision requiring the attendance of Members at both their relevant committee meetings and the full plenary sessions of Parliament (Rule 4, 1996); the EPP group has no such provision. Both groups now have formally established a "whips" office to monitor the attendance and voting behavior of Members.[51] There have additionally been increased informal attempts to monitor Member attendance at committee meetings and to use poor attendance as a reason to deny Members key *Rapporteurships* (interview March 1998).

Despite all of these efforts, there is little evidence that the group leaders have been able to surmount the increasing power of the national delegations. The most often cited example of elite control, voting cohesion, may be partially artificial. Keeping in mind that most of the decisions taken with the party groups are by simple majority of those present (EPP Rule 20, 1996; PES Rule 32, 1996), the role of the largest delegations once again becomes crucial. Working together, the two largest delegations can almost always sway the decisions of the group plenary. This means that the largest delegations within the groups will support the group stance. In the case of the UK and German delegations, these are also the individuals who participate most often in the full plenary (Brzinski, 1995; Kreppel and Tsebelis, 1999). In both groups the five smallest delegations make up less than 10% of total group membership. This means that even if one-third of the groups' national delegations consistently defected, the cohesion rating would still be above 90%.

It is difficult to know to what extent group dominance by the two largest delegations occurs because of the serious problem of absenteeism.

---

[51] The PES has employed a whip in one form or another since 1979. They now have a well-established "sessions unit" that monitors Members' attendance and voting record at important votes in the full plenary. The Sessions Unit can even request that the group call for a roll-call vote to aid in their monitoring.

Although the EPP and the PES tend to have higher participation than most groups (Chapters 6 and 7) they still suffer from high levels of absenteeism.[52] Members may prefer to be absent to avoid voting against the party line, but the steady level of internal group cohesion even when voting turnout increases suggests that this is not always the case (Chapter 7). What is clear, however, is that when the internal cohesion of a group does drop it is generally because of the defection of a national delegation, not a group of individuals from various national delegations (Corbett et al., 1995: 90).

This discussion should not be taken to discount the role of ideology in determining party group voting behavior. Broad nationally oriented coalitions across ideological lines are, and always have been, infrequent.[53] The point is that the groups have high levels of voting cohesion *not* because Members fear the retaliation of group leadership if they vote against the party line, but rather because Members of the same group do generally share similar values and ideals. If individual Members fear anyone, it is their own delegation leadership, which explains why internal national delegation cohesion tends to be even higher than group cohesion.[54]

The power of the national delegations to control the distribution of benefits among their own Members is significant, not only for its impact on the internal development of the party groups, but also for its effects on the evolution of the European Parliament itself. The limitations that national delegation power places on the party group elite to control members within the group structure has forced group leadership to attempt to impact Member activities through other means, in particular through the development of the Conference of Presidents (CoP). The CoP replaced the previous Bureau of the EP as a result of the 1992 Rules Revisions following Maastricht. The CoP was notable for its consolidation and centralization of powers within the EP as a whole and the introduction of weighted voting between the party groups (see Chapter 5).

---

[52] Only an average of 59% of EPP Members and 52% of PES Members participated in votes on resolutions between 1994 and 1996. The number was significantly higher for votes under the co-decision procedure, 76% and 74%, respectively.

[53] There are several exceptions where clear national interests tend to take over, such as the Common Agricultural Policy (CAP) and some budgetary issues.

[54] National delegation cohesion consistently averages over 95% for the votes analyzed in Chapters 6 and 7; however, levels of participation vary significantly between the national delegations.

Although it is impossible to know the original intentions behind the creation of the Conference of Presidents, it has come to be used today as an instrument of centralized control. There has been a growing tendency within the CoP to take decisions on behalf of the EP as a whole, despite these never going to the full plenary (a power that is nowhere stipulated in the EP's Rules of Procedure).[55] A contentious decision to link the daily allowance allotments of Members to their participation in at least 50% of all roll-call votes during a given day is an excellent example. The CoP and the Quaestors issued a memo to all MEPs stating that from February 1998 forward Members would have to actually vote (not just sign the attendance register) to obtain their full daily allowances.[56] As we have seen throughout, absenteeism is a tremendous problem within the EP, and the ability of the group leaders to cope with it through the use of sanctions within the groups is minimal at best. It is possible that as a result they have focused their energies within the CoP, where it is clearly the group leaders (and most importantly the leaders of the EPP and the PES) who control what gets decided while the national delegations have only marginal power.[57]

Conclusions

This understanding of the internal development of the party groups partially supports the macro and micro models, albeit not in the sense that was expected. The macro model merely predicted that internal changes would be linked historically to external changes. This connection was much more evident for the Socialists than for the EPP, although there was some connection between the addition of new legislative powers, increased legislative load, and the development of working groups and committee coordinators within the latter as well. It is also clear that the direct election of MEPs in 1979 had a significant effect on the internal development

[55] A recent example is a decision on free access to documentation that was published in the *OJC* as "a decision of the European Parliament" despite never having been voted on by the full plenary (*OJL*, 263 15/9/97).

[56] Members of the EP have vigorously protested this decision. In particular, Mr. Falconer objected to being forced to vote (even to voting an "abstention") and instead insisted on informing the presidency prior to every voting period that he was present but chose not to vote. See Minutes of the Sittings for February and March 1998 for the statements of Mr. Falconer and others.

[57] It should be noted that the CoP does not include the vice presidents, who effectively serve as national representation within the EP Bureau.

of the groups to the extent that this affected the evolution of the national delegations. Although the national delegations may have remained an informal aspect of at least one of the groups until 1985, most of those interviewed stated that they became significant actors within the groups after direct elections. Whether this was due to the technical difficulties incumbent with increased membership or a concerted effort on the part of the delegations leaders remains a mystery.

The power of the delegations has also increased as a result of the growing connections between national parties and the national delegations. The ability of the delegation leaders to potentially influence the electoral lists in the Member States cannot be overemphasized. This would allow for the establishment of a true "electoral connection" between the MEPs and at least their national parties if not their home electorate. The ability of the national parties to influence MEP behavior could be seen as both a negative and positive development. On the one hand, MEPs are supposed to be wholly independent; control by national parties would impinge significantly on that independence and would lend greater significance to national identity. On the other hand, stronger ties with the national parties might aid in reducing the infamous "democratic deficit." Either way there is a clear connection between broad environmental shifts, the development of the national delegations, and the absence of the development of significant group elite control over individual Members.

To what extent were the group leaders strategic in their adaptation to the rapid increase in the role and power of the national delegations? The micro model predicted that the party group elite would consolidate their authority within the groups to increase their control over Members as the EP gained legislative authority. As we have seen, they were effectively blocked from doing so because of the informal norms that placed control over benefits and sanction firmly in the hands of the national delegations. I would argue that to some extent the group leaders have responded by consolidating their powers (both official and unofficial) within the EP's hierarchy instead. The establishment of the Conference of Presidents and the recent informal expansion of that body's powers demonstrate an attempt by the group leaders to control Members' actions from within the EP hierarchy, as opposed to the party groups themselves.

This understanding of the internal development of the party groups gives a different significance to the steady increase of party group control over the internal organization of the EP as a whole (Chapter 5). The steady restriction of individual Member activities and the strengthening of the party groups within the EP may or may not have been a purposive attempt to circumvent the control of the national delegations within the groups, but it has served party group leaders well. The recent attempts by the CoP to influence Member activities have not gone unchallenged, however, as the debate over the new attendance rules demonstrates. The extent to which the group leaders will be able to effectively influence individual Member behavior through the Conference of Presidents and EP Rules of Procedure remains to be seen.

9

Conclusions: Understanding the Developmental Process

The primary goal of this research was to chart and explain the evolution of the European Parliament and the supranational party system. This was accomplished through the modification and then application of the macro and micro models of institutional development founded in the American congressional literature to the evolution of the EP's organizational structures, the supranational party group system, and the party groups. The macro model was used primarily to predict the timing of institutional change, while the micro model suggested the character of reform based on an understanding of the goals of the actors, the rules of the game, and who had the power to effectively pursue change.

As predicted by the macro model, the timing of the internal institutional development of the EP, as well as the transformation of the party group system, was connected to large exogenous increases to its political power and authority. The micro model was similarly successful in predicting the character of internal institutional reforms and the type of party group system based on an assumption of strategic action by the EPP and PES as they pursued their policy goals. Both models fell short of a satisfying explanation of internal party group reform; however, the reason for their lack of success lies more with the stunted nature of this evolution than with any inherent weakness in the models.

In this final chapter I briefly summarize the findings of the previous chapters and discuss some additional questions that arise naturally out of this research, in particular, to what extent are the macro and micro models of institutional development generally applicable beyond the American congressional context? How are the internal development of the European Parliament, the party groups, and party group system connected to the increased legislative authority of the EP as a whole and each other? Finally, how broadly applicable are the results of this research? Are the conclusions generalizable or applicable to other emerging democratic political systems?

The Macro and Micro Models: Beyond the American Legislative Context

One of the secondary, but important questions of this research was whether or not the macro and micro models of institutional development could be modified to allow their application beyond the American congressional context. This meant not only to other legislatures (the EP), but also to other institutions (the party groups and the party system). By and large, this research has demonstrated the predictive strength of both of these models, particularly when used simultaneously. The macro model, though generally applied within the American legislative setting, does not require much adjustment to be more generally applicable, and was quite successful in predicting the timing of institutional change within both the European Parliament and the party group system. The micro model, on the other hand, is much more closely linked to the American Congressional context, which includes a strong "electoral connection" and a majoritarian two-party system. With modifications, however, it too was successfully generalized to predict the character of institutional evolution in the EP and the party group system. Together these two models have proved extremely helpful in predicting the timing and character of the evolution of the internal organizational structures of the EP and the development of the supranational party group system. Does this mean that the models can be usefully generalized to apply to the development of political institutions in whatever setting?

I believe that the answer is "yes." A simplification of both models would allow for their more frequent use and facilitate comparisons between the development of political institutions beyond the American legislative context. The initial macro model grew out of an investigation of the impact of significant increases in the legislative workload of the Congress on its internal institutional structures (Polsby, 1968). Through simplification the model can be made more easily applicable to institutional development in general. The macro model requires only that internal institutional developments chronologically follow, and respond to, large exogenous changes in the role of the institution. There is no need to specify either

213

the precise character of the exogenous change or the nature of the internal reform beyond the requirement that the two should be logically connected. Thus, the macro model can be generalized in the following simple formula:

- Internal institutional development/reform will be logically and chronologically linked to significant exogenous changes in the political role or powers of the institution.

This maintains the requirement that internal evolution be inspired by large external shifts, and directly address these changes (public goods), while still allowing the model to be applied beyond both the American and the legislative contexts.

The micro model is more difficult to generalize. It is not entirely clear where the micro model originated, although perhaps the most well-known early application was David Mayhew's "Electoral Connection" (Mayhew, 1974). In this work Mayhew argued persuasively that the majority of the actions of Members of Congress could be understood in terms of their desire to get re-elected. Thus, preferences for committees, constituency work, position taking, and any number of other activities could be understood in terms of their impact on a Member's chances of re-election. Strategic action determined the behavior of both individual Members and political parties. The following predictive statement can generalize the basic concept of this body of work:

- Political actors (individuals or groups) will attempt to shape the institutions in which they work to maximize their ability to achieve their goals. Their action will be constrained by and reflect both the rules within the institution and the broader political environment.

This effectively generalizes the micro model and allows it to be applied beyond the American and the legislative contexts. It continues to require, however, that we know the goals of the actors and the rules of the game that potentially restrict internal institutional development.

Together both models can aid in predicting and understanding the internal development of numerous political institutions across a broad variety of political environments. To a limited extent, the patterns of institutional development that we have discovered in analyzing the European Parliament may already help us to understand or predict the character of institutional development in other settings.

Conclusions

The Internal Development of the EP and Supranational Party Groups

Given its inauspicious beginnings, the extent to which the European Parliament has evolved over the last forty years is remarkable. The character of the EP's internal development and the links between it, the party groups, and the exogenous increases in EP power are particularly interesting. While the empirical chapters (5, 6, 7, and 8) each dealt with these subjects in isolation, here I would like to attempt to draw together these various strands of internal evolution to underline the extent to which they are all related.

In Chapter 5 we learned that as the EP gained substantive direct legislative influence the character of its internal organizational structures was transformed from generally egalitarian to largely inegalitarian. Initially the Rules of Procedures of the EP were loose guidelines in which individual Members were the primary actors. After 1979 this began to change, and the party groups started to play an increasingly large role in the internal organization of the EP. Between 1979 and 1987, the groups assumed more and more responsibilities while the powers of individual Members were reduced correspondingly. Initially, the trend was for all groups to benefit equally to the detriment of the nonaffiliated Members, or those who wished to act independent of their party group. After the Single European Act, however, a shift occurred that began to privilege the largest parties to the detriment of everyone else. New rules were introduced with strict numerical requirements and weighted voting was instituted within the newly created Conference of Presidents, both of which limited the ability of small parties to act independently of the two largest party groups.

These trends closely coincided with exogenous increases in the legislative powers and political authority of the EP. They also benefited the only two groups that could ensure their passage: the EPP and the PES. Amendments to the Rules of the EP require an absolute majority. Since no single party has ever controlled an absolute majority and no ideological coalition was stable over time, the only coalition that could agree to mutually beneficial modifications of the Rules was the "grand coalition" between the EPP and the PES. The dominance of the EPP and the PES within the internal organizational structures of the EP coincided with similar shifts in the supranational party system and the internal evolution of the groups, which served to reinforce this trend.

At the same time, as the EPP and the PES were becoming hegemonic within the organizational structures of the EP, they were also realizing the need to cooperate within the legislative realm. In Chapters 6 and 7 the impact of the dramatic increase in the legislative power of the EP initiated by the Single European Act and the Maastricht Treaty was examined. The rules requiring an absolute majority to pass amendments and proposals in the later stages of the cooperation and co-decision procedures pushed the EPP and the PES toward cooperation if they wished to participate effectively in the final stages of the legislative process. The need to coordinate across ideological boundaries was compounded by the fact that all EP proposals had to be adopted by the other EU institutions. As a result, ideologically dogmatic proposals from the left or right would have only served to marginalize the EP, as they would have been unacceptable to the other EU institutions. Thus, the requirements of the cooperation and co-decision procedures combined with the institutional realities of the EU as a whole effectively pushed the EPP and the PES to cooperate in the policy process and led to a general tactic of coordination and compromise after 1987, the result once again being the creation of an alliance across ideological boundaries between the EPP and the PES and the general marginalization of the smaller party groups.

The pattern of cooperation between the EPP and the PES extended beyond what was required by the new legislative procedures. After 1987 there was an increasing tendency to cooperate in the passage of resolutions, which did not require any special majority and which did not have to be adopted by the other EU institutions. This does not mean that ideology has no impact on the decision-making process of the EP, but rather that the actors (primarily party group leaders) are constrained by the institutional structure of the EU itself. As was discussed in Chapter 7, the rules that require absolute majorities in some stages of the legislative process are not the only constraints on the actions of the EP. Because the Commission and the Council as well as the EP must agree to legislative proposals, all proposals must be moderate enough to garner broad consensus. Given the divergent ideological and national interests represented in the other institutions, the party groups are forced to produce moderate proposals if they are to have any influence at all. Combined with the majority requirements this constraint has also forced the EPP and the PES into a pattern of frequent cooperation. As was noted, however, this does not mean that there are no significant ideological divides in the EP. It does mean that when these cannot be overcome the EP is generally impotent to impact the policy process directly.

Adding to the general pattern of bipartisan cooperation, the leaders of the EPP and PES also agreed in a meeting, which took place outside the auspices of the EP, to rotate the presidency of the EP between them every two and a half years between 1989–1999,[1] thus effectively excluding the other party groups from the selection of the EP leadership for a decade. This increased, and not strictly necessary, cooperation between the leaders of the EPP and the PES might be connected to their inability to effectively control their Membership through the internal structures of their respective party groups. As we have seen, the power of the national delegations has effectively served to limit the ability of the party group elite to use benefits and sanctions to control their Members (Chapter 8). This trend has increased as the connections between the national delegation leaders and the national parties have grown. The potential, albeit still incipient, of the national delegations to influence the electoral lists at home lends them an indisputable upper hand in the battle over Member loyalty. This is exacerbated by the continued informal control of the national delegation leaders over the selection of specific Members to fill leadership positions within the EP hierarchy and the committees.

It is possible that the inability of the party group leaders of the EPP and the PES to control their Members from within their own groups is partially responsible for their increased control over the structures of the EP itself. As the powers of the EP have increased over time, the ability to control Member behavior has become more significant. Influence over rank-and-file Members has grown in importance, not only because of the new potential to actually impact legislative outcomes, but also because of the rules that regulate the process (majority requirements) and the growing public interest in the activities of the EP. The creation of a strong Conference of Presidents with an increasingly broad domain, dominated by the party group leaders and able to restrict the activity of Members, seems a logical response to the effective impotence of the leaders of the EPP and the PES within their own groups.

---

[1] This agreement was effectively annulled after the 1999 elections, when the EPP won the plurality of the seats and formed a "constitutive" coalition with the Liberals that would give the EPP the presidency during the first term of the legislature and the Liberals the office during the second term. If this agreement holds, it will mark the first time since 1984 that the PES has been blocked from the presidency for a full legislative term.

This is not to suggest that had the EPP and the PES leaders been able to better control their Members effectively within the groups they would have had no interest in also manipulating the structures of the EP as a whole to their benefit. Rather, I am suggesting that the lack of control over benefits and sanctions within the groups lent more urgency to the creation of a strong Conference of Presidents. The connection between the evolution of the internal structures of the EP and those of the party groups highlights the dynamic relationship between the different aspects of institutional development. Although the EP, the party system, and the party groups are dealt with individually in Chapters 5–8, their evolution is necessarily connected. In this sense, exogenous increases in the power and authority of the EP did not individually impact each aspect of the EP, but instead set in motion a dynamic process of evolution that included all three institutions. These relationships are represented graphically in Figure 9.1.

In this model of institutional evolution exogenous increases in the legislative authority of a parliament directly affect the development of the internal organizational structures, the party system (coalitions + number

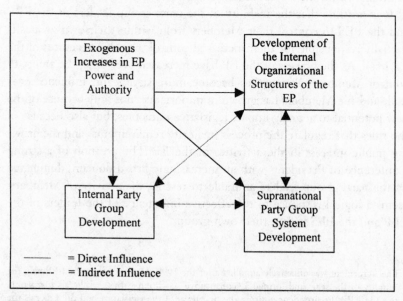

Figure 9.1 Dynamic Relationships Between Different Aspects of EP Evolution

of parties), and the internal development of the parties themselves (albeit weakly). Each of these in turn then indirectly affects the evolution of the others. The overall effect when the legislative powers of the parliament are not hegemonic is the centralization of power toward those with the ability to change the rules of the game. This means the marginalization of smaller parties or ideologically extreme groups, which are frequently of secondary significance within a legislature. Where other institutions with potentially different ideologies or interests must also agree to legislation there will also be an overall tendency to moderate proposals so that they are broadly acceptable.

In other words, granting a parliament legislative power has the potential to transform that parliament from a chamber of debate into a true legislative body. This requires the institution to become more streamlined, efficient, and frequently (where nonhegemonic) moderate. The cost of this type of internal reform is the marginalization of smaller groups/parties unable to manipulate or block the reform process. What do these conclusions tell us about the process of institutional evolution in general? How applicable are they to other emerging or newly democratizing political systems?

The Development of New and Emerging Legislatures and Party Systems

Several patterns of institutional development have been highlighted through this analysis of the evolution of the European Parliament that may be more generally applicable, in particular the effects of increased legislative authority on the character of a legislature's internal organizational development and the importance of ideology in the coalition formation process. Understanding how a legislature's political power and authority affect the character of its internal organizational structures and the nature of the party system can be extremely useful in planning or studying new and developing legislatures.

The apparent connection between a weak legislature and a consensual internal organizational structure could be important in developing democracies with significant regional or ethnic divisions. If a goal was to promote collegial behavior between potentially contentious groups, then unifying them through the common goal of increased legislative authority might prove helpful. At the same time, however, ideology appears to play a much more significant role in the policy process when a legislature is effectively only a debate chamber. This is a double-edged sword. On the one hand it promotes active ideological debate that can serve to interest and inform the electorate. On the other hand, legislative impotence can lead to ideological dogmatism and an inability to compromise or coordinate action across ideological barriers.

A political system not characterized by internal divisions might be better served by a legislature with effective control over the policy process. The transition to effective legislative influence in the case of the EP led to a systematic change in the character of the legislature as well as the party system. The internal organization of a legislature is likely to become more focused on efficiency, even at the cost of internal democracy, when there is a significant legislative role to play. This may lead to the marginalization of smaller parties (as in the EP) or the minority party in a two-party system. At the same time, however, significant control over the policy process can lead to ideological compromise and a general trend of co-operation between political parties. This tendency will be intensified where there is no single majority party or when the legislature constitutes only part of the legislative process.

As was demonstrated through this research, an important aspect of legislative development is the relative centralization of the political parties. In a federal or de-centralized system in which the official party elite have limited control over their members there may be a tendency for party leaders to circumvent the party apparatus through the manipulation of the internal organizational structures of the legislature itself. This will be particularly true when control over the realization of Member goals resides primarily outside the party elite. The EP is not the only example of this type of behavior. Gary Cox and Mathew McCubbins point to precisely this type of activity by the Democratic Party elite within the U.S. Congress (Cox and McCubbins, 1993). This tendency will be increased when the legislature is an effective legislative actor if policy outcomes are a central goal of Members and parties.

The desirability of a chamber of debate versus an active legislative body will depend on the specific political setting. Knowing the broader implications of both types, however, is a fundamental part of understanding institutional development in general and the connections between the internal organization of a legislature, the party system, and the effects of increased legislative authority.

Conclusions

This examination of the institutional development of the EP, the supranational party system, and the party groups served not only to provide a better understanding of the evolution of the EP, but also to suggest some general trends in institutional development. In particular, this research has demonstrated the crucial role of legislative power in determining the character of both a legislature's internal organization and the nature of the party system. The potential effects of decentralized party power on the institutional development of the legislature have also been highlighted. Finally, the applicability of the American-based macro and micro models to political institutions in general has been demonstrated. Together these conclusions suggest the significant influence of legislative power on the development of political institutions and the usefulness of the macro and micro models of development across different political environments.

Appendices

Appendix A

VERSIONS OF THE EP RULES OF PROCEDURE USED IN THE ANALYSIS

- 1st Edition Règlement, Luxembourg, September 1958.
- Modifications du Règlement de L'Assemblée Parlementaire Conformément à la résolutions du 25 Septembre et 21 Novembre 1959; 31 Mars et 28 Juin 1960; 26 Juin 1961; 30 Mars et 27 Juin 1962; 28 Juin 1963; et 20 Janvier 1965.
- Texte Modifiè Règlement Parlement Européen, 20 Novembre 1967.
- 1st English language version, Rules of Procedure, December 1972.
- Règlement, Janvier 1974.
- Rules of Procedure, July 1976.
- Rules of Procedure, December 1976 (as amended by Resolution of 17 November, 1976).
- Rules of Procedure, May 1977.
- Rules of Procedure, April 1979 (including the supplement to the rules pertaining to the General Instructions of the Bureau).
- Rules of Procedure, November 1979.
- Rules of Procedure, December 1981 (1st edition after general revision).
- Rules of Procedure, February 1983, 2nd Edition.
- Rules of Procedure, June 1984, 3rd Edition.
- Rules of Procedure, June 1987, 4th Edition.
- Rules of Procedure, July 1989, 5th Edition.
- Rules of Procedure, April 1991, 6th Edition.
- Rules of Procedure, September 1993, 7th Edition.
- Rules of Procedure, June 1994, 9th Edition.
- Rules of Procedure, February 1995, 10th Edition.
- Rules of Procedure, July 1996, 11th Edition.
- Rules of Procedure, September 1997, 12th Edition.
- Rules of Procedure, July 1998, 13th Edition.
- Rules of Procedure, June 1999, 14th Edition.

Appendix B

MAJOR AREAS OF RULES REFORM: I PERIOD

Area of Reform Period I (1970–1979)	Provisions/Rules in 1970	Provisions/Rules in 1979
Bureau	**Rule 5(1)** The Bureau shall consist of the President and eight Vice Presidents	**Rule 5(1)** The Bureau shall consist of the President and twelve Vice Presidents.
Election of President and Vice Presidents	**Rule 7(1)** The President and Vice Presidents shall be elected by secret ballot.	**Rule 7(1)** The President and Vice Presidents shall be elected by secret ballot on the nomination of a political group or at least ten Members; however, when the number of nominations does not exceed the number of seats, election may be by acclamation.
Quaestors	Does not exist.	**Rule 7A** After the election of the Vice Presidents Parliament shall elect at least three quaestors.
Agenda of Sittings	**Rule 12(1)** The Enlarged Bureau shall prepare the draft agenda on the basis of information passed to it by the Presidential Committee. This committee shall consist of the Enlarged Bureau plus the Chair or one Vice Chair of each Committee.	**Rule 12(1)** On receipt of the preliminary draft agenda prepared by the President, after consulting the Party groups, the party groups shall draw up the draft agenda. The draft agenda shall specify voting times for all resolutions down for consideration.
	Rule 12(2) The President shall lay before the Parliament, for its approval, the draft agenda for sittings, which Parliament may amend.	**Rule 12(2)** Parliament shall decide on the draft agenda submitted to it by the Enlarged Bureau without alteration other than those proposed by the President or proposed to him in writing by a political group, or at least ten members. All such proposals must be received by him at least an hour before the beginning of the part session. On such a proposal only the mover, one in favor and one person against may be heard.

Motion of Censure	**Rule 21(1)** Any representative may make a motion of censure against the Commission.	**Rule 21(1)** A political group or 1/10 of Parliaments membership can make a motion of censure against the Commission.
Speaking Time	**Rule 28(1–3)** The President in agreement with the chairmen of the political groups proposes the allocation of speaking time. Speaking time is allocated among the party groups with the proviso that it not exceed the time provided in the agenda.	**Rule 28(1–2)** The President, after consulting with the chairmen of the party groups, allocates speaking time in accordance with three provisions: a first fraction of time is divided equally among all groups, further fraction is divided based on the size of the groups. Nonattached Members are allocated the same time as that allocated equally to all party groups.
Tabling of amendments	**Rule 29(1)** Any representative may propose and speak in support of amendments.	**Rule 29(1)** Any Member may propose amendments. On a proposal from the President, Parliament may fix a time limit for the tabling of amendments. Parliament shall not debate an amendment unless it is moved during the debate.
Quorum requirements	**Rule 33(2)** A quorum shall exist when a majority of the current Members of Parliament are present	**Rule 33(2)** A quorum shall exist when one third of the current Members of Parliament are present.
Formation of Party Groups	**Rule 36(5)** A group shall consist of not less than fourteen Members.	**Rule 36(5)** A group shall consist of not less than fourteen Members. However, it may consist of not less than ten Members where these come from at least three Member States.
Disputes over Establishment of Committee Membership	**Rule 37(3)** Should any dispute arise [over committee appointments] Parliament shall decide thereon by secret ballot.	**Rule 37(3)** An amendment to the proposals of the Bureau shall be admissible only if tabled by at least ten members, Parliament shall vote by secret ballot.

MAJOR AREAS OF RULES REFORM: II PERIOD

Area of Reform Period II (1979–1986)	Provisions/Rules in 1979	Provisions/Rules in 1985
Term of office for President, Vice Presidents, and Quaestors	No specific provision existed. The norm was for a one-year term and a second by acclamation.	**Rule 16(1)** The terms of office of the President, Vice Presidents, and Quaestors shall be 2 1/2 years.
Functions of the Bureau	Not specified.	**Rule 22(2)** The Bureau shall take financial and organizational decisions on matters concerning Members, Parliament, and its bodies.
Functions of the Enlarged Bureau	Not specified.	**Rule 24(2)** The Enlarged Bureau shall take decisions on questions relating to Parliament's internal organization and on matters affecting relations with non-Community institutions and organizations.
Composition of the Enlarged Bureau	**Rule 5(3)** The enlarged Bureau shall consist of the Bureau and the chairmen of the political groups	**Rule 23(2)** The non-attached Members shall delegate two of their members to attend meetings of the enlarged Bureau, without having the right to vote.
Party Group Formation	**Rule 36(5)** A group shall consist of not less than fourteen Members. However, it may consist of not less than ten Members where these come from at least three Member States.	**Rule 26(5)** A minimum number of twenty-three Members shall be required to form a political group if all Members come from a single Member State. The corresponding number shall be eighteen if the Members come from any two Member States and twelve if they come from three or more Member States.

(continued)

Seating in the Plenary	Not specified.	**Rule 28** The bureau shall decide how seats in the chamber are to be allocated among Members of Parliament and the institutions of the Communities.
Delegation of power of Decision to Committee	Did not exist.	**Rule 33(1–4)** Where Parliament is consulted on a predominately technical matter of no general importance, the President may propose that the matter be referred to the appropriate committee with the power to take a decision. Where 1/10 of all Members or 1/3 of committee Members object, the proposal will be decided by the full plenary through the normal procedure.
Agenda of Sittings	**Rule 12(1)** On receipt of the preliminary draft agenda prepared by the President, after consulting the Party groups, the party groups shall draw up the draft agenda. The draft agenda shall specify voting times for all resolutions down for consideration.	**Rule 55(1)** Before each part session the draft agenda shall be agreed at a meeting between the President and political group chairmen on the basis of a program drawn up by the President after consulting the political groups and the committees. A representative of the non-attached members shall be invited to attend the meeting. The Commission and the Council may attend the meeting at the President's invitation.
Speaking Time	**Rule 28(1–2)** The President, after consulting with the chairman of the party groups, allocates speaking time in accordance with three provisions: a first fraction of time is divided equally among all groups, further fraction is divided based on the size of the groups. Nonattached Members are allocated the same time as that allocated equally to all party groups.	**Rule 65(3)** The speaking time of non-attached members shall be doubled so as to take account of the great diversity of political views among them and enable, as far as possible, each view to be expressed.

229

MAJOR AREAS OF RULES REFORM: II PERIOD *(continued)*

Area of Reform Period II (1979–1986)	Provisions/Rules in 1979	Provisions/Rules in 1985
Quorum	**Rule 33(2)** A quorum shall exist when one third of the current Members of Parliament are present.	**Rule 77(2)** A quorum shall exist when one-third of the current Members of Parliament are present in the chamber.
	Rule 33(4) If so requested before the voting has begun by at least thirty Members present, a vote shall be valid only if a majority of the current Members of Parliament have taken part in it; otherwise the vote will be taken during the next sitting.	Deleted.
Explanations of Vote	**Rule 26(3)** Once the general debate and considerations of the text have been concluded, only explanations of vote shall be given before the matter as a whole is put to the vote.	**Rule 80(1)** Once the general debate and consideration of the texts have been concluded, explanations of the vote may be given before the final vote, provided that a request to do so had been submitted to the President before the beginning of this vote.
		Rule 80(3) Explanations of the vote shall last not more than one and a half minutes, but each political group may give an explanation of vote lasting up to three minutes.
Closure of a Debate	Not specified.	**Rule 86(1)** A debate may be closed before the list of speakers has been exhausted on a proposal from the President, or at the request of the chairman of a political group or at least ten Members.

Composition of Committees	**Rule 37(2)** Committee Members shall be elected at the beginning of the session, which opens each year on the second Tuesday in March. Candidatures shall be addressed to the Bureau, which shall place before Parliament proposals designed to ensure fair representation of Member States and political views.	**Rule 92(1)** Committee Members shall be elected during the first part session following the re-election of Parliament and again 2 1/2 years thereafter. Nominations shall be addressed to place before Parliament proposals designed to ensure fair representation of Member States and political views.
Substitutes (on Committees)	**Rule 40(3)** Any Member of a committee may arrange for his place to be taken at meetings by another Member of Parliament of his choice. The name of the substitute shall be notified in advance to the chairman of the committee.	**Rule 93(1)** The political groups may appoint a number of permanent substitutes for each committee equal to the number of full members representing them on the committee. The President of Parliament shall be informed accordingly. These permanent substitutes shall be entitled to attend and speak at committee meetings and, in the event of the absence of the full member, to take part in the vote.
Committees of Inquiry	Not specified/did not exist.	**Rule 95(1)** Parliament shall, on a motion by 1/4 of its Members and without previously referring the motion to another committee, set up a committee of inquiry to investigate specific matters. The motion shall indicate the matter to be investigated which must fall within the sphere of activities of the Communities.
Creation of Sub-committees	**Rule 39(2)** A committee may, in the interest of its work, appoint one or more sub-committees, of which it shall at the same time determine the composition and competence. Sub-committees shall report to the committees that set them up.	**Rule 97(1)** Subject to prior authorization by the enlarged Bureau, a committee may, in the interest of its work, appoint one or more sub-committees, of which it shall at the same time determine the composition and competence, pursuant to rule 92 Sub-committees shall report to the committees that set them up.

MAJOR AREAS OF RULES REFORM: III PERIOD

Area of Reform Period III (1986–1994)	Provisions/Rules in 1986	Provisions/Rules in 1994
Nominations of Officers	**Rule 12(1)** The President, Vice Presidents, and quaestors shall be elected by secret ballot. Nominations shall be with consent. They may only be made by a political group or at least ten Members; however, when the number of nominations does not exceed the number of seats to be filled, the candidates may be elected by acclamation	**Rule 13(1)** The President, Vice Presidents, and Quaestors shall be elected by secret ballot. Nomination shall be with consent. They may only be made by a political group or by at least twenty-six Members. However, if the number of nominations does not exceed the number of seats to be filled, the candidates may be elected by acclamation.
Enlarged Bureau/ Conference of Presidents	**Rule 23(1)** The Enlarged Bureau shall consist of the Bureau and the chairmen of the political groups.	**Rule 23(1)** The Conference of Presidents shall consist of the President of Parliament and the chairmen of the Political Groups. The Chairman of a political group may arrange to be represented by a member of his group.
	Rule 23(3) Should voting in the Enlarged Bureau result in a tie the President shall have the casting vote.	**Rule 23(3)** The Conference of Presidents shall endeavor to reach a consensus on matters referred to it. Where consensus can not be reached, the matter shall be put to a vote subject to a weighting based on the number of Members in each political group.
Conference of Committee Chairmen	Did not exist.	**Rule 26(1–3)** The Conference of Committee Chairmen shall consist of the Chairmen of all the standing or temporary committees and shall elect its Chairman. The Conference of Committee Chairmen may make recommendations to the Conference of Presidents about the work of the Committees and drafting the agenda of part sessions. The Bureau and the Conference of Presidents may instruct the Conference of Committee Chairmen to carry out specific tasks.

Formation of Political Groups	**Rule 36(5)** A group shall consist of not less than fourteen Members. However, it may consist of not less than ten Members where these come from at least three Member States.	**Rule 29(2)** The minimum number of Members required to form a political group shall be twenty-six if they come from one Member State, twenty-one if they come from two Member States, sixteen if they come from three Member States, and thirteen if they come from four or more Member States.
Motions for resolutions	**Rule 47(1)** Any Member may table a motion for a resolution on a matter falling within the sphere of activities of the Communities. Such motions shall be printed and distributed in the official languages and referred to the appropriate committee, provided no request is made pursuant to Rule 48(1) [urgent debate].	**Rule 45(1)** Any Member may table a motion for a resolution on a matter falling within the sphere of activities of the European Union. The motion may not comprise more than 200 words.
Delegation of power of Decision to Committee	**Rule 33(1–4)** Where Parliament is consulted on predominately technical matter of no general importance, the President may propose that the matter be referred to the appropriate committee with the power to take a decision. Where 1/10 of all Members or 1/3 of committee Members object, proposal will be decided by the full plenary through the normal procedure.	**Rule 52(1–2)** The Conference of Presidents may refer a consultation, a request for an opinion, an own initiative report, or a report based on a motion for a resolution tabled pursuant to rule 45(1–5) to the appropriate committee for a decision. If after referral to committee pursuant to paragraph 1, 1/3 of the current members of the committee request that the power of decision be referred back to Parliament, the procedure for debate and amendment in plenary shall apply.

(continued)

233

MAJOR AREAS OF RULES REFORM: III PERIOD (*continued*)

Area of Reform Period III (1986–1994)	Provisions/Rules in 1986	Provisions/Rules in 1994
Agenda of Sittings	**Rule 55(1)** Before each part session the draft agenda shall be agreed at a meeting between the President and political group chairmen on the basis of a program drawn up by the President after consulting the political groups and the committees. A representative of the non-attached members shall be invited to attend the meeting. The Commission and the Council may attend the meeting at the President's invitation.	**Rule 95(1)** Before each part session the draft agenda shall be drawn up by the Conference of Presidents on the basis of recommendations by the meeting of Committee Chairmen and taking into account the agreed annual legislative program referred to in Rule 49. The Commission and Council may attend the deliberations of the Conference of Presidents on the draft agenda at the invitation of the President.
Allocation of Speaking Time	**Rule 65(3)** The speaking time of non-attached Members shall be doubled so as to take account of the great diversity of political views among them and enable, as far as possible, each view to be expressed.	**Rule 106(2c)** The non-attached Members shall be allocated an overall speaking time based on the fraction allocated to each political group under sub-paragraphs (a) and (b) [no longer doubled].
Principles governing voting	Not specified.	**Rule 114(1–2)** Voting on a report shall take place on the basis of a recommendation from the committee responsible. The committee may delegate this task to its chairman and *Rapporteur*. The committee may recommend that all or several amendments be put to the vote collectively, the collective vote on these amendments shall be taken first. It may also propose compromise amendments.

Explanations of Vote	**Rule 80(1)** Once the general debate and consideration of the texts have been concluded, explanations of vote may be given before the final vote, provided that a request to do so has been submitted to the President before the beginning of this vote. **Rule 80(3)** Explanations of the vote shall last not more than one and a half minutes, but each political group may give an explanation of vote lasting up to three minutes.	**Rule 122(1)** Once the general debate has been concluded, any Member may give an oral explanation on the final vote for not longer than one minute or give a written explanation of no more than 200 words, which shall be included in the verbatim report of the proceedings. Any political group may give an explanation lasting not more than two minutes.
Tabling Amendments	**Rule 53(1)** Any Member may table amendments. Amendments shall be tabled in writing and signed by at least one of their authors.	**Rule 124(1)** Any Member may table amendments for consideration in the committee responsible. Amendments for consideration in Parliament may be tabled by the committee responsible, a political group, or twenty-six Members. Amendments shall be tabled in writing and signed by their authors.
Referral back to Committee	**Rule 85(1)** Referral back to committee may be requested by any Member at any time.	**Rule 129(1)** Referral back to committee may be requested by a political group or at least twenty-six Members when the agenda is fixed or before the start of the debate, or the final vote.
Adjournment of a Debate	**Rule 87(1)** Before or during a debate on an item on the agenda, any Member may move that the debate be adjourned to a specific date and time.	**Rule 131(1)** At the start of a debate on an item on the agenda, a political group or at least twenty-six Members may move that the debate be adjourned to a specific date and time. Such a motion shall be put to the vote immediately.
Question Time in Committee	Does not exist.	**Rule 149** Question Time be held in committee if a committee so decides. Each committee shall decide its own rules for the conduct of Question Time.

Appendix C

EXAMPLES OF RULES REVISION CATEGORIES

Category	Original	Proposed Change
Increased Efficiency	**Rule 29(1)** Any Member may propose and speak in favor of amendments.	**Rule 29(1)** Any Member may propose amendments. <u>On a proposal from the President, Parliament may fix a time limit for the tabling of amendments. Parliament shall not deliberate on any amendment unless it is moved during the debate.</u> (doc. 335/76)
Increased Centralization	**Rule 92(3)** <u>Exceptionally,</u> the President may put the original text to the vote first, or give priority in the vote to a proposed amendment that departs less from the original text than the one that departs furthest from it.	**Rule 92(3)** The President may put the original text to the vote first, or give priority in the vote to a proposed amendment that departs less from the original text than the one that departs furthest from it. (doc. A3-390/91)
Increased Political Group Power	**Rule 7(1)** The President and Vice Presidents shall be elected by secret ballot. Four tellers chosen by lot shall count the vote.	**Rule 7(1)** The President and Vice Presidents shall be elected by secret ballot on the nomination of a political group or at <u>least ten members</u>; however, when the number of nominations does not exceed the number of seats to be filled, <u>the candidates may be elected by acclamation</u> (doc. 538/77)
Increased Large Political Group Power	**Rule 38(2)** The proposal, and where appropriate, the draft legislative resolution contained in the report shall be put to the vote without debate unless a political group or at least thirteen Members of Parliament lodge a protest in advance.	**Rule 38(2)** The proposal, and where appropriate, the draft legislative resolution contained in the report shall be put to the vote without debate unless at least <u>twenty–three</u> Members of Parliament lodge a protest in advance. (doc. A3-390/91)

Increased EP Powers	Did not exist.	**Rule 22A(1)** Where the Council intends to depart from the opinion adopted by the European Parliament, a procedure for conciliation with the Council of Ministers may be initiated by the European Parliament, when delivering its opinion with the active participation of the Commission, in the case of certain important Community decisions. (doc. 210/76)
New EP Powers	Did not exist.	**Rule 4(1)** A Member's term of office shall end pursuant to the provisions of the Act of 20 September 1976, on death or on resignation. (doc. 667/78)
Increased Non-Attached Powers	**Rule 111(1)** The political groups may appoint a number of permanent substitutes for each committee equal to the number of full Members representing them on the committee. The President shall be informed accordingly. These permanent substitutes shall be entitled to attend and speak at committee meetings and, in the event of the absence of a full Member, to take part in the vote.	**Rule 111(1)** The political groups and the non-attached Members may appoint a number of permanent substitutes for each committee equal to the number of full Members representing them on the committee. The President shall be informed accordingly. These permanent substitutes shall be entitled to attend and speak at committee meetings and, in the event of the absence of a full Member, to take part in the vote. (doc. A3-240)
Increased Small Political Group Powers	**Rule 36(5)** A group shall consist of not less than fourteen members.	**Rule 36(5)** A group shall consist of not less than fourteen members. However, a group may consist of 10 members where these represent at least three Member States (doc. 190/73).
Technical Revisions	**Rule 30(1)** A motion of censure on the Commission may be handed to the President of Parliament by one tenth of the current Members of Parliament.	**Rule 30(1)** A motion of censure on the Commission may be submitted to the President by one-tenth of the component Members of Parliament (doc. A3-240/93).

Appendix D

THE IDEOLOGICAL LOCATION AND SIZE OF THE PARTY GROUPS ACROSS TIME

Ideology	Party Group	1979	1980	1981	1982	1983	1984	1985	1986	1987	1988	1989	1990	1991	1992	1993	1994	1995	1996	1997	1999
Left	LU – Left Unity	***	***	***	***	***	***	***	***	***	***	***	14	14	13	13	13	***	***	***	***
Left	COM – Communists and Allies	44	44	45	48	48	43	43	46	48	48	48	***	***	***	***	***	***	***	***	***
Left	EUL/EUL-NGL – United European Left/Nordic Left	***	***	***	***	***	***	***	***	***	***	***	28	28	28	28 (?)	28	33	33	33	42
Left	Greens – The Greens	***	***	***	***	***	***	***	***	***	***	***	29	29	28	28	23	27	27	28	47
Left-C	PES – Socialists	113	113	120	124	124	130	130	172	165	165	166	180	179	179	198	198	217	217	214	180
Center	ELDR – Liberal and Democratic Reform	40	40	39	39	39	31	31	42	44	44	46	49	49	45	44	42	52	52	43	51
Right-C	ED – European Democrats	64	64	63	63	63	50	50	63	66	66	66	34	34	***	***	***	***	***	***	***
Right-C	EPP/EPP-ED – People's Party and European Democrats	107	107	109	117	117	110	110	118	115	115	113	121	122	162	163	157	173	173	181	233

	Group																				
Right	**EPD/EDA** – Progressive Democrats/Democratic Alliance	22	22	22	22	22	22	29	29	34	29	29	29	22	22	21	22	20	26	***	***
Right	**ER** – European Right	***	***	***	***	***	16	16	16	16	16	16	17	14	14	14	***	***	***	***	***
Right	**EN** – Europe of Nations	***	***	***	***	***	***	***	***	***	***	***	***	***	***	***	19	18	18	***	***
Right	**FE** – Forza Europe	***	***	***	***	***	***	***	***	***	***	***	***	***	***	***	27	***	***	***	***
Right	**UfE** (FE + EDA) – Union for Europe	***	***	***	***	***	***	***	***	***	***	***	***	***	***	***	***	54	55	56	***
Right	**UEN** – Union for a Europe of Nations	***	***	***	***	***	***	***	***	***	***	***	***	***	***	***	***	***	***	***	30
Other	**ERA** – European Radical Alliance	***	***	***	***	***	***	***	***	***	***	***	***	***	***	***	19	20	20	***	***
Right	**EDD** – Democracy and Diversities	***	***	***	***	***	***	***	***	***	***	***	***	***	***	***	***	***	***	***	16
Other	**TDI/ARC** – Technical	11	11	11	11	11	11	19	19	20	20	20	14	15	15	16	***	***	***	***	17
Other	**NA** – Nonaffiliated	9	9	25	10	10	6	6	7	15	15	14	10	12	13	22	27	31	31	33	9
	Total	410	410	434	434	434	434	434	518	518	518	518	518	518	518	518	579	626	626	626	625

Bibliography

Abeles, Marc. 1992. *La vie quotidienne au Parlement Europeen*. Paris: Hachette.

Agence Europe. Bruxelles. Belgium.

Aldrich, John. 1995. *Why Parties?* Chicago: University of Chicago Press.

Archer, Clive and Fiona Butler. 1996. *The European Union: Structure and Process* (2nd edition). New York: St. Martins Press.

Attina, Fulvio. 1990. "The Voting Behavior of the European Parliament Members and the Problem of Europarties." *European Journal of Political Research* no. 18: 557–579.

1992. "Parties, Party Systems and Democracy in the European Union." *The International Spectator* no. 3: 67–86.

1993. "Parties and Party System in the EC Political System." Paper presented at the ECPR Joint Sessions of Workshops, University of Leiden.

Bach, Stanley and Steven S. Smith. 1988. *Managing Uncertainty in the House of Representatives: Adaptation and Innovation in Special Rules*. Washington, DC: Brookings Institution.

Bardi, Luciano. 1992. "Transnational Party Federations in the European Community." In *Party Organizations: A Handbook on Party Organizations in Western Democracies*, Richard Katz and Peter Mair (eds.). London: Sage Publications.

1996. "Transnational Trends in European Parties and the 1994 Elections of the European Parliament." *Party Politics* no. 1: 99–114.

Bataille, Brigitte. 1990. "Le Groupe Socialiste au Parlement Europeen." Mémoire de Licence en Sciences Politiques, Universite Libre de Bruxelles.

Baun, Michael. 1996. *An Imperfect Union*. Boulder, CO: Westview Press.

Belgium and Current World Problems. 1953. New York: Belgian Government Information Center.

1956. New York: Belgian Government Information Center.

Belmont European Policy Centre. 1992. *The New Treaty on European Union*. Brussels.

Benelux Memorandum 1955 (1970). Reprinted in *Landmarks in European Unity*, S. Patijn (ed.). Leyden: A.W. Sithoff.

Benzecri, Jean Paul et al. 1973. *L'Analyse des Correspondances*. Paris: Dunod.

241

Bieber, Roland, J. Pantalis, and J. Schoo. 1986. "Implications of the Single Act for the European Parliament." *Common Market Law Review* vol. 23, no. 2: 767–792.

Bieber, Roland, Jean-Paul Jacque, and Joseph H.H. Weiler. 1985. *An Ever Closer Union: A Critical Analysis Of The Draft Treaty Establishing The European Union.* Luxembourg: Office for Official Publications of the European Communities.

Bieber, Roland. 1984. "The Evolution of the Rules of Procedure of the European Parliament." In *Le Parlement Europeen a La Veille de la Deuxiemme Election au Suffrage Direct: Bilan et Perspectives.* Bruge: College d'Europe.

Binder, Sarah. 1996. "The Partisan Basis of Procedural Choice: Allocating Parliamentary Rights in the House, 1790–1990." *American Political Science Review* no. 1: 8–20.

Blondel, Jean. 1973. *Comparing Political Systems.* London: Weidenfeld and Nicolson. 1990. *Comparative Government: An Introduction.* Hemel Hempstead: Philip Allan.

Bogdanor, Vernon. 1989. "The June 1989 European Elections and the Institutions of the Community." *Government and Opposition* vol. 24, no. 2: 199–214.

Bombardella, Pasetti. 1984. "Le Roles des Commissions." In *Le Parlement Europeen a La Veille de la Deuxiemme Election au Suffrage Direct: Bilan et Perspectives.* Bruge: College d'Europe.

Bonvicini, Gianni. 1974. *Interaction Between Parliamentary Institutions and Political Forces.* Luxembourg: European Parliament. 1987. "The Genscher-Colombo Plan and the 'Solemn Declaration on European Union' (1980–1983)." In *The Dynamics of European Union*, Roy Pryce (ed.). New York: Croom Helm.

Bourguignon-Wittke, R., E. Grabitz, O. Schmuck, S. Steppat, and W. Wessels. 1985. "Five Years of the Directly Elected European Parliament: Performance and Prospects." *Journal of Common Market Studies* no. 1: 39–59.

Bowler, Shaun and David Farrell. 1995. "The Organizing of the European Parliament: Committees Specialization and Co-ordination." *British Journal of Political Science* vol. 25, no. 2: 219–243. 1999. "Parties and Party Discipline within the European Parliament: A norms based approach." In *Party Cohesion, Party Discipline and the Organizing of Parliaments*, S Bowler, D Farrell and R Katz (eds.). Colombus Ohio: Ohio State University Press.

Bradley, Kieran St. C. 1987. "Maintaining the Balance: The Role of the Court of Justice in Defining the Institutional Position of the European Parliament." *Common Market Law Review* no. 24: 41–64.

Brzinski, Joanne Bay. 1995. "Political Group Cohesion in the European Parliament, 1989–1994." In *The State of the European Union: Building a European Polity*, Carolyn Rhodes and Sonia Mazey (eds.). London: Lynne Rienner Publishers, Chapter 6.

Bubba, Elena. 1970. *La Mission Du Parlement Europeen.* Namur: Editions UGA.

Burgess, Michael. 1989. *Federalism and the European Union.* New York: Routledge.

Capotorti, Francesco 1986. *The European Union Treaty: Commentary on the Draft Adopted by the European Parliament on 14 February 1984.* Oxford: Clarendon Press.

Bibliography

Chauchat, Mathias. 1989. *Le controle politique du Parlement europeen sur les executifs communautaires*. Paris: Librairie generale de droit et de jurisprudence.

Churchill. Winston. 1970. Statement by Mr. Winston S. Churchill at the Consultative Assembly of the Council of Europe. In *Landmarks in European Unity*, S. Patijn (ed.). Leyden: A.W. Sithoff.

Cocks, Barnett, Sir. 1973. *The European Parliament; Structure, Procedure & Practice* London: H.M. Stationery Office.

Colomer, Josep and Madeleine Hosli. 1997. "Decision-Making in the European Union: The Power of Political Parties." Paper presented at the annual meeting of the American Political Science Association, Washington, DC.

European Commission. 1966. *Compromis de Luxembourg*. European Bulletin 3/66.

Conference Des Ministres des Affaires Etrangeres, February 12, 1957, MAE 498 f/57 gd.

Conference Intergouvernementale pour le Marche Commun et L'Euratom, December 27, 1956, MAE 838 f/56 in.

January 14, 1957, MAE 101 f/57 in.

Coombes, David. *The Future of the European Parliament*. 1979. London: Policy Studies Institute.

Cooper, Joseph and Cheryl Young. 1989. "Bill Introduction in the 19th Century: A Study of Institutional Change." *Legislative Studies Quarterly* no. 1: 67–105.

Cooper, Joseph and David Brady. 1981. "Institutional Context and Leadership Style." *The American Political Science Review* no. 2: 411–425.

Cooter, Robert and Josef Drexl. 1994. "The Logic of Power in the Emerging European Constitution." *International Review of Law and Economics* no. 14: 307–326.

Copeland, Gary and Samuel Patterson (eds.). 1994. *Parliaments in the Modern World*. Ann Arbor: University of Michigan Press.

Corbett, Richard. 1987. "The 1985 Intergovernmental Conference and the Single European Act." In *The Dynamics of European Union*, R. Pryce (ed.). New York: Croom Helm.

Corbett, Richard. 1989. "Testing the New Procedures: The European Parliament's First Experiences with its new 'Single Act' Powers." *Journal of Common Market Studies* no. 4: 359–372.

1996. "Governance and Institutional Developments." In *The European Union 1995: Annual Review of Activities*, Neill Nugent (ed.). Cambridge: Blackwell Publishers.

Corbett, Richard, Francis Jacobs and Michael Shackelton. 1995. *The European Parliament* (3rd edition). London: Cartermill Press.

Cox, Gary and Mathew McCubbins. 1993. *Legislative Leviathan: Party Government in the House*. Berkeley: University of California Press.

Cox, Gary. 1987. *The Efficient Secret: The Cabinet and the development of political parties in Victorian England*. Cambridge: Cambridge University Press.

Crombez, C. 1996. "Legislative Procedures in the European Community." *British Journal of Political Science* vol. 26, no. 2: 199–228.

de Gaulle, Charles. 1970. Excerpts of the press conferences of General de Gaulle at the Elysee Palace; Paris, 9 September. In *Landmarks in European Unity*, S. Patijn (ed.). Leyden: A.W. Sithoff.

  1971. *Memoirs of Hope: Renewal and Endeavor*, Translated by Terence Kilmartin. New York: Simon and Schuster.

Deering, Christopher J. and Steven S. Smith. 1997. *Committees in Congress* (3rd edition). Washington, DC: CQ Press.

Dehousse, Fernand. 1967. *L'avenir Institutionnel des Communautes Europèenes*. Nancy: Centre Europeen Universitaire, Universite de Nancy.

Devuyst, Youri. 1999. "The Treaty of Amsterdam: The Community-Method after Amsterdam." *Journal of Common Market Studies* vol. 37, no. 1: 109–122.

Dinan, Desmond. 1994. *Ever Closer Union?* London: Macmillan Press Ltd.

  1994a. "The European Community, 1978–1993." *Annals of the American Academy of Political and Social Science* no. 531: 10–24.

Draft Treaty Establishing the European Union, Bull. EC. 2/1984.

Duverger, Maurice. 1954. *Political Parties*. New York: John Wiley and Sons Inc.

Earnshaw, David and David Judge. 1993. "The European Parliament and the Sweetners Directive: From Footnote to Inter-institutional Conflict." *Journal of Common Market Studies* no. 1: 103–116.

  1996. "The European Parliament's path to Legislative Power." In *European Union: Power and Policy-Making*, Jeremy Richardson (ed.). London: Routledge.

Eijk, C. van der and Mark N. Franklin with Johan Ackaert. 1996. *Choosing Europe?: The European Electorate And National Politics In The Face Of Union*. Ann Arbor: University of Michigan Press.

Elles, Baroness D-L. 1984. "The Role of the Presidency of the European Parliament." In *Le Parlement Europeen a La Veille de la Deuxiemme Election au Suffrage Direct: Bilan et Perspectives*. Bruge: College d'Europe.

Eurobarometer. 1994. *Trends and Variables 1974–1993*. Brussels, Belgium: Commission Directorate General for Research and Analysis.

European Commission. *Bulletin of the European Union*. Luxembourg: Office for Official Publications of the European Communities.

European Community Information Service. 1965. *The European Parliament*. Brussels.

European Court of Justice. *Rulings of the European Court of Justice*. Luxembourg: Office for Official Publications of the European Communities.

European Parliament. 1988. *Parliamentary control of community finances* (3rd edition). Luxembourg: Office for Official Publications of the European Communities.

  1989. *Forging Ahead: The European Parliament 1952–1988* (3rd edition). Luxembourg: Office for Official Publications of the European Communities.

  1968. *Dix annees, 1958–1968*. Luxembourg: Secretariat General du Parlement Europèen.

  1972. *The European Communities' Own Resources and The Budgetary Powers of the European Parliament: Selected Documents*. Luxembourg: European Parliament.

244

Bibliography

1978. *Minutes of Proceedings, Action Taken on Resolutions: 1952 to 1976–1977.* Luxembourg: Directorate General for Sessional and General Services.

1980. *The European Parliament, its Powers.* Luxembourg: Office for Official Publications of the European Communities.

1982. *Growing Together.* Luxembourg: Office for Official Publications of the European Communities.

1983. *Fact Sheets on the European Parliament and the Activities of the European Community.* Luxembourg: Office for Official Publications of the European Communities.

1984. *Forging Ahead: Thirty Years of the European Parliament, 1952–1982.* Strasbourg: Directorate-General for Research and Documentation.

1984. *On The Right Road: A Report On The First Legislative Period, 1979–1984.* Luxembourg: European Parliament, General Secretariat, Directorate-General for Research and Documentation.

1988. *The Impact of The European Parliament on Community Policies.* Luxembourg: European Parliament, Directorate General for Research.

1988. *The Impact of the European Parliament on Community Policies.* Luxembourg: Office for Official Publications of the European Communities.

1989. *Europe's Parliament and the Single Act.* London: European Parliament.

1989. *Forging Ahead: European Parliament, 1952–1988: 36 Years* (3rd edition). Luxembourg: Office for Official Publications of the European Communities.

Fiorina, Morris. 1987. "Alternative Rationales for Restrictive Procedures." *Journal of Law, Economics and Organization* no. 6: 1–20.

Fitzmaurice, John. 1975. *The Party Groups in the European Parliament.* Westmead, England: Saxon House.

1978. *The European Parliament.* Westmead, England: Saxon House, Teakfield Limited.

1988. "An Analysis of the European Community's Co-operation Procedure." *Journal of Common Market Studies* no. 4: 389–400.

Fouchet Plans I and II. 1965. *Projets de Traité en Vue d'Une Union Politique Européenne.* Luxembourg: Directorate General for Research.

Fowler, Linda, Pieter Polhuis, and Scott Paine. 1983. "Changing Patterns of Voting Strength in the European Parliament." *Comparative Politics,* 159–175.

Franck, Christian. 1987. "New Ambitions: From the Hague to Paris Summits (1967–1972)." In *The Dynamics of European Union,* Roy Pryce (ed.). New York: Croom Helm.

Gamm, Gerald and Kenneth Shepsle. 1989. "Emergence of Legislative Institutions: Standing Committees in the House and Senate, 1810–1825." *Legislative Studies Quarterly* no. 1: 39–65.

Garrett, Geoffrey and George Tsebelis. 1996. "An Institutional Critique of Intergovernmentalism." *International Organization* vol. 50, no. 3: 269–299.

Genscher-Colombo Plan. 1981. Bull. EC 11/1981.

Gerbet, Pierre. 1987a. "In Search of Political Union: The Fouchet Plan Negotiations (1960–1962)." In *The Dynamics of European Union,* Roy Pryce (ed.). New York: Croom Helm.

245

1987b. "The Origins, Early Attempts and the Emergence of the Six (1945–1952)." In *The Dynamics of European Union*, Roy Pryce (ed.). New York: Croom Helm.

Greenacre Michael J. 1984. *Theory and Applications of Correspondence Analysis*. London: Academic Press.

Gueguen, Daniel. 1992. *A Practical Guide to the EEC Labyrinth*. Rennes: Editions Apogee.

Guidi, Guido. 1983. *I gruppi parlamentari del Parlamento Europeo*. Rimini: Maggioli.

Haas, Ernst. 1958. *The Uniting of Europe*. London: Stevens Press.

Haggar, Mark and Martin Wing. 1979. "The Deconcentration of Legislative Power: The Development of Committees in the European Parliament." *European Journal of Political Research* no. 7: 117–146.

Hallstein, Walter. 1958. *United Europe, Challenge and Opportunity*. Cambridge, MA: Harvard University Press.

1964. *A New Path to Peaceful Union*. New York: Asia Publishing House.

1972. *Europe in the Making*, Translated by Charles Roetter. London: George Allen and Unwin Press.

Hayes-Renshaw, Fiona and Helen Wallace. 1997. *The Council of Ministers*. New York: St. Martin's Press.

Henig, Stanley (ed.). 1979. *Political Parties in the European Community*. London: George Allen and Unwin Press.

Henig, Stanley. 1980. *Power and Decision in Europe*. London: Europotentials Press.

Herman, Valentine and Juliet Lodge. 1978. *The European Parliament and the European Community*. New York: St. Martin's Press.

Hix, Simon and Christopher Lord. 1997a. *Political Parties in the European Union*. New York: St. Martin's Press.

1997b. "The making of a President: The European Parliament and the Confirmation of Jacque Santer as President of the Commission." *Government and Opposition* vol. 31, no. 1: 62–76.

Hix, Simon. 1995. "Parties at the European Level and the Legitimacy of EU Socio-Economic Policy." *Journal of Common Market Studies* no. 4: 527–554.

Houdbine, Anne Marie and Jean-Raymond Verges. 1966. *Le Parlement Europèen dans la construction de l'Europe des six*. Paris: Presses Universitaires de France.

Hubschmid, Claudia and Peter Moser. 1997. "The Cooperation Procedure in the EU: Why was the European Parliament Influential in the Decision on Car Emission Standards?" *Journal of Common Market Studies* vol. 35, no. 2: 225–241.

Hurwitz, Leon (ed.). 1980. *Contemporary Perspectives on European Integration: Attitudes, Non-Governmental Behavior, Collective Decision-making*. Westport, CT: Greenwood Press.

Jackson, Robert Victor. 1977. *The Powers of the European Parliament*. London: Conservative Group for Europe.

Jacobs, Francis. 1991. "The European Union Parliament and Economic and Monetary Union." *Common Market Law Review* no. 28: 361–382.

Bibliography

1997. "Legislative Co-decision: A Real Step Forward?" Paper presented at the Fifth Biennial ECSA Conference in Seattle, WA.

Jacque, Jean-Paul. 1984. *Le Parlement Européen*. Paris: Economica.

Journal Officiel. 1951–1973. Luxembourg: Office for Official Publications of the European Communities.

Judge, David and David Earnshaw. 1994. "Weak European Parliament Influence? A Study of the Environment Committee of the European Parliament." *Government and Opposition* no. 2: 262–276.

Judge, David, David Earnshaw, and Ngaire Cowan. 1994. "Ripples or Waves: The European Parliament in the European Community Policy Process." *Journal of European Public Policy* vol. 29, no. 2: 27–52.

Katz, Johnathan and Brian Sala. 1996. "Careerism, Committee Assignments and the Electoral Connection." *American Political Science Review* no. 1: 21–33.

Keatinge, Patrick and Anna Murphy. 1987. "The European Council's Ad Hoc Committee on Institutional Affairs (1984–1985)." In *The Dynamics of European Union*, Roy Pryce (ed.). New York: Croom Helm.

Keohane, Robert. 1984. *After Hegemony: Cooperation and Discord in the World Political Economy*. Princeton, NJ: Princeton University Press.

Keohane, Robert O. and Stanley Hoffman. 1991. "Institutional Change in Europe in the 1980s." In *The New European Community: Decisionmaking and Institutional Change*, Robert Keohane and Stanely Hoffman (eds.). Boulder, CO: Westview Press.

Kirchner, Emil Joseph. 1984. *The European Parliament: Performance and Prospects*. Aldershot, Hampshire, England: Gower.

Klepsch, Egon. 1995. *The Period After Maastricht: The Major Challenges Facing Europe – the Role of the European Parliament*. Florence: European University Institute.

Koelble, Thomas. 1996. "Economic Theories of Organization and the Politics of Institutional Design in Political Parties." *Party Politics* vol. 2, no. 2: 251–263.

Krehbiel, Keith, 1991. *Information and Legislative Organization*. Ann Arbor: University of Michigan Press.

Kreppel, Amie. 1999a. "The June 1999 Elections, Amsterdam and the Perils of Ideology." *The European Community Studies Association Review*, Fall.

1999b. "The European Parliament's Influence over EU Policy Outcomes." *Journal of Common Market Studies* vol. 37, no. 3: 521–538.

2000a. "Procedure and Influence: An Empirical Analysis of EP Influence Under the Cooperation and Co-decision Procedures." Paper delivered at the annual meeting of the American Political Science Association (APSA), Washington, DC.

2000b. "Rules Ideology and Coalition Formation in the European Parliament." *European Union Politics* vol. 1, no. 3: 341–363.

Kreppel, Amie and George Tsebelis. 1999. "Coalition Formation in the European Parliament." *Comparative Political Studies* no. 8: 933–966.

Ladrech, Robert. 1996. "Political Parties in the European Parliament." In *Political Parties and the European Union*, John Gaffney (ed.). London: Routledge.

1997. "Partisanship and Party Formation in European Union Politics." *Comparative Politics* vol. 29, no. 2: 167–188.

Laprat, Gerard. 1985. "Le Groupes Politiques au Parlement Europeen: La Dialectique de l'Unite et de la Diversite." *Marche Commun* no. 286: 220–230.

Laruelle, Annick and Mika Widgrén. 1997. "The Development of the Division of Power Among EU Commission, EU Council and European Parliament." Paper presented at the annual meeting of the American Political Science Association, Washington, DC.

Lawson, Kay. 1976. *The Comparative Study of Political Parties*. New York: St. Martin's Press.

Legrand-Lane, Raymond. 1988. "Quelques Observations sur le Secretariat du Parlement." *Marche Commun* no. 313: 29–33.

Lijphart, Arend. 1969. *Politics in Europe; Comparisons and Interpretations*. Englewood Cliffs, NJ: Prentice-Hall.

1975. *The Politics of Accommodation: Pluralism And Democracy In The Netherlands* (2nd edition). Berkeley: University of California Press.

1977. *Democracy in Plural Societies: a Comparative Exploration*. New Haven, CT: Yale University Press.

1984. *Democracies*. New Haven, CT: Yale University Press.

Lindsay, K. 1958. *Towards a European Parliament*. Strasbourg: Secretariat of the Council of Europe.

Lipset, Seymour Martin and Stein Rokkan. 1967. *Party Systems and Voter Alignments: Cross-National Perspectives*. New York: Free Press.

Lodge, Juliet. 1984. "European Union and the First Elected European Parliament: the Spinelli Initiative." *Journal of Common Market Studies* no. 4: 375–402.

1986. "The Single European Act: Towards a New Euro-Dynamism?" *Journal of Common Market Studies* no. 3: 203–223.

1994. "The European Parliament and the Authority-Democracy Crisis." *Annals of the American Academy of Political and Social Sciences* no. 531: 69–83.

Lodge, Juliet and Valentine Herman. 1982. *Direct Elections to the European Parliament: A Community Perspective*. London: The Macmillan Press LTD.

Loewenberg, Gerhard and Samuel Patterson. 1979. *Comparing Legislatures*. Boston: Little Brown and Company.

Londregan, John and James Synder Jr. 1994. "Comparing Committee and Floor Preferences." *Legislative Studies Quarterly* no. 2: 233–266.

Louis, Jean-Victor and Denis Waelbroeck. 1988. *Le Parlement Europèen dans l'evolution institutionnelle*. Bruxelle: Editions de l'Universite de Bruxelles.

Manzanares, Henri and Jean-Pierre Quentin. 1979. *Pourquoi un Parlement Europeen?* Paris: Berger-Levrault.

Marjolin, Robert. 1980. *Europe in Search of its Identity*. New York: Council on Foriegn Relations.

Marquand, David. 1979. *A Parliament for Europe*. London: J. Cape.

Maurer, Andreas. 1998. "Co-Governing After Maastricht: The European Parliament's Performance 1994–1998." Working Paper Poli104EN. Luxembourg: European Parliament, Directorate General for Research.

Bibliography

Mayhew, David. 1974. *Congress: The Electoral Connection*. New Haven, CT: Yale University Press.

Mayne, Richard. 1962. *The Community of Europe*. New York: W.W. Norton & Company Inc.

1968. *The Institutions of the European Community*. London: Chatham House.

Mezey, Michael. 1979. *Comparative Legislatures*. Durham, NC: Duke University Press.

Michels, Robert. 1962. *Political Parties: A Sociological Study of the Oligarchical Tendencies of Modern Democracy*. New Brunswick, NJ: Transaction Publishers.

Monnet, Jean. 1978. *Memoirs*, Translated by Richard Mayne. New York: Doubleday & Company. Inc.

Moravcsik, Andrew. 1993. "Preferences and Power in the European Community." *Journal of Common Market Studies* no. 4: 473–524.

1999. "Explaining the Treaty of Amsterdam: Interests, Influence and Institutions." *Journal of Common Market Studies* no. 1: 59–88.

Morgan, Roger and Clare Tame (eds.). 1996. *Parliaments and Parties: The European Parliament in the Political Life of Europe*. New York: St. Martin's Press.

Morlino, Leonardo. 1980. *Come Cambiano I Regimi Politici: Strumenti di Analisi*. Milano: Franco Angeli Editore.

1981. *Dalla Democrazia all'Autoritarismo*. Bologna: Il Mulino.

Moser, Peter. 1996. "The European Parliament as a Conditional Agenda Setter: What are the Conditions? A Critique of Tsebelis." *American Political Science Review* vol. 90: 834–838.

Nickel, Dietmar. 1997. "The European Parliament's Impact on the IGC Process." Paper presented at the Fifth Biennial ECSA Conference in Seattle, WA.

Nicoll, William and Trevor Salmon. 1994. *Understanding the New European Community*. New York: Harvester Wheatsheaf.

Nicoll, William. 1996. "The European Parliament's Post-Maastricht Rules of Procedure." *Journal of Common Market Studies* vol. 32, no. 3: 402–410.

Niedermayer, Oskar. 1985. "Transnational Party Co-operation." In *European Elections 1979/1981 and 1984: Conclusions and Perspectives from Empirical Research*, Karlheinz Reif (ed.). Berlin: Quorum, Chapter 5.

Noel, Emile, OBE. 1992. *Working together: the institutions of the European Community*. Luxembourg: Office for Official Publications of the European Communities.

Noel, Emile. 1995. *La conference intergouvernementale de 1996 vers un nouvel ordre institutionnel*. Florence: Robert Schuman Centre.

Norton, Philip. 1993. *Does Parliament Matter?* New York: Harvester Wheatsheaf.

Nugent, Neill. 1994. *The Government and Politics of the European Union* (3rd edition). Durham, NC: Duke University Press.

Official Journal of the European Communities. Series A – Annexes. Luxembourg: Office for Official Publications of the European Communities.

Series C – Information and Notices. Luxembourg: Office for Official Publications of the European Communities.

Series L – Legislation. Luxembourg: Office for Official Publications of the European Communities.

Ollerenshaw, Steve. 1993. *The European Parliament: More Democracy or More Rhetoric?* Essex: University of Essex, Centre of European Studies, Occasional Papers.

Olson, Mancur. 1971. *The Logic of Collective Action: Public Goods and the Theory of Groups*. Cambridge, MA: Harvard University Press.

Ostrogorski, Mosei. 1964. *Democracy and the Organization of Political Parties*. Chicago: Quadrangle Books.

P.E.P. 1961. *France and the European Community*. Occassional Paper No. 11, January. London: Chatham House.

1969. *Action Committee For the United States of Europe: Statements and Declarations 1955–1967*. London: Chatham House.

Palmer, Michael. 1981. *The European Parliament: What it Is, What it Does, How it Works*. New York: Pergamon Press.

1983. "The Development of the European Parliament's Institutional Role within the European Community, 1974–1983." *Journal of European Integration* no. 2: 183–202.

Panebianco, Angelo. 1982. *Modelli di Partito*. Bologna: Il Mulino.

Peters, Guy. 1992. "Bureauractic Politics and the Institutions of the European Community." In *Euro-Politics: Institutions and Policymaking in the "New" European Community*, Alberta Sbragia (ed.). Washington, DC: Brookings Institute.

1996. "Agenda-Setting in the European union." In *European Union: Power and Policy-Making*, Jeremy Richardson (ed.). London: Routledge.

Pinder, John and Stanley Henig. 1969. *European Political Parties*. London: Unwin Brothers Limited.

Pinder, John. 1991. *European Community: The Building of a Union*. Oxford: Oxford University Press.

Polsby, Nelson. 1968. "The Institutionalization of the U.S. House of Representatives." *American Political Science Review* no. 1: 144–168.

1975. "Legislatures." In *Handbook of Political Science*, F.I. Greenstein and Nelson Polsby (eds.). Reading, MA: Addison Wesley Press, pages 277–296.

Polsby. Nelson, Miriam Gallaher, and Barry Spencer Rundquist. 1969. "The Growth of the Seniority System in the U.S. House of Representatives." *The American Political Science Review* no. 3: 787–807.

Poole, Keith and Howard Rosenthal. 1991. "Patterns of Congressional Voting." *American Journal of Political Science* no. 1: 228–278.

Pridham, Geoffrey and Pippa Pridham. 1979. *Towards Transnational Parties in the European Community*. London: Policy Studies Institute.

1980. *Transnational Party Co-operation and Direct Elections to the European Parliament*. London: Allen and Unwin.

Pridham, Geoffrey. 1986. "European Elections, Political Parties and Trends of Internalization in Community Affairs." *Journal of Common Market Studies* no. 4: 279–296.

Radoux, Lucien and Jean-Guy Giraud. 1977. *Les Pouvoirs du Parlement Europeen*. Bruxelles: Institut Emile Vandervelde.

Bibliography

Raunio, Tapio. 1996. *Party Group Behaviour in the European Parliament: An analysis of Transnational Political Groups in the 1989–94 Parliament.* Tampere: University of Tampere Press.

Reif, Karlheinz (ed.). 1985. *European Elections 1979/1981 and 1984: Conclusions and Perspectives from Empirical Research.* Berlin: Quorum.

Remington, Thomas and Steven Smith. 1995. "The Development of Parliamentary Parties in Russia." *Legislative Studies Quarterly* no. 4: 457–489.

1996. "Theories of Legislative Institutions and the Organization of the Russian Duma." Paper presented at the Annual Meeting of the American Political Science Association, San Francisco.

Resolution of Foriegn Monisters at Messina. 1955 (1970). In *Landmarks in European Unity*, S. Patijn (ed.). Leyden: A.W. Sithoff.

Robinson, Ann and Adrian Webb. 1985. *The European Parliament in the EC Policy Process.* London: Policy Studies Institute.

Robinson, Ann and Caroline Bray. 1986. *The Public Image of the European Parliament.* London: Policy Studies Institute.

Sartori, Giovanni. 1973. *Correnti, Frazioni e Fazioni nei Partiti Politici Italiani.* Bologna: Il Mulino.

1976. *Parties and Party Systems: A Framework for Analysis.* Cambridge: Cambridge University Press.

1979. *La Politica: Logico e Metodo in Scienze Sociali.* Milano: SugarCo Edizioni.

Sasse, Christoph, Edouard Poullet, David Coombes, and Gerard Deprez. 1977. *Decision Making in the European Community.* New York: Preager Publishers.

Sbragia, Alberta (ed.). 1992. *Euro-Politics: Institutions and Policymaking in the "New" European Community.* Washington, DC: Brookings Institute.

Scalingi, Paula. 1980. *The European Parliament: The Three Decade Search For A United Europe.* Westport, CT: Greenwood Press.

Schmitt, Hermann. 1990. "Party Attachment and Party Choice in the European Elections of June 1989." *International Journal of Public Opinion Research* no. 2: 169–185.

Schmuck, Otto. 1987. "The European Parliament's Draft Treaty Establishing The European Union (1979–1984)." In *The Dynamics of European Union*, Roy Pryce (ed.). New York: Croom Helm.

1991. "The European Parliament as Institutional Actor." In *The State of the European Community*, Leon Hurwitz and Christian Lequesne (eds.). Boulder Colorado: Lynne Rienner Publishers.

Schneider, Gerald. 1995. "The Limits of Self-Reform: Institution-Building in the European Union." *European Journal of International Relations* no. 1: 59–86.

Scholl, Edward. 1986. "The Electoral System and Constituency-Oriented Activity in the European Parliament." *International Studies Quarterly* no. 30: 315–332.

Scully, Roger M. 1997. "The European Parliament and the Co-decision Procedure: A Reassessment." *Journal of Legislative Studies* vol. 3: 52–74.

Shackelton, Michael. 1997. "The European Parliament's New Committees of Inquiry: Tiger or Paper Tiger?" Paper presented at the Fifth Biennial ECSA Conference in Seattle, WA.

Shaw, Malcolm T. and John David Lees. 1979. *Committees in Legislatures: A Comparative Analysis.* Durham, NC: Duke University Press.

Shepsle, Kenneth A. and Barry R. Weingast. 1995. *Positive Theories of Congressional Institutions.* Ann Arbor: University of Michigan Press.

Sinclair, Barbara. 1989. *The Transformation of the U.S. Senate.* Baltimore: Johns Hopkins University Press.

——— 1995. *Legislators, Leaders and Lawmaking.* Baltimore: Johns Hopkins University Press.

Single European Act (SEA). 1987.

Sloot, Thomas and Piet Verschuren. 1990. "Decision-Making Speed in the European Community." *Journal of Common Market Studies* no. 1: 76–85.

Smith, Julie. 1994. *Citizens' Europe? The European Elections and the Role of the European Parliament.* London: The Royal Institute of International Affairs.

——— 1995. *Voice of the People: The European Parliament in the 1990s.* London: The Royal Institute of International Affairs.

——— 1996. "How European are European Elections?" In *Political Parties and the European Union,* John Gaffney (ed.). London: Routledge.

Smith, Steven S. 1987. *Sequence, Position, Goals, And Committee Power.* Washington, DC: Brookings Institution.

——— 1989. *Call To Order: Floor Politics In The House And Senate.* Washington, DC: Brookings Institution.

Spaak, Paul-Henri. 1967. *Face to Face with Europe.* London: Conservative Political Centre.

Spinelli, Altiero. 1983. *Towards the European Union.* Florence: European University Institute.

——— 1987. *Battling for the Union.* Luxembourg: Office for Official Publications of the European Communities.

Steunenberg, Bernard. 1994. "Decision-Making Under Different Institutional Arrangements: Legislation by the European Community." *Journal of Institutional and Theoretical Economics* vol. 150: 642–669.

Steunenberg, Bernard, Dieter Schmidtchen, and Christian Koboldt. 1997. "A Method for Evaluating the Distribution of Power in Policy Games: Strategic Power in the European Union." Paper presented at the annual meeting of the American Political Science Association, Washington, DC.

Stewart, Charles, III. 1992. "Responsiveness in the Upper Chamber: The Constitution and the Institutional Development of the Senate." In *The Constitution and American Development,* Peter Nardulli (ed.). Urbana, IL: University of Chicago Press.

Stuttgart Solemn Declaration. 1983. Bull. EC 6/1983.

Swinbank, Alan. 1989. "The Common Agricultural Policy and the Politics of European Decision-Making." *Journal of Common Market Studies* no. 4: 305–322.

Bibliography

Taylor, Paul. 1983. *The Limits of European Integration*. London: Croom Helm.

Terranova, Giovanni. 1978. *Miraggio Europa: il Parlamento europeo e l'improprio esercizio del potere*. Firenze: Vallecchi.

The Bulletin of the European Commission (Bull. EC).

The Official Journal of the European Communities, Series C and L (*OJC*) 1958–1999.

Tindemans Report. 1976. *Bull. EC* 1/1976.

Treaty on European Union. 1992, 1997.

Tsebelis, George and Amie Kreppel. 1998. "The History of Conditional Agenda-Setting in European Institutions." *European Journal of Political Research* vol. 33, no. 1: 41–71.

Tsebelis, George. 1994. "The Power of the European Parliament as Conditional Agenda-Setter." *American Political Science Review* no. 88: 128–142.

1995a. "Conditional Agenda-Setting and Decision-Making *Inside* the European Parliament." *The Journal of Legislative Studies* no. 1: 65–93.

1995b. "Decisionmaking in Political Systems: Veto Players in Presidentialism, Parliamentarism, Multicameralism, and Multipartyism." *British Journal of Political Science* vol. 25: 289–326.

1996. "More on the European Parliament as a Conditional Agenda Setter." *American Political Science Review* vol. 90: 839–844.

1997. "Maastricht and the 'Democratic Deficit.'" *Aussenwirtschaft* no. 52: 29–56.

Tsebelis, George and Geoffrey Garrett. 1997. "Agenda-Setting, Vetoes and the European Union's Codecision Procedure." *Legislative Studies* no. 3: 74–92.

2001. "The Institutional Foundations of Intergovernmentalism and Supranationalism in the European Union." *International Organization* vol. 55, no. 2: 357–390.

Tsebelis, George, Christian Jensen, Anastassios Kalandrakis and Amie Kreppel. forthcoming. "Legislative Procedures in the European Union: An Empirical Analysis." *British Journal of Political Science*.

Van Oudenhove, Guy. 1965. *The Political Parties in the European Parliament: The First Ten Years*. Leyden: A.W. Sijthoff.

Van Zeeland, Paul. 1953. "The Future of Europe." Speech delivered at the Conference of Ambassadors, reprinted in *Belgium and Current World Problems*. New York: Belgian Government Information Center.

Vandamme, Jacques. 1987. "The Tindemans Report (1975–1976)." In *The Dynamics of European Union*, Roy Pryce (ed.). New York: Croom Helm.

Vedel, Georges. 1972. *Rapport du groupe ad hoc pour l'examen du probème de l'accroissement des compétences du Parlement européen* "Rapport Vedel." Bruxelles: Office des Publications Officielles des Communautés Européennes.

Vido, Lina. 1975. *Evolution et perspectives des groupes politiques du Parlement europeen: travail de recherche*. Luxembourg: Groupe Democrate-Chretien du Parlement Europeen.

Vinci, Enrico. 1968. *Il Parlamento Europeo*. Milano: Giuffre.

Ware, Alan. 1996. *Political Parties and Party Systems*. Oxford: Oxford University Press.

Weiler, J.H.H. 1993. "Journey to an Unknown Destination: A Retrospective of the European Court of Justice in the Arena of Political Integration." *Journal of Common Market Studies* no. 4: 417–446.

Weiler, Joseph H.H. 1991. "The Transformation of Europe." *Yale Law Journal* vol. 100: 2403–2483.

Welsh, Michael. 1996. *Europe United?* New York: St Martin's Press.

Westlake, Martin. 1990. *The Origin And Development Of The Question Time Procedure In The European Parliament.* Florence: European University Institute.

1994. *A Modern Guide to the European Parliament.* London: Pinter Publishers.

1995. "The European Parliament, the National Parliaments and the 1996 Intergovernmental Conference." *The Political Science Quarterly* vol. 66, no. 1: 59–73.

Wigny, Pierre Louis. 1958. *L'Assemblee parlementaire dans l'Europe des six.* Luxembourg: Service des publications de la Communaute Europeenne.

Wille, Emilio. 1984. "The Conciliation Procedure and the European Parliament's Pursuit of Legislative Powers." *Il Politico* no. 3: 489–500.

Wood, David and Birol Yesilada. 1996. *The Emerging European Union.* New York: Longmann.

Index

absenteeism
  in analysis of coalition formation
    (1980–96), 134, 138–40, 147–8
  high levels in EP of, 21, 37n14, 174,
    206n50, 207–9
  influence on coalition behavior, 133
absolute majority
  no political group controls, 20
  requirement in EP for, 8, 21–2, 215
  requirement under Maastricht
    Treaty, 86
acquis communautaire, 76
Adenauer, Konrad, 53
amendments
  absolute majority requirement for,
    21, 158
  adopted by EP (1987–93), 80
  adopted by EP (1987–97), 80
  adopted by EP (1993–97), 87–8
  categorization of, 103
  under co-decision, 158
  under cooperation, 158
Amsterdam Intergovernmental
    Conference (IGC), 19, 87–8
Amsterdam Treaty (1999), 7, 9, 11, 34,
    87–9
  co-decision process under, 87–8, 129–
    30, 176n15
assent
  of absolute majority, 8
  EP power under SEA, 85–6

procedure for, 130
Assizes, 81, 82n9
association agreements, 86
Austria, 86

Belgium, 56
Benelux Memorandum (1955), 56
Brandt, Willy, 66–7
budget
  correcting mechanism of, 67
  of European Commission, 66
  partial EP control over, 20, 23, 96
Budget Act (1970), 18–19, 66–7, 89,
    96, 120
Bureau and Enlarged Bureau of the
    EP, 95
Bureaus of political groups, 195–8,
    202n43, 203

CAP. *See* Common Agricultural Policy
    (CAP)
Catherwood Report, 80
censure (motion of), 58
coalition formation
  analysis of RCVs for information
    about, 127–32
  changing character of, 7, 176
  correspondence analysis in EP of,
    129–32
  of EP party groups, 127
  grand coalition, 170, 174, 215

255

Index

Dehousse Report, 60
Denmark
  becomes member of EEC, 68, 96–7
  opposition to majority rule, 77
  opt-outs for, 82n30
d'Hondt method
  to distribute internal positions, 46–
    7, 95, 188
  for EP committee position
    distribution, 189
  used by political groups to
    distribute positions, 203–4
Dooge, James, 75
Dooge committee report (1985), 75–6
dual mandate, 61
Dublin summit (1990), 81
Duverger, Maurice, 40–1

Economic and Monetary Union
  (EMU), 69n18, 82
ECSC. *See* European Coal and Steel
  Community (ECSC)
EEC. *See* European Economic
  Community (EEC)
elections, European, 71
EPP. *See* European People's Party
  (EPP)
Euratom Treaty, 56–8
European Coal and Steel Community
  (ECSC)
  attempted expansion of, 56
  Common Assembly of, 52–57
  Council of Ministers, 54
  Court of Justice, 54
  formation of (1952), 53
  High Authority of, 54–5, 57
  See also Common Assembly of
    ECSC
European Commission
  censure of, 58
  independence of, 38
  under Maastricht Treaty, 84–7
  proposal for financing of CAP, 63–4
  role in adoption of legislation, 174
  under Rome Treaties, 61
  under SEA rules, 78–9

European Council, 69
  calls Intergovernmental Conference
    (ICG), 76
  direct elections for EP introduced
    by, 96
European Court of Justice (ECJ)
  creation of, 57
  Isoglucose case, 72–3, 113
European Democratic Alliance (EDA),
  95, 101n9, 144, 146
European Democratic Group (ED,
  EDG), 132, 135
  in analysis of coalition formation
    (1980–96), 136–8, 140–51
  formation of, 183n12
European Economic Community
  (EEC)
  British entry into, 67–8
  budget of, 66
  CAP in budget of, 66
  effect on political groups with
    expansion (1973), 183
  European Parliamentary Assembly
    of, 1, 56, 57
  formation of (1957), 57
  political cooperation among
    Member States, 69
European Economic Community
  (EEC) Treaty, 56–8
European Monetary System (EMS),
  69n18
European Parliament (EP)
  bipartisanship in, 10
  Budget Act (1970), 66–7, 89, 96
  Bureau and enlarged Bureau, 95
  co-decision procedure in, 129–30,
    153
  Committee on Institutional Affairs,
    74
  committee position allocation in, 189
  consultation procedure, 58–9
  cooperation procedure in, 77–90,
    129–30, 151, 153
  creation of Conference of
    Presidents (CoP), 99–100, 102,
    118–21

257

Index